VERTIGO

VERTIGO

A Memoir

Louise DeSalvo

A DUTTON BOOK

B
DES

DUTTON
Published by the Penguin Group
Penguin Books USA Inc., 375 Hudson Street, New York, New York 10014, U.S.A.
Penguin Books Ltd, 27 Wrights Lane, London W8 5TZ, England
Penguin Books Australia Ltd, Ringwood, Victoria, Australia
Penguin Books Canada Ltd, 10 Alcorn Avenue, Toronto, Ontario, Canada M4V 3B2
Penguin Books (N.Z.) Ltd, 182–190 Wairau Road, Auckland 10, New Zealand

Penguin Books Ltd, Registered Offices:
Harmondsworth, Middlesex, England

First published by Dutton, an imprint of Dutton Signet,
a division of Penguin Books USA Inc.
Distributed in Canada by McClelland & Stewart Inc.

First Printing, August, 1996
1   3   5   7   9   10   8   6   4   2

Lyrics from "Show Me the Way to Go Home" by Irving King and Hal Swain
copyright © 1925 (Renewed) by Campbell Connelly, Inc. International copyright
secured. All rights reserved. Reprinted by Permission.

🅓 REGISTERED TRADEMARK—MARCA REGISTRADA

LIBRARY OF CONGRESS CATALOGING IN PUBLICATION DATA:
DeSalvo, Louise A.
Vertigo : a memoir / Louise DeSalvo.
p.   cm.
ISBN 0-525-93908-3
1. DeSalvo, Louise A.—Childhood and youth.   2. English literature—Appreciation—
United States.   3. Women—United States—Books and reading.   4. Italian American
families—New Jersey.   5. New Jersey—Social life and customs.   6. Italian American
women—Biography.   7. Critics—United States—Biography.   8. Women and literature.
I. Title.
PR55.D47A3   1996
809—dc20
[B]   96-678
CIP

Printed in the United States of America
Set in Sabon
Designed by Jesse Cohen

To Rosemary Ahern
for whom I wrote this book

CONTENTS

ver-ti-go, noun. 1. a disordered condition in which one feels oneself or one's surroundings whirling about. 2. the dizzying sensation caused by this. 3. a disease marked by vertigo. (derived from Latin *vertigo*, whirling movement, dizziness = *vert (ere)* to turn (see verse) + *igo* noun suffix.)

verse, noun, verb. 1. one of the lines of a poem. 2. to versify, that is, to turn a phrase. (derived from Latin *versus*, a row, literally, a turning toward = *vert (ere)* to turn + *tus* suffix of verb of action; akin to -ward, worth.)

Remembering the past gives power to the present.
Fae Myenne Ng, Bone

PROLOGUE

IT IS 1956, and I am thirteen years old. I have begun my adolescence with a vengeance. I am not shaping up to be the young woman I am supposed to be. I am not docile. I am not sweet. I am certainly not quiet. And, as my father tells me dozens of times, I am not agreeable. If he says something is true, I am sure to respond that it is most certainly not true, and that I have the evidence to prove it. I look up at the ceiling and tap my foot when my father and I argue, and this makes him furious.

In the middle of one of our fights, the tears hot on my cheeks, I run out of the house, feeling that I am choking, feeling that if I don't escape, I will pass out. It is nighttime. It is winter. I have no place to go. But I keep running.

There are welcoming lights a few blocks away. It is the local library. I run up the stairs. I run up to the reading room, sink into one of its comforting, engulfing brown leather chairs, pull an encyclopedia down from the shelf, hold it in front of my face so that no one can see me, so that no one will bother me, and pretend to read so that I won't be kicked out. It is warm and it is quiet. My shuddering cries stop. My rage subsides.

VERTIGO

Soon, though, I become restless. Decide to go downstairs to my favorite room, the one where they house fiction. I've already decided that I will stay here until closing time because here, I know, no one will bother me. The librarians have very strict rules. So, while I'm here, I think, I might as well read something, might as well not waste my time.

I pick a book off the "New and Noteworthy" shelf. Sloan Wilson's *The Man in the Gray Flannel Suit.* I read a few pages here and there so I know it will interest me, know that I'm not wasting my time. It's about a family; it's about the war—two subjects about which I want to know more.

I take the book back upstairs. The hours pass. The lights flicker off and on, off and on, the signal that the library is about to close.

I take my book downstairs, cruise the fiction room again, pull down a few other books to check out just in case I run out of books to read. It's time to go home. If worse comes to worst, I tell myself, I can sneak into the house through the coal chute, and hide out in the coal cellar. It's the best hiding place in our house because nobody thinks to look for me there. But there's just space enough, behind the coal bin, for a smallish girl to hide. Often, when my mother and grandmother fight, I read there. It's quiet and I don't mind the dirt.

What drives me, what impels me to be so disagreeable, my father has often asked me. I don't know how to answer this question. But I am restless, questing, trying to find something that I want that I don't have, but I don't yet know what that something is. I am certain, though, that I will find it, and that when I find it, it will make me happy. I know that I'm not happy now, and that I haven't been happy for a very long time, though I don't know why. When I try to remember the last time I was happy, I think back to when my father was away at war, and when my mother and I lived in Hoboken, New Jersey. Then, I tell myself, I was happy, so I know I can be happy again. Somewhere, I tell myself, I will find this something that will make me happy.

It is 1957. I am fourteen years old, standing behind the window of the bakery where I work to earn my spending money. What I do inside the bakery is fold paper boxes before I put the pastries and cakes inside. And then I tie up the boxes with the red-and-white string that always tears into my flesh.

Across the street there is a park where all my friends hang out while I work. Through the window, I can see them fooling around. There is one special boy I care about. He's there with his girlfriend. I see him put his arm around her, kiss her. I stop paying attention to what I'm doing. My boss yells at me.

On Halloween, children come and paint the plate glass window. They paint witches and goblins in black and in primary colors. Now I can't even see what is going on in the park across the street. But I still put the buns in bags, the coffee cakes in boxes. Work is work. And work permits no play. I have to work. That is the way it is. But I know that someday I want to find work that I will enjoy, someday I want to learn what it is like to play. What I don't know, can't anticipate, is how long this will take me.

It is spring, 1986, some two years after my sister Jill kills herself. My sister's suicide in 1984 surely has been the most important and traumatic event I have experienced in my adult life. But I have tried hard to put it behind me, to keep it out of my mind, though, often, I try to explain to myself the mystery of why Jill died yet why I have survived—for, like our mother, both Jill and I were inclined to depression.

My life, as usual, is too busy, too near chaos. I am always tired, irritable, and fearful—it is just after the nuclear accident at Chernobyl, just after the United States bombs Libya. I seem to have no emotional resilience these days because I am not sleeping well. And

I am not sleeping well because a family of ducks has taken up residence in a huge puddle of water in our next-door neighbor's backyard. These ducks are insomniacs, I think. They quack all night long, and I can't get any sleep. I need my sleep because I am trying to restore order and balance into my life and this takes energy. (It seems that I am always trying to restore order and balance into my life.) I am also trying to enjoy the spring. I haven't enjoyed a spring since my sister's death.

One night, in a fury, after being awakened yet again by the quacking of the ducks, I leap out of bed, run outside, grab a handful of stones from our garden, and start flinging them over our fence. It is a clear night with a bright moon. I can see the ducks clearly. My aim is perfect. I tell myself that I am merely trying to scare the ducks away. But I also know that I am angry enough to want to hurt them.

"Some pacifist you are," my husband chides wearily, when I come back inside, when I explain what I've been up to. "I think you better do some writing," he tells me.

"I can't," I tell him. "The kids have stolen all my pens."

This is true. My sons *have* stolen all my pens. But I know it's a ridiculous excuse. I can reclaim my pens. I can buy some new ones. My husband knows what I always seem to forget. That I am happier when I am writing, more tolerant, easier to live with. I need to write my way out of pain. If I were in the midst of writing something, the ducks would be safe. (I would be safe.) I better start writing something soon, my husband says, or I'll go off the deep end, cook up some crazy scheme, kill the ducks, get arrested, be shipped off to Sing-Sing. Our home will be torn apart, our children will be motherless.

"Stop," I beg. "I get it. I'll start writing."

As I pull the pillow over my head—for the ducks have already returned to the puddle that has become their home—I am grateful, now, for this husband of mine, though I have not always been.

* * *

A few days later, as I am taking a walk, I suddenly know what I will write next. It will be a book about how my sister killed herself, about how and why I survived. This has been prompted by my seeing a wild rosebush on my walk, like one that, years before, had grown in my backyard. I had loved that neglected bush. I had never given it rose food. Never pruned away its dead branches. Never put a trellis behind it to support its growth. Yet somehow it had survived, and it gave me pleasure. I loved its profuse blossoms, its heady scent. One day, when I wasn't home, my father came over to our house and chopped it down. He thought he was doing me a favor because it had taken over much of our tiny back garden. I considered my father's action a terrible violation, and I suspected, privately, that he had cut it down because, like me, it had overstepped its bounds.

I run home. Pick up a yellow pad and a pen, sit on the sofa in my study, tuck my knees up, and begin. Fortunately, my children are occupied. I give the work a title. I call it *My Sister's Suicide*. I write for an hour; I am beginning to write a novel that is not really a novel because it is the story of my life and yet I don't know what form it should take. I write about how I have to write about my life to give it some shape, some order.

Even as I write, though, I am wary of what I am writing. I am, inescapably, an Italian-American woman with origins in the working class. I come from a people who, even now, seriously distrust educated women, who value family loyalty. The story I want to tell is that of how I tried to create (and am still trying to create) a life that was different from the one that was scripted for me by my culture, how, through reading, writing, meaningful work, and psychotherapy, I managed to escape disabling depression. It is the unlikely narrative of how a working-class Italian girl became a critic and writer.

* * *

I wish I could say that I wrote steadily at the story of my life after that sudden burst of inspiration. But I did not. I stopped after about thirty or so pages. Instead, for seven years, I wrote the story of other people's lives, and taught, and lived a woman's life—I saw both of my sons through college, watched my mother die, saw one of my sons marry, did about three thousand loads of laundry, took care of my father after his open-heart surgery, and cooked about four thousand dinners (each, delicious, like the sauteed pork chops with Cajun spices, baby spinach with garlic and balsamic vinegar, and yams with candied ginger that I will cook tonight).

But every few months, I would haul out the manila envelope and read through my tentative start and decide, yet again, not to throw it away. Sometimes I would scribble a sentence or two into a notebook, or onto a napkin, to remind myself of what I wanted to write. Some subjects required just a word or so to jog my memory. "Fights." "Food." "Fires." "Fainting." "Long Island." "Depression." "Mom." "Despair." "Jobs/Work/Reading/Writing." "Jill."

One Saturday, in September 1995, my pulse races, I get dizzy, and feel faint. I have come to the end of a big writing project. This is a dangerous time for me. I know I need to start writing something soon. But I don't know what I want to write. I'm tired of doing research. Weary of libraries. Tired of delving into other people's lives. If I see another note card, I have told my friend Kate, I'll scream.

That day, when I get a telephone call from a friend, I tell her what I'm feeling, tell her I need a big project. Why don't I write that memoir we've talked about? she asks me. She makes it sound so simple. I should start with a few pages describing what I want to write. Maybe begin a small piece. The one about my sister's suicide. See how it goes. Send it to her to read.

Sure, I tell her, I'll give it a try. And soon I'm at my desk, and though the words I am putting down aren't yet making very much sense, I am writing, blessedly, writing.

That night, to celebrate, I cook myself a special meal of roasted chicken stuffed with artichokes, roasted potatoes with rosemary, and steamed asparagus. I have begun to work, though I don't yet know where the work will take me.

The next morning, I go downstairs to my basement. And begin to unpack one of the many boxes I have stored down there since my mother's death. Boxes containing my sister's clothing, her treasures, her pottery, her kitchen utensils. And others containing my mother's collection of family photographs, and recipes, the letters I have written her, the ones she has written my children. I work awhile, until it is time for me to write, and then, go back to my desk, and begin. This is, I think, a good place to start.

"My basement is a complete mess," I write, "and has been, for years." And it is through the contents of these boxes in my basement that I piece together my family's history. In the two years it takes me to write this book, each day, as I go to my desk between the hours of one and five in the afternoon, I feel revitalized, as I take up the work, as I reclaim my past, as I learn who I am.

Fixing Things

IT IS A little more than a month after my sister's suicide in January 1984. I think that I am doing well. I am going through the motions of living a normal life, pretending that her death hasn't made much of an impact on how I am feeling. My diary entries are filled with prosaic happenings. About my children. About teaching at Hunter College. About trying to find time for my writing. I write that I wish I could work harder (though I later realize that I have been keeping to an excruciating schedule). I reassure myself that I'm handling my sister's death very well. I hope for a far more tranquil future.

But there are warning signs that all is not well with me. I start to break out in enormous hives that cover my whole body. My eyelids ache. My wrists, breasts, and neck are covered with angry red volcanic craters. They are so itchy that I scratch myself hard. I make myself bleed. Trickles of blood like lava seen at night run down my body. When I notice what I am doing, I stop myself, try to staunch the flow of blood, and apply another of the healing lotions someone has recommended. I can't understand why this is happening. I don't connect it with my sister's suicide.

I start swallowing antihistamines; they give me some relief. They make me sleep, and I need to sleep. They stop the itching, and I need to stop scratching. But when I awaken, I feel drugged, disoriented, depressed. I'm terrified of feeling depressed. Have always been terrified of it. To me depression is like a locked dark room I can't escape. It has no windows, no books, no doors, no hope, no paintings on the wall, no telephone, no handknit sweaters, no sex, no pasta, no reading, no writing.

Depression is a place I have visited more than once; I don't want to visit it again. Some people are lucky and get out. Others don't. I've gotten out. My mother, my sister didn't. I'm afraid that I'll wind up like my sister. Dead, at the end of a rope. Or like my mother. In a hospital, having shock treatments. So I stop taking antihistamines. Try to control the urge to scratch. Can't. The only color I feel comfortable wearing, now, is red. A red sweater won't show the blood.

One day, while I'm preparing to enter a class that I teach at Hunter College, I have a crisis. I describe it the next day in my diary.

"Yesterday I had an attack of nerves—anxiety. Broke out yet again in monstrous hives and then just before class got light-headed, afraid I was going to pass out. There's a wonderful student in my class who is a nurse. She helped me compose myself, and soon I could go on teaching. I think that I have been way too hard on myself, expecting myself not to be affected by Jill's suicide, and, at a difficult time in my life, I've stopped doing the things that keep me sane—good, hard, intellectual work, writing that matters to me, swimming, taking walks."

Mother's Day 1984 is a glorious day, and I have vowed to take a whole weekend off for rest and reflection. I write in my diary, to focus myself, to see where I have been, to chart where I will be going.

In no special order, I list the crises that I have lived through within the last few months. 1) My mother's hospitalization for an acute psychotic depression and her shock treatments. 2) My sister's breakdown and her suicide. 3) My father's anger at me for not being as available as he would have liked through these crises. 4) My hospitalization in the wake of a fainting episode. 5) A legal wrangle over one of my books. 6) My two sons' emotional crises in the wake of my sister's death and their grandmother's institutionalization. 7) My husband's knee operation. 8) My husband's business being in serious difficulty. 9) My car's being hit by a truck while I'm commuting to work; luckily, I'm not hurt, though the incident scares me.

I pause to take stock. Until I have written these events down in my diary, I have been unaware that I have lived through so many crises in such a short period, that I have been in the middle of a vortex of events and emotions.

This has been no ordinary period in my life, I tell myself. So why haven't I recognized this? Why do I expect myself to carry on as if nothing extraordinary has happened?

It's like I have amnesia. Something terrible happens. After, I feel stressed, or agitated, or depressed. Or I faint. But I don't connect these emotions or my fainting to what has happened. I can't figure out what I'm feeling or why until I start to write things down in my diary.

In the winter of 1980, as I am reading Virginia Woolf's early diaries, I start to keep a diary, in direct and somewhat sheepish imitation of her lifelong practice, which she began at the age of fifteen. My first entries are halting, nothing more than lists of things I've done or read, or of things I need to do or read for the various writing projects in which I am engaged.

From the start, though, I list in great detail the delicious things I have cooked or that I have eaten. (French squash soup; oysters with

VERTIGO

Gruyère; duck with orange stuffing and Cumberland sauce; crème
brûlée for New Year's Eve.) Life, I have always believed, is too
short to have even one bad meal.

By the end of the next year, I am experimenting with examining
my life, with charting the course of my feelings, with giving my
work purpose and direction, through remembering where I have
been, through seeing where I am now, through writing about what I
want to do.

Unlike Woolf, who was taught early that the events in her life
and her thoughts were significant and worth recording, as an Italian-
American woman with working-class parents, my experience was
very different. Diary writing was certainly not encouraged by my
family. Though I had scribbled away as a child, during my adolescence, I had never kept much of a diary. Writing anything that I was
doing, anything that I was feeling or thinking, was dangerous in a
household like mine in which one did not have a right to privacy, in
which the contents of one's bureau drawers were routinely riffled
through and inspected. It was apparently dangerous, too, for Virginia Woolf. I have noticed that the diary she kept at sixteen had a
lock and a key, and that she also sealed sheets from another diary
between the pages of a book she had purchased especially for the
purpose (Dr. Isaac Watts's *Right Use of Reason*) to hide them from
the prying eyes of her household.

Noticing these things in Virginia Woolf's life helps me understand my adolescent need for privacy, and how it was thwarted: it
makes me think her household was not so different from mine, and
that in understanding her household, I might understand mine.

Writing in my dairy, I am discovering, like studying Virginia
Woolf's diary and her life, helps me understand my life. I think, as I
write, that my journal acts as a kind of "fixer," as in photography.
Like the chemical that you use to stabilize an image, to make it permanent. But I begin to see, too, that the other meanings of "fixer"
also apply to why I write. I use my journal, my writing, as a way of

making things better, of fixing things, and of healing myself, and as a way of taking a "fix" on my life. Of seeing where I am, and plotting a course for the future.

Doing intellectual work, I have always known, also makes things better for me. Thinking about novels has always helped me with the problems in my life.

In the summer of 1956, I am thirteen years old. I sit on the curb outside my house, talking about books with my best friends, Freddie and Susan. In an important way, what will become my life's work—studying literary creativity, studying the relationship between writers' lives and their work, and the relationship between their lives and works and our own as readers—is nothing but an extension of these childhood conversations. (I think of the opportunities young people miss when they construe the world from television, from movies, when they don't engage with one another, as we did, in hard talk, in painful talk, about what we are reading, and about the relationship between our lives and what we are reading.)

By now, each of us has discovered that the roofs of our houses and the closets of our basements are sometimes, though not always, safe hiding places from our parents' rages. We have each lived through years of separation from our fathers during World War II, through years of our mothers' terror during wartime. So far as we can tell, as a group of adolescents we are not extraordinary. We have survived the death of family members: Freddie's grandfather has died; so has mine; so has Susan's mother and five other members of her family in a fiery automobile crash that has burned the image of charred bodies into our brains through the pictures on the front pages of local newspapers. And we have just recently endured the suicide of a friend's mother, who, we are told, hanged herself by tying a rope around a doorknob, looping it over the top of the door, and kicking the chair out from under herself. My sister, particularly, is fascinated by this death, wants to hear its details repeatedly, even as I wish our friends wouldn't talk about it so much. I want to talk about *A Farewell to Arms* and how I am trying to find out what it is like to be in a war, something my father has lived through, but won't talk about. I want to talk about *Raintree County*, a novel that so terrifies me, I can't keep it in my room when I go to bed at night. (Many years later, I meet the author's son, and learn that the author committed suicide.)

As we sit on the curb, popping bubbles of tar with our sneakers, and sucking noisily on quickly melting ice pops as we talk about our friend's mother, and, at last, about the books we are reading, and the heat seduces us into lethargy and comradeship, I learn that I have lived through many of the same things as the heroes and heroines of these fictions. Talking about books verifies, for me, that the feelings I have struggled with alone in the solitary space of my private suffering are shared by other people, and that I am powerful enough and resilient enough to withstand hardship, and hardy enough to endure and to prevail. That I have already endured, already prevailed.

Without books, without talking about books, where would I be now? Without *Of Mice and Men, Crime and Punishment, History: A Novel, Ghost Dance, Ceremony, The Bone People, Surviving the Wreck, Praisesong for the Widow, Woman Warrior, The English Patient, The North China Lover, Sons and Lovers, All Passion Spent, Housekeeping, Dreaming in Cuban, The Bluest Eye, I Know Why the Caged Bird Sings, A Farewell to Arms, Silences*, would I have created a life for myself so different from my mother's, from my sister's? Filled with pain, yes, but not disabled from pain as they were? I don't think so.

Books were, at first, solid objects to hide behind. *Hawaii, The Brothers Karamazov, Exodus* were substantial books I could get lost in, safe screens to prevent me from watching my family. Something to hold in front of my face so that I could not see what was happening. I could hold *Atlas Shrugged* up in front of my face to ward off the blows.

"Louise is always hiding her face in a book," my family's words. True words. But hiding was necessary. A strategy for survival.

Events in books became a universe against which to measure what I was living through, a world through which I sought understanding.

The Voyage Out, To the Lighthouse, Jacob's Room, Ryder, The Antiphon, Women in Love, Crazy Cock, Tropic of Cancer, Feel the Fear and Do It Anyway, Learned Optimism, Trauma and Recovery, Thou Shalt Not Be Aware, Legacy of the Heart. It is as simple as this. Reading, and writing about what I have read, have saved my life.

I have read somewhere that the opposite of depression is not happiness but vitality. Somehow, knowing this helps me. Inscribed on a note card, this saying is tacked above my desk. It has become an avatar to staunch my chronic terror, which only dissipates the moment that I settle myself into reading and note taking, the moment that I put pen to paper, the moment that I tap out sentences, no matter how ragged or incomprehensible, on a keyboard.

Knowing that the opposite of depression is vitality serves as reminder that, for me, no matter how difficult, the act of turning toward whatever causes my pain, of reading about it in works of literature, and of trying to find the words to describe it, helps me modulate the feeling that I am in the middle of a vortex of events that is sucking me under and threatening to overwhelm me.

Once, a long time ago, when as a teenager I see Alfred Hitchcock's *Vertigo*, I understand that, like the hero played by Jimmy Stewart, I too suffer from vertigo. I look the word up in the dictionary that was my parents' gift to me the previous Christmas.

> **ver-ti-go**, noun. 1. a disordered condition in which
> one feels oneself or one's surroundings whirling
> about. 2. the dizzying sensation caused by this.
> 3. a disease marked by vertigo.

Because I have taken Latin in junior high school, I am curious about the derivation of this word that so accurately describes a condition I suffer from (which they call a disease), and so I read on.

> **vertigo.** (derived from Latin *vertigo* whirling move-
> ment, dizziness = *vert(ere)* to turn (see verse) + *igo*
> noun suffix.)

I have been trained well in dictionary skills by the nuns in my Catholic grammar school. I know how to use it to nail down the precise meanings of words I encounter in my reading, to learn their histories, to explore their roots and derivations. The entry says "see verse," and so I turn to the entry for "verse." I know that the word has something to do with poetry. But will it tell me more?

> **verse**, noun, verb. 1. one of the lines of a poem.
> 2. to versify, that is, to turn a phrase.

Nothing new here. But what about the word's derivation?

> **verse.** (derived from Latin *versus* a row, literally, a
> turning toward = *vert(ere)* to turn + *tus* suffix of
> verb of action; akin to -ward, worth.)

I ponder the differences. Vertigo: dizziness, an endless turning. Verse: an act of turning toward, somehow linked to the word "worth."

* * *

Vertigo; verse. The one, then the other. The one or the other. These words, through the years, become linked for me at a very deep level. To turn a phrase in the midst of my instability. By versifying, to transmute my instability, my vertigo into something that is worthwhile.

At an earlier point in my life, I had imagined that, one day, I would have my difficult emotional work behind me, and that I would know, once and for all, the secrets of serenity. That my vertiginous self would be conquered; that my instability would be behind me.

Now, though, I am beginning to see that the act of understanding is a lifelong, ongoing, shape-shifting process. One that is never over; one that I have to enact as often as I am able; one that I must try to enact especially when I feel I am unable, when meaning seems too elusive to grasp. And understanding, for me, means reading, means writing about what I read. And now, finally, writing about myself.

"The opposite of depression is not happiness but vitality." Next to this talisman above my desk is another. A water-stained arrow-shaped piece of cardboard with the words YES YOU CAN inked in enormous black letters.

I found it on a table while visiting a friend at the National Arts Club in Gramercy Park in New York City sometime around 1974, just before beginning work on the dissertation I was afraid I would never write. The National Arts Club intimidates me; it is filled with testimonies to lives of fame and achievement. As a working-class girl, born and raised in Hoboken, New Jersey, how could I hope to fulfill a life's ambition, to do serious intellectual work, to become a critic, a writer? Though I had read scores of books, not one had been written by an Italian-American woman. I had no role model among the women of my background to urge me on, though I had

9

found inspiration in the works of African-American and Jewish-American writers.

I was thirty-two years old; wife, mother, daughter, sister, friend, teacher, student, cook, knitter, no writer yet.

YES YOU CAN.

Sheepishly, I looked around the room, saw that no one was watching, tucked it into my purse.

I was not in the habit of stealing things. And I would have been mortified if anyone had seen me take it. But it seemed as if someone had left this behind so that I could find it. A foolish, simple saying. But I knew, as I snatched it, that I needed it, that I wanted to have it with me, to see it before me all the days of my life, as I see it before me now, on this beautiful autumn day in 1994, as I am writing, still writing.

YES YOU CAN. An antidote to the toxicity of the words the world flings at aspiring working-class girls: YOU CANNOT, YOU CANNOT, YOU CANNOT.

I stop for a while, before continuing to write in my journal, on Mother's Day, 1984, to paint my toenails red. A ritual that signals for me the beginning of the outdoor season. I am glad that I have written out the long list of what I have endured in the last several months. I realize that I must slow down, take stock, and begin the work of mourning my sister's death.

An enormous Mother's Day barbecue is in the offing, and I have finished my preparations. We will have barbecued steak. Beer-basted spareribs. My mother's noodle salad (which she is well enough, thank God, to make). My husband Ernie's green salad. My french-fried onion rings. My son Justin's pigs in blankets. My son Jason's garlic bread. My Queen of Puddings with a blackberry sauce made by one of my students. Though my sister is dead, though the wounds from her death are still fresh for each of us, though each of us is still locked in the intense privacy of grief, our surviving family will come together for this meal.

Today, all seems peaceful enough, at least for now, and I continue to write, to reflect, to plan.

I have sworn, after about ten years of working on Virginia Woolf, that I will never work on her again. That I have done enough work on her for a lifetime.

I have published three books and many essays about her life. And I have written a memoir trying to explain my ongoing fascination with her life and work.

Still, I am drawn to her. I believe that there is more to say about her. Issues in her work, in her life, that I have avoided.

When I started my work on Woolf, I did not realize how similar her family was to mine—did not know my sister would kill herself as Woolf had; did not see depression as the core of my mother's life as it was the core of Woolf's and her mother's; did not realize that I, too, would fight depression; did not see that we were both abuse survivors. And that I would learn, through studying her, the redemptive and healing power of writing.

When my friend Frank asks me, at our weekly lunch to discuss our work in progress, what I'm going to begin next, my immediate reply to him surprises me, though I have been toying with the idea for some time.

"Incest," I say. "I'm going to write about Virginia Woolf and incest." It is the first time I mention this idea to anyone, though I have been thinking about it for a few months now. "But someday," I tell him, "I also want to write about my sister's suicide."

"You should write about both," he says. "But now is not the time. Wait awhile. Wait until you can put some emotional distance between yourself and what you've lived through."

Although I value Frank's advice, I don't agree with him now and I tell him so.

I know I can't wait; that I won't wait; that waiting will be too dangerous. I will begin, now, and do as much as I am able. I know that, for me, there is an ongoing dialectic between my work and my life, that my life informs my work, and that, conversely, my work changes because of my life. That the ivory tower doesn't exist for me. That I will never have enough spare time or free time or quality time to do my work in this way. That my insights will come as I wait for Justin to finish his speech therapy, while I listen to Jason practice his guitar, while I do laundry or knit or chop garlic or walk or disagree with Ernie about what kind of pasta we should make for dinner. I know that my work must be accomplished in the face of uncertainty and chaos, when instability threatens to engulf me, to spin me out of control, for only then will I achieve a clarity of vision that comes when I try to integrate my life's work with my life.

Now is the time for me to understand Virginia Woolf as an incest survivor. In the wake of my sister's suicide. I will never have another such time. Woolf killed herself; so did my sister. Are the two related, and how? Only time and study will teach me some answers to those questions. Now, and not later, I will try to understand.

My intellectual work, I now know, is an outgrowth of the life I've led. It has transformed whatever traumas I've survived into something useful for myself, and, I hope, for others. My work has changed my life. My work has saved my life. My life has changed my work.

Vertigo; verse. The tug between these two poles remains, is very real. Right now, it feels good to be where I am. Safe. Secure. Centered. At my desk, writing these words down, my YES YOU CAN clear before me. Keeping the terror at bay, at least for now.

My Sister's Suicide

MY BASEMENT IS a complete mess, and has been, for years.

After my mother's death, when my father remarries, he sells the house that I grew up in, and most of its furniture, except three pieces that I take. He packs up our family's mementos, and tells me that if I don't want them, he will dispose of them.

I am furious that he has chosen to bring very little from his first life—his clothes, his tools, a few photos of my mother (but none of my family or me or my sister)—into his new and happy life, though, in part, I understand. The last several years have not been pleasant ones for him. My sister's suicide. My mother's depression. Her terrible, inexplicable terminal illness.

I sense that he wants to leave behind anything that will remind him of those years. I would too. I tell him that I will take everything, go through the boxes, and decide what to keep, what to give away, and what to throw away.

"My father goes off to Florida to get married," I tell my friend Kate. "And he leaves me behind to deal with all his shit." I make it sound like he's forced me into taking these discards. He hasn't. I take them because I can't bear to think of these boxes being heaved atop a pile of trash at the town dump. I will take what I want. Discard the rest. I will take care of it right away.

But that was three years ago.

Every morning, when I go downstairs to throw in a load of laundry—a ritual that helps me think about what I will write that day—I pass the pile of cardboard boxes. I think that, someday, I will make time for sorting through them, I really will, but that, today, I don't have the time, or the energy, or the courage.

"Clean the basement." These words have appeared on hundreds of my "To do" lists.

"Today I have to deal with what's downstairs," I say to my husband, over coffee, almost every morning. Using a studied irreverence to mask my fears and feelings, I have started to refer to the boxes in the basement as "my mother's death stuff."

"When I take care of my mother's death stuff," I tell him, "we can put the Lifecycle down there, get some dumbbells, put down indoor/outdoor carpeting, make it into an exercise room."

What has stopped me from cleaning out the basement, I know, are the three cardboard boxes marked with my sister's name, "Jill," in the barely legible handwriting of the last months of my mother's life.

It is not that I expect that when I open these boxes, I will find documents—my sister's letters, or diaries—that will explain the reasons for my sister's suicide some seven years before. I know my mother too well. Had these existed, she would have destroyed them.

What I know I will find, and what will be painful for me to see, are the few, trivial objects that my mother has chosen to save from my sister's thirty-seven years of life. The objects that will tell me what it was about my sister that my mother wanted to remember.

When I let myself remember Jill, I always see her in work clothes. In her country house in the Pacific Northwest. Or in the backyard of the tiny house she and her husband lived in for a year on a coastal island when he was doing work for his Ph.D. (There, the strains on their marriage had already begun to show. She often wrote me of trying, and failing, to please her husband, to win his approval. Of wanting meaningful work of her own that would pay well so that she could have some self-respect, but not knowing what that might be, for the pottery she loved earned her next to nothing. Of days when she couldn't summon enough energy to get up in the morning, though she insisted on baking her own bread, and growing her own vegetables to keep their costs low.)

I see Jill bending over her potter's wheel, her long, honey-colored hair covering her face. I see her hands, red as raw meat from working with clay. Blunt, powerful fingers. A worker's hands. My father's hands.

I see my sister's hands arranging delicate teapots in the kiln. Preparing it for firing. Harvesting vegetables. Feeding her numerous pets—dogs, cats, and, once, a pig.

Remembering my sister's hands at work is harder than remembering anything else about her.

Summer 1983

My sister is living on the West Coast. Her marriage has long since dissolved. Her most recent love affair has ended, and she begins "freaking out," as I phrase it in my diary. She wants to sell her house and move back East.

"I have no reason to stay here," she tells us.

I am worried about her, and my husband and I offer help. We'll find an apartment, she can take a job in my husband's medical company, and take some time to get her life together.

After my sister starts coming apart, I begin noticing, and recording, into my diary, disasters that I read about in the newspaper, or hear about on the radio.

"People hurt when the ceiling of a shopping mall fell in. People hurt when someone doused them with gasoline in a supermarket and set them on fire," I write. My children start to call me DEW. "Distant Early Warning."

August 1983

"Jill has moved here from the West Coast," I record, "and it isn't as bad as I thought it would be. I've been keeping her busy and helping her out."

Against my advice, and for no good reason—she has plenty of money from the sale of her house—Jill has moved back into our parents' house.

"A surefire recipe for disaster," I tell my husband.

December 1983

My life has been a shambles since soon after my sister's arrival. Several telephone calls a day, from my mother, my father, and Jill. My mother, insisting that I should include Jill in my life. Take her along when I go for a swim, have her over for lunch. My sister, complaining about my parents. About my father's condemnatory attitude—how he disapproves of her seeing this man or that one, how he gives her little lectures on how she can improve her life. About my mother's jealousy of the time she spends with my father. My father, telling me that Jill spends too much time in bed, telling me to call her, to give her a pep talk. Calling my husband for advice, and, in exasperation, watching the three of them deteriorate. Trying to help. But trying to keep my distance.

Late one night, when Jill has come over to our house to talk to us, I excuse myself to go to bed. My husband is involved in conversation with her and I am too exhausted to go on.

After a time I awaken, and discover that he is not in bed with me. I pull on my bathrobe and prepare to join him and Jill in the living room.

As I approach, I hear my sister's sultry laugh. I don't like this, so I stop and listen to what she is saying, to test whether my premonition is true. And it is. She is flirting with my husband. It is clear to me in that moment that she's dangerous, and that she's out of control. A door slams against her in my heart.

I enter the living room, threaten her, tell her to get out, tell her to leave my husband alone.

"What has come out so far," my mother tells me one day, after a family therapy session, "is how happy we were, as a family, and how close." What has not come out, I think to myself, is the violence. (I see myself at fourteen, running away after a furious fight with my father about how late I've stayed out the night before; he picks up a knife and threatens me; my grandmother rushes to protect me; I bolt out the front door to escape, sure that he's trying to kill me; I'm choking, charging down the street, shirttails flapping, wondering where I'll go.)

I am teaching full-time at Hunter, finishing two books, raising two teenage boys. I have no time for this, I say to myself. I wish they would leave me alone. "I have just about been worn out by everyone's needs," I write.

I believe that I have kept my sanity by keeping my distance from my family. I don't want to be drawn back into their orbit. It's too dangerous for me. Sometimes I feel I'm living my mother's life and not my own, or my mother's version of what my life should be.

My own battle against depression has been an ongoing struggle that I finally believe I am winning with the help of a wonderful woman therapist. I know I need help when I am so unhappy that I can't get out of bed; when I find myself in the middle of a street in New York City, standing in front of a car, and I don't know how I've gotten there; when I see my son Justin fall off a swing in our backyard, and I can't propel myself out the door to go help him; when I urge myself to work harder and harder, though I am already working harder than I should; when I dissolve in tears for no reason at all; when I can't sleep; when I find myself becoming sexually provocative to just about anyone, obsessed with trying to have a love affair to end all love affairs, with loving and losing, though I know that, should that happen, it would just cause even more problems, endanger my marriage, compromise my children's well-being.

Throughout the early part of December, my sister's moods vacillate wildly, the swings get wider, and become more frequent. She is depressed and can't get out of bed. Then she has a great day. She meets a man she takes to immediately; she likes him so much she thinks she can marry him. She gets a job. She asks me how I'm doing, and seems to mean it—the first time in months. Then the man disappoints her, and she is very depressed.

In the middle of December, my mother is in very bad shape. She checks herself into the psychiatric ward of our local hospital.

My sister gives me her perspective on my mother's deterioration. "She's doing it to get back at me."

I listen. Wonder if Jill is exaggerating. What is happening with my mother and my sister seems connected in some dangerous way that I don't want to understand.

"Before she decides to go crazy," my sister says, "she writes out her menu for Christmas, and makes a shopping list for food. She

balances her checkbook, and leaves a note about the bills that will
have to be paid."

She also finds, and goes through, all my sister's mail. She reads
the sexy letters my sister has received from a lover during her marriage. Then, according to my sister, she begins swallowing Valiums,
goes to bed, and refuses to get up.

At first, the doctors try drug treatment. But it has to be stopped. My
mother quickly develops a serious allergic reaction to the drugs.
Shock treatment, the doctors say, is the only alternative. We find
out, from my father, something we have never known: my mother
has been hospitalized for depression before, as a young girl. And
she has received shock treatment before. These are the only details
my father shares. I don't press him for more information because he
is very distressed. But when I find out, I am not surprised that my
parents have kept this secret. Mental illness, after all, is not something anyone discussed openly when we were growing up. My sister
is furious that we haven't been told before. I wonder whether this
was the reason that Jill and I were so often sent off to Long Island
to spend our summers with relatives.

As my mother gets worse, my sister gets better. She seems more
cheerful. Full of plans. Sure, now, that if she sets her mind to it, she
can control her life and make it work. Craziness is a ball that is being passed back and forth between them.

My father comes to my house to spill out his sorrow, bewilder-
ment, and rage. He tells me that what sent my mother over the edge
was her finding my sister's love letters. That, and my going away
for Christmas with my husband and children.

"That isn't why Mom's in the hospital," I say.

His rage spills over. He bangs my kitchen table with his fists. I
plan an escape route, think of what I'll do if his anger escalates. For
now, I think, I'm safe enough.

"All your mother ever wanted from you," he tells me, "was a

little love, which you never gave her." Nothing has changed. Whenever anything goes wrong, he blames it all on me. Blames it on my not loving her, or him.

I control myself. Don't say much. My husband isn't home. He's caught me off guard, come over unannounced, when I'm home alone.

He talks about my sister. Weeps about how rotten her life is. Begins telling me what she's told him about her sex life with her ex-husband.

"I don't want to hear this," I say. What he's telling me is not something Jill has revealed to me. This isn't right, I think. No father should know this much about his daughter's sex life. I wonder where and when my father and my sister have had such intimate conversations. I wonder whether my mother was with them while this was going on. I suspect that she wasn't.

Before I go away on my vacation, I plan on visiting my mother in the hospital. I want to bring her a Christmas present, but I don't know what to do about it, for I have been told that she's really not in contact with reality. I have visited the local craft and hobby shop, the bookstore, some clothing stores, searching for something to buy, but stopping myself from buying anything. Clothing, puzzles, books, jewelry—all seem grotesque presents, like sick jokes, in light of my mother's hospitalization. (I am reminded of how my friend Kate's mother-in-law gave her a set of sheets with just one pillow case the year her husband left her. "The perfect gift," Kate said. "I'm surprised she didn't send me a set of crib sheets the year I lost my baby." For days after, to ease the pain of her mother-in-law's sadistic gesture, we regaled one another with ideas for "perfect" gifts for friends in disastrous circumstances.)

One day, when I'm out shopping for food, I spy a tiny potted Christmas tree with miniature plastic ornaments of snowmen and snowflakes and tiny red velvet bows fastened to its branches with pieces of wire, its base wrapped in garish magenta tinfoil. I consider buying it, but waver. I know it's a stupid present to give someone who's gone crazy, but I can't figure out what wouldn't be a stupid present to give someone who's gone crazy. I look at the rack of women's magazines that abut the cash register. No help, I'm sure, in those pages. The problems they deal with are not the problems I am dealing with. I imagine the articles inside: "What to Give the Man Who Has Everything"; "A Thoughtful Gift for a Thoughtful Secretary"; but not one entitled "A Timely Gift for the Mother Who Has Lost Her Mind."

I am about to go ahead with my purchase, but then wonder whether the nurses will allow her to have it. My father has told me of the very strict rules the hospital enforces about presents for patients on my mother's ward. Nothing potentially harmful is permitted, and with good reason. (When I see my mother, I am shocked by the damage that she has already inflicted on herself with nothing more than her blunt fingernails.) I decide to buy it anyway—if they won't let her have it, so be it.

There is a special elevator to my mother's ward, and two sets of locked doors to go through. I pass through the second set of doors into another country, into the world of the insane, where space, time, and objects exist in ways that I can't even imagine. My son Jason has insisted on coming to see his grandmother; I have tried to discourage him, afraid of what he'll see and hear, afraid of how I'll behave, afraid of how he'll react, but he has insisted. He loves his grandmother, who has helped him grow up, who has interacted with him more than she ever interacted with me, coloring Easter eggs with him, giving him sprinkler showers on her back lawn during heat waves, making Christmas cookies with him in years past. He wants to know what she's going through; what he'll see, he explains to me, can't be as bad as what he's imagining. But I'm not so sure.

There is a woman with blowsy yellow hair pushing along an orange plastic chair as she mutters obscenities to herself. There is a man sitting on a plastic chair tied in restraints, rocking back and forth. A young woman, my age, rushes down the hall, arms upraised, shrieking, with two nurses chasing after her.

Oh my God, I think, what has happened to my mother, and what is my mother doing in here, and will she ever get out?

Thoughts about my mother have been ever present since I heard she is in the hospital. Now, though, I begin to worry about myself. I wonder whether I will ever snap as she has snapped, whether I, too, will wind up in here. From now on, I will spend much of my life taking my mother's and my emotional temperatures, reading books about depression, doing everything that I can to stay sane, trying to help keep my mother on an even keel. And I will write about it. As if thinking about depression, knowing about it, learning about it, writing about it in the lives of famous writers will give me the powerful weapons I need to ward it off.

We stop at the nurses' station and find out, after a careful inspection, that yes, my mother can have the Christmas tree, that her room is down the hall. We walk there very, very slowly, keeping our eyes straight ahead, not wanting to look into anyone else's room, into anyone else's horror.

And there she is, sitting on the edge of her bed, in her bathrobe, looking like someone else's mother, eyes vacant, eyes darting, holding herself, rocking back and forth, muttering about money, about not having enough money, never having enough money, and about not being able to find her way home.

(A recurrent dream my mother has shared with me. She is in an unfamiliar landscape. There are no landmarks she can identify. She has been trying to make her way home for a very long time. But she has no idea where home is. There is no one to ask. No one to help. And she's terrified that she'll never find her way home.)

My mother turns and looks at us, doesn't seem to know who we are. Jason says nothing but hello. What can he say? I say hello, tell her I've brought her a present, hold out my insubstantial offering of the Christmas tree, which she ignores, so I put it on her dresser. I sit next to her, at the edge of the bed, wary of her, wanting to touch her, to hold her, not wanting to touch her or to hold her.

I think of how foolish I have been to bring her this present. There is nothing to celebrate here.

This, I think, is too hard for anybody. Too hard for her. Too hard for Jason. And too hard for me.

Christmas 1983

I am in the Cayman Islands, with my husband and children, having the scuba-diving holiday that we had planned for months. It is a difficult time, and I feel I shouldn't be here.

My mother is still in the hospital, undergoing shock treatment. Every day, we make a call to see how she's doing. She isn't doing well.

My father is angry at me for going away with my family at this terrible time. My husband and I almost canceled this trip. I almost stayed home. But my husband insisted that I need to get away, that we need to get away, after the strain that we have been living with for months.

In Cayman Brac, I try to relax, try to get some rest, but it's not easy. I walk to the end of the pier in the wind, and wonder if I'll fall off or be blown away. I have a moment of exquisite pleasure watching a sunset, but panic when I see a toddler running on the pier, unattended. I am happy to see my sons together in a paddle boat, but worry if they'll run aground on the reef. I notice a waterspout at the horizon, and watch it until it moves out of sight. And I can't enjoy my dives or my swims. I know there are sharks and moray eels and

23

barracuda and spiny sea urchins. After an instructor tells a story of a diver swallowed by a seven-hundred-pound grouper (which everyone but me regards as apocryphal), I stop diving.

What soothes me is lying on my belly at the edge of the water, watching hermit crabs. I do this for hours, while my husband and sons dive. The sea grass is filled with them. They have red and blue bands around their legs. Their parade across the sandy bottom amuses me. Their fights do not seem connected to territoriality. I notice that they sometimes hitch rides atop one another.

I see a small one, struggling under the weight of a huge shell. A large one, just barely protected by a small shell. I wonder how they select the shells they haul around on their delicate bodies for protection. Is it accident? Some aesthetic sense? Do some feel a greater need for protection than others, and so look for shells that are far larger than their bodies? Are there brave hermit crabs who don't mind being exposed? And timid ones who need the largest shells they can carry?

I have taken my diary to Cayman Brac. Its cheerful cover of purple and white irises in bloom is out of keeping with the family tragedy I am recording in its pages, the family history of violence and insanity that I am trying to recall and to understand. Writing in my diary, as always, helps me immeasurably. It is, by now, a five-year-old habit.

"What I see clearly," I write, "is how, as a child, I was blamed for their bad times, how they expected me to make them feel good, and how unfair that was, and how impossible it would be for any young child to do what they expected." I remind myself of my mother's history of being unmothered, of its consequences in her care for me.

I write, too, about my work. About how work, for me, is salvation. I wonder whether I have chosen to work on Virginia Woolf because of the similarities between her family's history and mine. In making out a work plan for my return home (which is an activity that always makes me feel good), I write, "Think about Virginia Woolf and incest." This idea comes as a surprise. I have vowed never to work on Woolf again.

My sister, my father has told me in a telephone conversation, is returning to the West Coast. He's taking her to the airport. He's afraid that something terrible will happen if she leaves, but my mother, in her moments of lucidity, insists on it. She says she won't come home from the hospital if Jill is still there.

For a time after I get this call, I feel bad for him, and for my sister. Feel bad that the weight of my mother's and sister's illnesses is all on his shoulders. But I am fighting to stay clear. In my journal, I write that I am fighting for my life.

January 1984

My mother is home. She's not back to normal (and will never be), but she is functioning. She has begun to cook, and to clean. The last report from my sister from the West Coast has been good. She has gotten an apartment in Oregon to share, and a job, and a car. Everything seems to be returning to what passes for normal in our lives.

One morning, I am cutting an orange for breakfast. I am, as always, distracted. I slice a piece out of my finger, see the blood pour out, and lose consciousness. I have a history of blackouts. I've had them since childhood. They terrify me. I'm always afraid that the next one will be the last one. Afraid that I'll die. My family has always called what I do "fainting," but I'm not so sure.

This one is scarier than most. My husband tells me that, this time, I stopped breathing for a long time, and he thought he would have to resuscitate me. He knew that if he did, he would break my ribs, so he waited through one, two, three, four, five interminable seconds to see if I'd start breathing on my own. Just as he decided not to wait any longer, he tells me, I start taking deep, shuddering breaths.

The ambulance comes. My sons watch me taken away on a stretcher. The doctors, as usual, can't find anything wrong with me. "Stress," my husband says. "It's all the stress you're under."

This is a danger sign that I cannot ignore. I call my therapist and get back into therapy. In time, I learn that when I'm angry, I cut myself, hurt myself in some way, hold my breath, make myself faint (all without realizing what I'm doing), because hurting myself is safer than showing my rage.

February 1984

A few weeks after, I record into my diary, in very controlled prose, that my sister has killed herself.

"Jill killed herself at the end of January—January 29, to be exact," I write. "What to record here about it? The feeling I have, of having escaped. The distance I put between myself and my family, necessary, because it saved me. Sadness, certainly. But also, . . . a sense of freedom, almost of euphoria, that I was no longer responsible for her, and that I had been responsible for her for so very, very long, as long as I can remember. . . ."

There is a family photograph of the two of us, taken when I am about thirteen and she is ten. I am sitting in my nightgown, in my mother's rocking chair. Jill is on my lap, pretending to be a baby. I hold a toy bottle to her lips. I pretend to feed her. My father is taking this picture, and we are posing for it. I look like I have been pressed into this against my wishes though I wear a phony smile. My glassy eyes look past her, past the camera, and past my father, into the far, far distance. Jill looks straight into the viewfinder. She, too, wears a phony smile, pretending she's having a good time. But I can see the sadness in her, the sadness that was always there.

"Did you have to bring *her*?" These words from one or another of my friends, or boyfriends, throughout my teenage years, whenever I arrive at a basketball game, or the park, or the Sweet Shoppe where we all hang out. My parents don't often allow me out of the house without my sister. I can't stand being in the house where someone is always yelling at someone else—I need to get out of the house as often as I can. I nearly always accept my parents' condition that I take my sister with me. But I make her pay.

I race to wherever I'm going so fast that it is a terrible struggle for her to keep up with me. When we get to where we're going, I ignore her, pretend she isn't there.

She stands at the edge of the crowd. My mother hasn't wanted her at home. I don't want her with me. My friends think she's a royal pain in the ass. She looks the way she always looks, like she's on the verge of tears.

The call comes, as these calls do, around midnight, while I am sleeping. The phone awakens me. My husband answers it. He is in his study, a room that adjoins our bedroom. I can hear him talking and I know, from the tone of his voice, that something is wrong. The first part of the conversation is muffled. Then I hear him say, "Yes, I'll tell Louise. I'll tell her parents. I'm sorry, so very, very sorry."

I hear my husband's footsteps. I sit up in bed. Prepare myself. I know what his news will be, though I have kidded myself into thinking that because Jill seems better, I can have some breathing space, some time to catch my breath, until the next crisis. I can get on with my life, and not worry so much about hers.

My sister has hanged herself in the basement of the apartment that she has shared for less than a month with the woman who has called us. She has used a belt to do it. She has killed herself early in the morning. "It is a beautiful, sunny morning," she has written in

27

the note in which she tells us that she can't go on, and that she has decided to take her life.

This is not the first time this woman has found someone dead, she tells my husband. Her brother killed himself, and she is the one who found him.

When my husband tells me this, I feel sorry for her, and furious at my sister for putting someone so vulnerable through this again. But then I think, "I'm glad she didn't do it here. I'm glad I wasn't the one who found her."

My husband makes the telephone call to my parents. My father answers the phone. I can hear his screams. "No! No! No! No!" Then my mother's cries.

I get on the telephone with them. I don't remember what I say. My husband takes the phone out of my hand, and says we'll be in touch throughout the night. I hear him tell my father that, no, Louise can't come. He is protecting me. "She has to tell the boys. She has to be here with me and with them," I hear him say.

I go up into my study to call my friend Kate to share the news with her. As I'm talking, I see that the light is blinking on my answering machine; I haven't checked my messages all day; I wonder if there could be a last message from Jill. I'm stunned by this possibility; I tell Kate; ask her what I should do.

She thinks for a minute, then says, "What do you want to do?"

"Erase the messages," I say.

"Then erase the messages," she counsels.

"I can't do that," I say. "What if there's a message from Jill?"

"Erase the messages," Kate says. "Follow your instincts. If there's a message from your sister, what's in that message can only hurt you. Erase them. I'll wait while you do it."

I know that Kate is right. I know that this is something I have to do. To protect myself.

Kate waits. As I push the erase button I start screaming. I continue to scream until all the messages have been erased. If Jill has left me a final message, it is gone, and it can't hurt me now.

When I tell my friends about my sister's death, I tell them that the belt she used to strangle herself had been a gift from me. I don't know if this is true—I *had* given Jill a belt—but I am compelled to say it, and, at the time, I don't know why. Now, though, it seems to have been my way of taking responsibility for what happened to her, though I have never admitted to myself that I have felt guilty about her death. And there is this too. My telling the story in this way links us, binds me to her, even in death.

Summer 1984

It is the summer after my sister's death, and I am beginning to re-claim my life. I am feeling much better, though there are many times when I feel a dull ache. I am working well: I have finished an essay on Virginia Woolf's adolescence; I have begun reading about incest to prepare for writing about Woolf's childhood. But I am also spending many afternoons sitting by the ocean, watching the gulls and the plovers, mesmerized by children building ambitious sand castles, too close, I think, to the water's edge.

My children are healing. Jason has a girlfriend, and her ener-getic, cheerful presence has enlivened our household. Justin is on a cross-country trip. He writes us that he is thinking about his future.

But just as I am feeling much better, my mother brings boxes of my sister's personal effects over to my house. She wants to give them to me.

"I don't want them," I tell her. "I have plenty of stuff of my own. Take them away."

"I don't know what to do with them," my mother says.

"Neither do I," I counter. "Take them back. I don't want Jill's stuff in my house."

Nonetheless, there comes a day after my husband and I have taken a holiday when I open a cupboard and discover that there are two sets of stacking glass bowls where, before, there had been only one. There are two saucepans, identical in size and shape, where, before, there had been only one. And there are two wire whisks, two sets of Tupperware bowls, two quiche pans, and two bread baskets. Two cutting boards, two waffle irons.

My kitchen has become a demented household version of Noah's Ark.

Christ, I think to myself, she's brought Jill's shit over and stuffed it in my closets while I've been away. What do I do now?

I call Kate.

"Guess what?" I say.

"I don't want to guess," she replies. "Just tell me. Something must have happened to upset you."

"Do you believe in ghosts?" I ask her.

"No, why?" Kate asks.

I tell her about the objects I have found. I joke that either, in my household, objects have discovered how to reproduce themselves or my mother has been responsible for the invasion.

I ask Kate what to do, whether I should confront my mother or what.

"Pack up all the stuff in a box," Kate suggests, "and call Goodwill. You can't confront your mother. It won't do you any good."

"But what if there's more?" I ask.

"We'll take care of that when the time comes. One thing at a time. Just do this for now."

I take Kate's advice, do what she suggests. Trying to discuss this with my mother will get me nowhere. I know that all this clutter is threatening to overwhelm the trusty vessel I have made of my home and I have to get rid of it.

November 1994

I am in Portland, Oregon, on a book tour. It is in this city, some ten years before, that my sister killed herself.

A year or so after her death, I cleaned out my Rolodex, as I do each year, discarding the cards bearing the names and telephone numbers of people with whom I've lost contact.

When I came to my sister's name, and her last address in Portland, I took the card out of the Rolodex and tossed it away. I told myself I wouldn't be needing it anymore. I was still in a state of numbness about what she had done, still unable to feel.

I tossed this card into the garbage as unthinkingly as I would toss away the name and address of someone who has meant absolutely nothing to me.

When I am told that I will be speaking in Portland, I wonder whether I'll have the courage to go to this city. I've been there only once, with Jill. We spent the day walking around downtown, visiting the city's famous rose gardens, going for a treat at Rose's. I haven't been back since her death. Imagine that it's a city I'll never return to because of my sister's death, though I loved it on my first visit.

For a few days, I consider asking my publisher to delete Portland from the list of cities I'll visit, but I decide not to, because I know I don't want to explain why.

I have a few hours between appointments in Portland, so I decide to take a walk, alone. It is a beautiful, sunny day. There are still some leaves on the trees.

This walk is hard for me. I wonder whether any of the clapboard houses I wander past is the house where it happened, where Jill killed herself. Whether Jill ever shopped in this store. Ate in this restaurant.

The tears come, unbidden. In this city where she ended her life, so far from where I live mine, her death finally becomes a reality to me.

I find a park, a bench, and sit to mourn her. Close by, I see a garden with riverbed rocks and stones in several sizes. I take a few of these and make a small pile of them in the park, in imitation of a Native American ritual that I have read about for remembering the dead.

February 1, 1984

Throughout my sister's wake, I remain detached and controlled. I don't cry. I store up incidents to tell my friend Kate, who comes with her husband and children the first night. It is the only way I can get through this.

When my parents, my husband, and I are brought up to the casket by the undertaker to view the body, my mother kneels down on the pew, looks at Jill, then turns to me, and says, "Doesn't she look beautiful?"

"Mmmm," I say. I don't contradict her. Jill doesn't look beautiful. Her face is disfigured. Later, Ernie, who is a doctor, explains why.

My mother gets up. "See," she says to me. "She came home to us, after all. She came home to be with us on her birthday."

This is the craziest thing my mother has said so far. I can't stand it. But I tuck it away in my memory to tell Kate.

It *is* the first of February, my sister's birthday. She would have been thirty-eight years old. But, I think, wouldn't it be better if Jill was away, and still alive?

I remember something that happened with Jill in the autumn, soon after she came east.

She is walking away from me in the parking lot of the Y, where I have taken her swimming, toward her car. She is tossing something she is saying offhandedly, over her shoulder.

It is, I recall, a beautiful October evening. The sun is setting.

The sky is glowing fuchsia, orange. In less than three months she'll be dead.

I don't want to hear her; I'm really not listening; I want to drown out her crazy talk. This day, she has gone on and on and on about the new man she has met, and how they have "clicked," and how she is thrilled that he has a daughter, how she's always wanted a daughter, and how, this time, she knows it's going to work, she's going to make it work. I've heard this before. I want to be alone; I wish she wasn't here.

"Who wants to be forty?" she says. I'm forty-one, and think it's just a dig at me. Then she says, "Me, I'll never be forty." I think this is just another crazy remark. Or Jill telling me she's afraid to grow old. When she's not wearing her overalls to do her pottery or her gardening, she still dresses as if she's fifteen. Cute little outfits. Foolish little-girl shoes. Proud when she's thin enough to buy her clothes in the preteen shop.

Jill is still talking. Now she is talking about my father, and how my mother hates them for spending so much time together alone.

"She's jealous of us," my sister says. "Jealous of how well we get along."

I don't answer. I climb into my car. Give a wave. She heads for hers. I am relieved that, inside my car, there is silence. As she walks away from me, I see, she is still talking. But now she is talking to the air.

Two nightmares I have about this time. In one, I am in a house with boglike floors. If I try to walk into a room, I know I will get sucked in and I won't get out. In another, I am in a house that is also a school, and someone is hitting me and hitting me and hitting me, and no one will come to help me.

Though there is a church-filled candlelit service for my sister in Oregon, organized by her close friends, not many people come to her wake in New Jersey. Mostly, our relatives. My parents' friends. My sister's life in the East ended when she moved west with her husband just after her marriage in 1968. Her ex-in-laws, who live nearby, don't come. My eldest son is not there. He has refused to come to the wake or to the funeral. Jill has killed herself during the week of his final exams. He has to get good grades to get into a good college, and he is angry with her for, as he put it, "fucking everything up."

I have picked out the casket. "Make it plain," I say to the undertaker. "She was not a pretentious woman."

I have picked out the clothes that she'll be buried in. An ordinary plaid blouse, and slacks, I decide. My parents let me have my way. They are barely functioning.

I have picked out the flowers. Daisies. She used to pick wild ones in the fields near her home when they came into season.

I have chosen a few poems to read. Innocuous ones. Anything appropriate will reveal too much. I have said a few words about my sister's gift for working with her hands, for making pottery, and for turning humble things into works of art.

Before the undertaker closes the casket, he asks us if we want to say good-bye.

My mother takes my hand. She wants me to join her, and my father, at the side of my sister's casket. She wants us to say good-bye to my sister as a family. I pull my hand away.

"No," I say. "I want some time with Jill alone." My mother tries to grab my hand again, tries to pull me with her up to my sister's body, but I pull away. She gives up when she realizes that I won't give in, and that I am stronger than her, and willing to make a scene to get my way.

At last alone, I kneel down, and look at Jill. I try to look beyond the misshapen face in the casket to the Jill I remember. The Jill I shared a bed with for fourteen years because my mother, who practiced economies, determined that it was far cheaper to buy a double bed for the two of us than to buy each of us a bed of our own.

Of course, Jill is not there in the casket. The only place, now, that she will ever be for me is in my memory. And now, in these pages that I write about her.

I reach into my purse and pull out an envelope. In it is a picture of her and the man who left her, when they were happy. They are clowning for the camera. It is Halloween, and she has carved a pumpkin. It stands beside them on the counter. As with everything my sister did with her hands, there is wonder and magic in her work. The pumpkin looks like a demon mask, the kind that is used to ward off danger and evil. In the envelope, too, is a card on which I have written the words "I love you," even if I'm not sure they're true.

I put the envelope, and one of the first pots my sister made, into the casket. I can't, I won't say good-bye.

Late Summer 1993

I have had a good, work-filled summer. Finished the book about revenge I've been working on for years. Finished revising my second novel, about two teenage sisters. For its epigraph, I have chosen lines from Sylvia Plath's "Two Sisters of Persephone": "Two girls there are: within the house/One sits; the other, without. . . ."

I have cleared my desk. Filed away my notes, and manuscripts. Sent everything off to my agent. For the first time, since 1974, I have no writing to do, although I have some ideas about what I want to turn to next. This has been my plan: to give myself some breathing room.

My asthma, which has been disabling for close to a year and a half, is under control. My hard work—daily fast walking, meditation, therapy—is paying off. I feel better, in every way, than I have for years, though, of course, there are still problems. My chronic fears. My terror of losing consciousness, of fainting while I am in my car, stuck in a traffic jam, so that no one can get to me.

In therapy, we chip away at this, bit by bit. We look at the similarity between this and the way my sister chose to die. We develop strategies for me to try when the feeling comes over me. We talk about my fear, my rage, my fury, and what I have to be so angry about. We talk about how what I'm having is a kind of temper tantrum. We talk about the difference between the way things were for me in childhood and the competent adult I have become, something I keep forgetting, something I need to relearn daily. I can see myself making progress.

And on a day like any other day, I go down to do the laundry, but wind up, instead, in the basement, and I go straight to the back, to the boxes marked with Jill's name. My friend Kate has come over, and I have excused myself for a minute to run downstairs to throw a load of laundry in the drier.

Sooner or later, I tell myself, I have to see what is in those boxes. It might as well be now.

I call up to Kate and ask her to come downstairs. I tell her what I'm about to do, and ask her if she'll stand by me while I do this.

The first box contains some clippings. An announcement of my sister's being "lady in waiting" to the high school prom queen. News items from her graduations, from her induction into an honorary society. The announcement of her engagement. And of her wedding. (In each picture, Kate observes, she smiles a forced smile.)

Underneath the clippings, carefully folded, and wrapped in tissue paper, are my sister's Girl Scout beret and her merit badges. We find it strange that my mother has saved them.

In the next box, a set of measuring cups and one of measuring spoons. A few wooden spoons, one of which has a burnt handle.

"Worthless stuff," I think to myself. "Why on earth did my mother save it?"

In another box is my sister's collection of porcelain dolls. I take them out, and we look at them. "They're ugly," Kate says.

Under the dolls, though, are the clothes that my sister has made.

And now I can see her, in memory, bending over my mother's Singer sewing machine, honey hair falling into her eyes, peering through her thick glasses, at the garment she is making. I hear the rat-ta-ta-tat of the foot pedal, as she stitches along. All the doll clothes that my sister makes are dressy. Cocktail dresses with matching headbands. Evening gowns. The kind of dresses suitable for a life my sister will never know.

"Of all the things to keep," Kate says. "Of all the things to treasure," I think, "my mother has chosen these."

But in keeping these things, I know, my mother has tried, desperately, to hold on to the memory of the happy child. The happy child that my sister had never been.

When I find them, and hold them, I start crying. At last, at last, I am crying for my sister, I am crying for my mother, and I am crying for myself. I am glad that Kate is here for comfort. I know that I am ready to begin to give my sister up. I am ready to begin the long process of saying good-bye.

Combat Zones

1942

ON SUNDAY, SEPTEMBER 27, the rainy day that I am born at the Margaret Hague Maternity Hospital in Jersey City, New Jersey, toughened, sunburned Marines cling tenaciously to a beachhead on Guadalcanal; leaders of the Czech Orthodox Church are sentenced to death by the Nazis; gasoline rationing is announced in the United States; Soviet troops push forward into German positions northwest of the smoking city of Stalingrad, giving hope that the fascist siege of that city might now be repulsed; Allied bombers attack three Japanese transports east of New Guinea; five Axis ships are sunk in the Mediterranean; the Bureau of Vital Statistics predicts a bumper crop of ten thousand new babies in New York City for October; Bloomingdale's department store in New York City is selling warm and cozy quilted bathrobes (in a choice of solids, big prints, or little prints) for $3.98, on sale; and Abraham & Straus announces a special on a four-pound box of cookies (including butterscotch, caramel, and lemon), perfect for men in the service for just $1.19, including mailing—also a sale on Harris adjustable headlight hoods for automobiles, for only $1.98, designed to meet all official blackout and dimout regulations.

My mother's labor is long and difficult, but she considers herself fortunate nonetheless. Unlike many other women on the maternity floor, my mother has her husband with her; her husband hasn't yet gone off to war. My father, though he has received his orders to go into the navy before my birth, is unwilling to leave his pregnant wife. He wants to help care for me during my infancy because he knows how she worries about becoming a mother, about whether she can do a good job. Because he has already served one tour of duty in the navy, before the war, my father can strike a bargain: in return for delaying his entry for close to a year, he signs on for an extended tour of duty.

My parents are so sure that I'm a boy that they've already chosen my name. Louis. For my father. But that I am a girl comes as a shock. They quickly decide that they can still name me after my father. They will call me Louise. My mother gives me the middle name Anita because she likes it, and because it has the same first letter of Annunciata, her own middle name.

The specter of my father's leaving hangs over our family during the first year of my life, a year during which, among other wartime events, Germany renews its air attacks on London, the Russians destroy the German army southwest of Stalingrad, the Royal Air Force begins to bomb Berlin, the massacre in the Warsaw ghetto occurs, United States' forces capture the Aleutians and land in New Guinea. Unless the war ends quickly, and no one thinks it will, my father, like so many other fathers, will be assigned to go off to one combat zone or another, and my mother and I will stay behind to wait and see whether he will survive the conflagration. (In consequence, I will spend much time studying the lives of writers profoundly affected by war.)

*   *   *

What do I know of my parents' lives before they became my parents, before they married on Sunday, July 6, 1941? Not very much at all.

We were not a family inclined to sit for hours talking about ourselves, sharing intimacies, sharing personal histories. What I learned about my parents' histories came to me piecemeal. Usually, it was something I overheard when I entered a room, when I walked past an open door, or when I listened to an argument.

What do I know about my mother's life? I know that her proudest moment was when she won a prize in high school in 1929, for writing. I know that she wanted to go to college, and that she had been awarded a scholarship to attend one in New York State, but that she couldn't go because her parents were too poor to send her. I know that my mother worked as a salesperson for W. T. Grant's in Hoboken, New Jersey, after she graduated high school, before she married my father. (She stands on the edge of a group portrait of Grant's workers in 1940, wearing a tweed jacket, sweater, and short skirt, looking tense.) I know that she sold shoes. I know that she developed a strong, lifelong friendship during her years at Grant's. I know that she taught herself to become a fine seamstress.

I know that my mother adored her father, and that she had a very difficult childhood. That her mother died during the influenza epidemic of 1918, when she was two years old. That her father, an Italian immigrant, who spoke no English, who worked for the railroad as a day laborer, had a difficult time finding adequate child care for her, and that he farmed her out to neighbors or relatives who probably either abused or neglected her. I know that she nearly died after her mother's death and that her father remarried a peasant woman newly arrived from Italy, primarily to provide a mother for his child. I know that my mother hated her stepmother. And that, at some point in her life, my mother experienced a depression so severe she had to be hospitalized.

Much of this I learned from my father as an adult. It was not something my mother talked about. As a child, I was never told that my grandmother was my mother's stepmother. This was a secret, although it was alluded to by my parents and other relatives in close whispers, or by my mother and stepgrandmother in heated arguments.

I was told of my mother's birth mother, and shown her picture only after I had married. I was astonished to see that I looked just like her. Same heart-shaped face. Same small eyes. Same wide brow and upturned nose. Same dark, wavy hair. Same prideful look on her face as on mine.

Learning that my stepgrandmother was not my mother's birth mother was a great shock I experienced as a young bride. The other, that my mother had taken the $5,000 I had saved during my years of work from our joint bank account to pay for my wedding reception. I had worked hard, lived frugally, denied myself material pleasures to save enough money to feel financially secure and to be independent. I was furious when I discovered she had spent it on my wedding without asking me.

For years I have wondered why no one told me that my mother's birth mother was dead. It would have explained so much. Why my mother and grandmother always shouted at one another in Italian about love, and about respect. Why our household was always a pitched battleground after my grandmother came to live with us after my grandfather's death. "You're not my blood," the mysterious words my stepgrandmother flung at my mother routinely.

Sometimes I think that my mother's mother's death was kept a secret from me because she hadn't died from influenza, she had really killed herself. I have no evidence for this. But what else could explain this shroud of secrecy? Why else would they have tried to obliterate her memory?

The greatest gifts I get from my mother are her fierce loyalty to family, her sense of justice and fairness.

And what do I know about this man who became my father? I know that his being the only son in a family with four daughters was a source of irritation to him. That, as a boy of six or seven, he helped his mother at her piecework job by buttoning the buttons on the shirts that she folded. I know that my father was required by his parents to drown the kittens that the family cat would periodically deliver. I know that this disturbed him. I know that, as a teenager, he was caught stealing copper pipe from a construction site and put in jail. I know that his mother, not his father, came to bail him out.

I know that my father graduated from eighth grade when he was sixteen years old because his family moved around so much that he was always getting left back. (He lived in Italy, Brooklyn, New York City, North Bergen in New Jersey.) I know that my father was dyslexic, and that going to school was agony for him. I know that he wanted to go to high school, but decided that since he would be more than twenty years old when (and if) he graduated, he would quit school to work to help his family. That his father was a barber, and that he owned his own shop, but that he was irresponsible—he would return to Italy periodically after the family moved to the United States, leaving his wife and five children behind without an income.

An early memory: I am on a pier in New York City waving good-bye to my paternal grandfather, who is in the bow of the ship waving a white handkerchief. He is off on another of his jaunts to Italy. I wonder why we have come to say good-bye to him because I have heard the family arguing heatedly about these periodic sojourns of his. When I am older, I think that he must have had another woman, perhaps even another family, in Italy. Only this can explain to me why he comes and goes, comes and goes.

I know that my father had a spectacular untrained operatic voice, that he wanted to become a singer (he had the raw talent, and the temperament, to become a star), but that he couldn't afford the lessons, and, besides, he didn't have sufficient schooling to make that possible. I know that my father, without much formal education, had decided that he could get the training he needed to become a skilled laborer if he enlisted in the service, and so he did, spending the years from 1935 to 1939 in the navy. I know that he was good at fixing things. I know that he loved to travel and that that's another reason why he joined the navy. In the navy, his secret ambition was to become a pilot, but he soon learned that he didn't have the necessary education to fulfill his dream. Throughout his life, he will read hundreds of books on flying. Whenever there is a space launch televised, he will sit in front of the screen watching the entire event intently. He will try to get the rest of the family to join him, but we're not as interested in these things as he is. I know that when my father left the navy the first time, he had become a gifted machinist, and that he could figure out how to fix just about anything, an ability that was put to good use by the navy during the war.

The greatest gifts I get from my father are his capacity for finding joy in whatever comes his way, his engagement with life, and his voracious curiosity for discovering how things work.

I saw a movie, once, in which a character played by Humphrey Bogart said, "The world is inhabited by two classes of people. Those who are alive. And those who are afraid." My father was alive. My mother was afraid.

July 1941

My parents' honeymoon photos chronicle their auto tour through the Revolutionary War battlefields of Massachusetts, and their stay in Maine. In them, my father is relaxed and happy, grinning broadly, proud to have married such a hard-working woman, such a serious woman, such a well-dressed woman, such a faithful and loyal woman, such a beautiful woman (who, everyone says, is the spitting image of Ingrid Bergman), such a well-spoken woman (who, everyone remarks, does not seem working-class, she sounds college-educated, she is a woman who uses words well, both when she speaks and when she writes letters, her special skill, which will enrich her grandchildren's lives when they are away at college some forty years later).

In one picture my father is slender and gorgeous in his new suit, posing with one foot perched on the running board of the car he has borrowed for this first journey with his new bride. In another, he is rakish, wearing sunglasses, sitting in his bathrobe, on the wooden bench outside their rented cottage on a beach in Maine.

But there seems no gaiety, no pleasure at all in my mother in the pictures my father has taken of her on their honeymoon, though she manages a weak smile. She is perfectly attired in a polka-dotted dress with dark cummerbund as she stands stiffly next to the car, one hand resting timidly on the door handle. In wide-legged trousers and turban, posing in front of an inn, or looking up at a statue of a musket-bearing soldier, my mother does not smile, and I wonder why. Could it be that marriage is making her anxious? Or that this honeymoon journey is causing her distress? Is she as sad on her honeymoon as she seems?

Throughout their life together, my father will adore travel, and my mother will despise it, for any break from her normal routine will unnerve her. Perhaps this is why she does not smile in these pictures that he has taken of her on their honeymoon; she is too nervous. And although she will travel with him (to see my sister when she lives in Michigan, St. John, Catalina, and Oregon, and to Italy and Hawaii), I know that she would have preferred to stay at home. To keep my mother happy, our family will take fewer vacations than my father desires—driving trips to Niagara Falls, Lake George, the Finger Lakes, the St. Lawrence River, the Ausable Chasm. On these trips, my mother will hold her mouth in a tight grimace; the snapshots in our album will capture how disconsolate my sister and I are, standing in front of this or that body of water, clutching at our dolls, me not even managing the wannest of smiles, my sister, trying. On a trip to Canada, my father will try, but he will fail, to persuade my mother to climb to the top of a lock that overlooks a canal. Attired in black foul-weather gear, she will accompany us on the *Maid of the Mist*, as it makes its way under Niagara Falls, but, for the duration of the voyage, she will be miserable, and her knuckles will turn white as she clenches the boat's rail.

Most evenings, my father will sit in his easy chair and pore over one issue or another of *National Geographic*. He will imagine himself in deserts, high sierras, tropical rain forests, and Arctic wastelands. His favorite presents will be books about explorers, about naval or land battles in distant lands.

After my mother's death, when he marries again, his second wife, though she too prefers routine, tries to accommodate his Wanderlust. In less than three years, when he is in his late seventies and early eighties, they journey to France, Alaska, Bermuda, the Pacific Northwest, Florida, Virginia, Long Island. They repeat some trips he and my mother have taken. His new wife, though, is thrilled by his daring, and never tells him to come down from the tops of towers or lighthouses; instead, she trips gaily along behind him. She is content to stand next to him for hours and watch barges making their way from one lock to another; she is happy to go whale-watching in Alaska; and she goes to bed and doesn't worry when their ship encounters dangerously high seas even though, while she sleeps, she knows my father stands in the bow of the ship so he can experience the full force of the storm.

In one photo of my mother, which my father has taken of her on their honeymoon, she is oblivious to him and the camera as she sits on a bench on a rock-strewn beach in Maine, wearing sunglasses and a bathing suit with huge daisies. She is concentrating intently on a piece of writing—a letter to a friend—that she balances on her lap. She is choosing her words so carefully that her friend can picture the dueling waves that she describes. One ample thigh is crossed over the other, and her head is cocked to the side.

There are innumerable photographs my husband has taken of me throughout my life in precisely this pose, photos in which I am writing, always writing, as my mother does in this one—and I too am wearing sunglasses and a bathing suit, I too am on one beach or another, in one chair or another, ample thighs crossed, staring down at the current piece of writing in my lap, refusing to look at the camera, choosing my words carefully, so carefully, oblivious to my husband, to my children, to the world.

1 9 4 2 – 4 3

While my parents wait for my father to depart, their lives are far from serene. Of course, they worry about the war. But I am a difficult infant, I am always crying, and my mother feels distressed that she seems unable to comfort me. Her mother has died so young. What does she know about being a mother? And will she live long enough to raise me? Or will she, too, die young? These are the questions that run, always run, through my mother's mind.

My mother has read Dr. Spock, who tells parents that babies should be fed on a strict schedule, every four hours. Feeding babies "on demand" or comforting them or even picking them up to quiet them between feedings, my mother reads, will spoil them.

My mother, to both her and my detriment, complies with the doctor's directions. (My father has told me that he disagreed strongly, and that he and my mother fought about this issue constantly.)

My mother, under the best circumstances, was timid. She was always uncertain whether she was doing the right thing, so, initially, it might have been comforting for her to have such a strict set of rules given to her by an authority. This way, she won't have to make an ongoing series of decisions about what to do for me; she won't have to read my moods, to guess my needs.

"Feed the baby every four hours, even if it cries between feedings. Do not pick the baby up between feedings or you will spoil the baby. Sooner or later, the baby will learn that it will need to eat at these scheduled times." This is the gist of the routine she practices.

But I don't learn sooner, and I don't learn later. Instead, I continue to always cry. And I suspect that my mother, whose sense of her own worth is always fragile, believes that my crying means that she is an incompetent mother, and that, the more powerless she feels, the more depressed she becomes.

Feed the baby every four hours, whether or not the baby is hungrier earlier. Watch the baby while it cries. Watch the baby splutter and gasp. Hear the baby scream for hours on end. Stand by the crib and watch the baby howl. But under no circumstances comfort the baby, or hold the baby. The baby must learn to take its feedings every four hours. If you give in to the baby's whims, you will create a monster.

My mother tells me that sometimes I scared her and my father because I cried so hard that I seemed to lose my breath. When my mother reports this to the doctor during a visit, the doctor tells her that some babies are more willful than others, that it is important to stick to the regimen, and that, in time, I will learn that I am not going to get my way by crying.

But I don't learn, and I cry, my father tells me, for the better part of the first eight months of my life. Throughout these long, agonizing months, their lives are accompanied by the unending cacophony of my screaming. I howl with the blaring of the air raid sirens. I continue to howl as the sirens signal "all clear." Still my mother dutifully enacts the program she has read about. Still my parents wait it out, still they let me cry. And still they feed me on schedule, as Dr. Spock directs, every four hours.

Their household on Fourteenth Street in Hoboken near the

shipyard turns into an agony, for there is no place in our small apartment to which they can escape. They can afford only a three-room apartment (without hot water), and my crib is in their bedroom, directly next to their bed. It complicates their relationship with one another, and with their neighbors.

"The people in the building stopped looking at me on the landings," my mother tells me. "You always cried. You kept our neighbors up all night long. You kept us up all night long. You had your days and your nights all mixed up."

To my parents, I am a "difficult baby." In time, I become a difficult child, and an even more difficult adolescent.

I learn that my parents are not to be trusted, that my needs will not be met, and that if I need comfort or care, I will have to provide it for myself.

In my very earliest memories, I am hungry, always hungry. I suck the edge of a pillow or blanket for comfort. Or I take deep, shuddering breaths, trying to get enough air into my lungs. But no one comes to take care of me. No one comes to relieve my distress.

In the first pictures taken of me as an infant, I am lying on my back in my crib, looking dazed, wearing far too many clothes. Or my mother is balancing me on her lap, uneasily. There are no pictures taken of my father and me until I am eleven months old, but in the first picture of us together, he is dangling me, to my delight, in the waters of Lake Hopatcong, New Jersey, our family's favorite summertime destination. By this time, in my pictures, I am a cheerful and satisfied baby. Sitting on a blanket by the beach, my difficult infancy behind us, we seem a very contented family.

But this doesn't last for long.

Before my father leaves for the war, my mother and he devise an elaborate code so that she will know where he is. They know that his letters home will be read by censors, and that any indication of his whereabouts will be expunged. They take a map of the world, and divide it up into sections. Each section will be denoted by a reference to an item in my wardrobe—a polka-dotted dress; a pair of Mary Janes; a set of white gloves.

My father takes the time to memorize the code; my mother quizzes him on it to make sure there will be no slipups.

When he's gone, my mother will rip open his letters eagerly.

"Did Louise enjoy going to her cousin's birthday party?" he will write to her in the months to come. "And did you dress her up in her nice white eyelet dress?" By this reference to a piece of my finery, my mother will know that my father's vessel is somewhere to the east of Hawaii in the Pacific Ocean. She will move the pin with which she marks his whereabouts to that spot on the globe. As she reads or hears the news reports of battles, she can ascertain whether he is in mortal danger. She worries about him all the time.

1 9 4 3

I am fourteen months old when my father goes away to war. I have no memory of this event. In the pictures that are taken of me just after my father goes to war, I look shell-shocked. The real father whom I experienced has been wrenched away from me and will be replaced by a father whom I will know only through my imagination.

I know that children who lose caregivers at this young age can become withdrawn and there is something of that look about me. I have the feeling that I experienced the loss of him profoundly, that I mourned his loss as surely as if he had died, and, to protect myself, I locked him out of my heart.

As I grew older, I told myself stories about how we were happier without him, better off without him, about how all the mothers and children were better off without their husbands and fathers, and that all the trouble started in my life when my father came back from the war a changed man, an angry man, a man against whom I will wage my own war. But I know my stories aren't all true.

From time to time, during the war, my mother shows me a picture of my father so that I won't forget him, so that I will remember what he looks like.

He is standing in his navy uniform, on deck. Giant coils of rope are behind him. He is clowning around. His cap is pulled back on his head so that you can see his curls. He has a silly grin on his face.

Now, so many years after this picture was taken by one of his buddies, so many years after my mother received it, so many years after she has shown me this picture of my father in his bell-bottoms for the last time, before he returns home from war, I detach the tape that holds it in place, and take it out of the album, carefully, and turn it over, wondering whether, so many years ago, he wrote any message to his wife on the other side.

"Me trying to look funney," he wrote, misspelling that word, as he has misspelled it throughout his life.

I experience an almost unbearable surge of love for him, for his ability to feign happiness, to try to look "funney" for the family he has left behind, for the family that he knows he might never see again.

1 9 4 3 – 4 5

This is how I remember the war years, though I know that it is not altogether true, and, maybe that it is not true at all. Maybe this is the story that I tell myself about that time in my life because it is too difficult to remember what I really lived through.

Soon after all the husbands in our working-class apartment building in the Italian section of Hoboken, New Jersey, left for the war, the geography of the place changed so completely that life itself took on an antic, festive, tribal quality. Anarchy prevailed, and it was good.

Before, each family was locked together to carry on its claustrophobic life in its tiny three-room cell. There was a funeral-parlor-like quiet to the building, though if you listened closely enough, you could hear raised voices or howls or sometimes even smacks and screams behind closed doors. Parents and children were stuffed together in single bedrooms in the apartment's center; meals were taken at predictable hours at kitchen tables; laundry was done on Mondays in kitchen sinks with washboards (and, always, no matter how careful the mothers were, there were far too many suds, which made the rinsing a horror) and hung outside to dry on lines strung like a giant's version of cat's cradle, one of our favorite games played with string.

Before the war, hellos between women and children were exchanged, politely and briefly, as we passed one another on the stairs, or on the streets outside (the men merely grunting, or nodding in grudging recognition). Families went to church on Sundays when everyone dressed up in their best to show how affluent they wished they were, and parents trundled their children in perambulators or strollers up and down sidewalks.

But after the men left for war, the women, who were left behind to raise their families single-handedly, threw open all the doors to their apartments, and children began to clatter up and down the five flights of stairs at all hours of the day and night. Women and children wandered from one apartment into another without ceremony or invitation. Children played together on landings, and in the weedy enclosed courtyard, which was completely off limits when the men were in residence—the sound of shrieking voices was too trying for them after their long, hard day's work.

Meals were taken, picnic-style, in the strangest places—on fire escapes and parlor floors, in the cellar where my grandfather made wine at Easter, on the stoop out front, or in other people's kitchens.

Bedtime, naptime, came whenever you were tired and you fell asleep wherever you were, and not necessarily in your own bed.

Mothers ducked into churches for prayers for the safe return of their husbands on their way to and from markets or playgrounds and they generally avoided the place on Sundays.

Children, even girl children, were allowed to play hard enough to get dirty and rip their clothes. Heads, examined for lice regularly, were found to contain them more often than not; children with infestations were gathered into one kitchen or another and lined up for the gasoline shampoos that were guaranteed to kill the lice. Skating contests were held routinely on the sidewalk out front. Mr. Albini, the owner of the drugstore on the corner of Adams Street, where we now live, too old for the war, tended to our cuts and bruises with neither panic nor warnings that, next time, we should be more careful.

Gangs of women—five, six, or more—gangs of children—nine, ten, or more—would gather together in the tiny parlors of apartments during birthday parties (which seemed to occur weekly) or holiday celebrations or for no good reason at all, except for the pleasure of being together.

The children, when they think of these years, will remember the happy press of hordes of bodies in one tiny place or another; they will remember drinking juice without being afraid they will spill it; they will remember licking the icing off the cake before it was cut and not getting yelled at for it; they will remember their mothers' thinking that jumping up and down on someone else's bed was the funniest thing in the world.

After the party, the women scrunch together, happily, on the sofa, for a picture-taking session. They have had their sherry; they are very happy. They lean against one another's knees, lean into one another's bodies, caress one another's shoulders. They are all smiling; they are always smiling. They decide to have six copies of the picture made to mail to their men at war.

(In various combat zones, on battlefields and battleships throughout the world, six men will later open their letters, look at this picture, and wonder to themselves, what is going on, and why on earth these women look like they're having such a good time.)

Then, it is the children's turn to take pictures to be sent off to their darling daddies away at war. The four smallest toddlers stand in front, holding hands. The bigger children stand behind, making faces. The tiniest babies hang off their mothers' laps, their mothers aglow with female talk and companionship. One child decides to walk out of the picture; something else has captured his fancy. No mother bothers to stop him. The mothers do not care whether he appears in the picture or he doesn't.

Although the women say they miss their men (and try to teach their children to miss them as well), and although they spend hours of every day penning long accounts of their brave and unhappy lives alone to their husbands in combat, their lives, and those of their children, are far happier than either before their husbands go to war or after their husbands return home.

This is my story about the war, and, as I have said, I'm sure it can't be all true. Yet, in many photographs that my mother sends to my father during the war, she smiles broadly and she seems happy. In one, deeply tanned, hair atop her head, she is gathering me close, as she kneels next to me in the surf of a beach. In another, on a snowy winter day, in winter coat and scarf, she kneels behind me; I am all bundled up, sitting on my new sled, my Christmas present. In still another, I am perched atop her knee in an armchair in our parlor and I am wearing my sailor dress; again, she smiles (though I do not).

It may have been that she doesn't want to show her sorrow, which would demoralize him, and so she feigns her wide smiles. Or, released from wifely responsibilities for the duration of the war, she is, from time to time, truly satisfied.

* * *

At regular intervals throughout the war, my mother rounds me up, washes away my scruffiness, clothes me in my best clothes, arranges my banana curls perfectly, and poses me for a picture to be sent to my father so that he can see how well I am doing and how big I am growing.

It is Christmas Day, 1944, and I am standing in our parlor, in front of the tabletop Christmas tree, in my brand-new pajamas with feet attached to them. They are way too big for me—so big that every time I try to walk in them, I fall down. My mother has already begun what becomes a habit with her—buying clothes a size too big for me so that I'll grow into them. Under the tree, on the fern-patterned carpet, there are four Christmas presents. Under my right arm and in my right hand I clutch two more. I am neat, clean, and my hair is combed. I am as clean and neat as if I am going to church, or to a party.

Behind the chair my mother sits in, against the fern-patterned wallpaper, is a bookcase filled with a set of books, all with the same blue-gray binding. I think it is my mother who has bought them, on time, from a traveling salesman, either for decoration or to establish the image of her household as literarily minded—neither she nor my father reads them. Yet ours is the only parlor I know with books in it.

When I am little, I take one of these books down from the shelf and pretend to read it. Often, I hold the book upside down, but my mother corrects my mistake. "Don't bother Louise, she's reading," my mother jokes to a friend when I do this. Later, in my early teens, I read each of them—the first of my many self-imposed reading programs. They are a strange agglomeration: Oscar Wilde's *Picture of Dorian Grey*; Samuel Butler's *The Way of All Flesh*; Sir Walter Scott's *Ivanhoe*; Fyodor Dostoyevsky's *The Possessed*; some plays by Yeats; some poems by Frost. I am the only one in my family to read these books; I am the only one of my teenage friends to read books like these, even though I don't really understand all of what they're about.

Less than a month after Christmas, my mother fixes me up to pose again. This time, I am standing in our kitchen, dressed in my sailor dress, feet crossed, demurely, bow in my hair. On my chalkboard, my mother has penned the message HELLO DADDY. WE LOVE YOU. On the counter behind me is our new telephone.

After the photo is developed, my mother writes a message on the back of it from me to my father.

"January 17, 1945. Dear Daddy:—How do you like our telephone. Gosh mommie & I are just wishing we get a call from our favorite sailor real soon. We love you daddy. Louise."

Easter Sunday, 1945. I am standing next door to our apartment in front of Albini's Drugstore in my Easter finery. Behind me, there is a prominent display of Kotex napkins and an advertisement for a special sale on Ex-Lax. I am wearing a new baby-blue coat with a Peter Pan collar that my mother has made for me, and a wonderful hat with a feather that is drawn down onto my forehead. I am very proud to be wearing it because it is such a grown-up hat. I am wearing white gloves and carrying a little pocketbook. My socks have little embroidered hearts on them.

"It won't be long now," my mother tells me when I ask her when my father will return. "Daddy's coming home soon. And then we can all get back to normal."

August 5, 1945

When my mother heard about how we had dropped the atom bomb on Hiroshima, she wept. She did not join the people celebrating in the streets sure, now, that the war would soon be over. All she could think about was all of those innocent people dying. She was ashamed of what her country had done, even if it meant that her husband would be coming home soon. She couldn't look at the newspapers.

1 9 4 5

When the men came storming back from the war, I remember staring at them in their uniforms as they walked down the street, and I remember not liking what I saw. From as far back as I could remember, the streets of Hoboken were inhabited only by women, children, and old men. Men my father's age were a species I hadn't grown up with, didn't remember, wasn't familiar with, and now there was an invasion of these men into what I had come to consider my private territory.

Everything changed for me when the men came home from the war. It was harder to see my friends. Gangs of cheerful women and exuberant children stopped getting together for the impromptu potluck suppers that were a mainstay of the war years. All the doors in our apartment building were, again, closed. All children were cautioned to play quietly, if we were allowed to play at all, because the fathers needed their peace and quiet after what they had been through. Nighttime story hours were shortened or curtailed altogether. Snacks were forbidden. Mothers hushed their voices, and hushed us, to listen with deference and awe to whatever the men had to say. And, as if it weren't bad enough that we had lost our mothers, that our fathers had displaced us, a year or two years later, there was a spate of squalling babies who came along to complete the separation of us wartime children from our mothers. Many of us wartime children tried our best to pretend that our fathers and those babies weren't really there.

I can remember my mother telling me "Daddy is coming home soon," but I can't remember what I felt when I heard those words. I can remember her taking me to the movie theater on Washington

Street to see the newsreels showing jubilant sailors waving franti-
cally, tossing their caps into the air, as they stood on the decks of
naval vessels as they sailed past the Statue of Liberty, making their
way home, at last, to the wives and children they had left behind a
very long time before, to resume their lives.

My father is lucky to be coming home alive and unharmed. Although he was in constant danger from submarine attacks on the
way to where he was stationed, he spent the war on an island in the
Pacific at a seaplane base after the Japanese had left the island. His
job was to repair seaplanes that had been damaged in battle or ma-
neuvers. And, although he saw a man crushed by a truck, rescued a
buddy engulfed by flames from a gasoline fire, and watched a ship
transporting munitions explode, killing all four hundred men
aboard, he himself made it through the war years without injury.
He knows he has gotten off easy.

Of the several hundred daily letters that my mother wrote to my father in the evenings after she had put me to bed, none have survived. She penned them at the kitchen table, or in an easy chair in
the parlor, the blackout curtains preventing the overhead lights
from being perceived by the enemy, or sitting in her rocking chair in
a corner of the kitchen.

Of the several hundred daily letters that my father wrote to my
mother at nighttime after his duties for the day were completed,
hunched down on the beach, by the flickering light of a gasoline-
soaked pail of sand, none have survived.

Years later, when I ask my father what happened to this corre-
spondence, he tells me he doesn't know. He tells me that he thinks
my mother had saved the letters for a while—he remembers a box of
some kind, stored in the top of some closet or other—but thinks
that at one point my mother destroyed them because she didn't
think they were worth saving, that they were "only collecting dust,"
as she would have put it.

* * *

I remember staring at the rows of buttons on my father's navy pants as he walked through the door of our apartment on Adams Street in Hoboken, back into a life that would never be the same for me. I don't remember whether I thanked him for the cowrie-shell bracelet he had made for me or for the baby doll he was thoughtful enough to buy though he was in a rush to get back home, or whether I liked his presents.

But not too long after he came back home, I took to "punishing" this doll for being a very bad girl by scraping her face against the bricks of the building across the street. When I got finished torturing her, she looked as if she had been through the war herself. When I realized that I had damaged her permanently, and that it was impossible for her to heal, I mourned her lost perfection.

To appease my pain, I plastered her battered face with an elaborate assemblage of Band-Aids, and I prayed to the picture of the Sacred Heart that was tucked into the corner of my mother's chifforobe mirror, that one day I would wake up in the morning to find that the ugly scars on Patricia's face had miraculously disappeared.

I never forgave my father for coming back from the war. For looking so handsome as he came through the open door in his navy dress uniform into the apartment that was mine and my mother's, not his. For shutting the door behind him with a resounding smack. For gathering my mother (*my* mother) into his arms for a long, ardent kiss. For saying the stupidest thing he could have said to me as he handed me his presents: "My, how you've grown; what a big girl you are." For not understanding that we were better off without him. For banishing me to my grandparents' apartment (just next door but on the other side of the ocean as far as I was concerned) so that he and my mother (*my* mother) could have some private time together. I never forgave my mother for letting him invade our space, our life, our world. For putting him first. For turning our idyllic world upside down. For having a new baby so soon after he came home. (They named her Gilda, for my paternal grandmother, and for the opera heroine; her husband later nicknamed her Jill, the name we all remember her by, the name I now use when I think of her, even when she was a little girl.)

I never forgave my mother for loving him more than she loved me. I never forgave her for letting him make the rules as soon as he came home.

"No backtalk."

"No means no."

"No slouching at the dinner table."

"No playing with food."

"Bedtime at seven o'clock."

"No wise remarks."

"Do as you're told."

"Clean up that mess immediately."

"Did you hear what your mother just told you?"

"What are you, deaf? stupid? or just not listening?"

"No means no."

"Wipe that stupid look/grin/smirk off your face."

"I'll teach you a thing or two."

"My word is law."

"This is *my* house." (If this is your house, where, then, is my house?)

"How often do I have to tell you that no means no?"

I thought that the luckiest girl in the world was the girl at the end of our block whose father was killed during the last days of the war. Everyone else thought it was a disaster. Thought that she'd never recover. I knew better.

When I saw her on the street with her mother dressed all in black, to me she looked happier than those of us with fathers who had come home all safe and sound. In my imagination, I trade

59

places with her. I pretend that it is my father who hasn't come home from the war. I pretend that he has gone down in a ship at sea, down into waters populated with sharks and octopuses and eels and crabs and other sea creatures whose names I do not know.

This is how I remember I felt when my father came home, but the photos taken of my father and me after the war tell a different story.

In them, I am euphoric. I wear an expensive tweed coat and jodhpurs, a new hat with earflaps, a purse and gloves that my mother has bought for me to celebrate his return, and so that he can see me looking my best.

He kneels behind me, wearing his new Borsolino hat. He has pulled me close to him, and I am smiling more broadly than in any of the pictures my mother has taken of me during the war years.

My daddy is home.

Perhaps I really did miss him. Perhaps I was angry with him for leaving me to go to war. Perhaps it was he that I wanted, and not my mother. Perhaps his gaiety had protected me from my mother's sorrow, and when he was away I saw my mother slip away into that other place she inhabited, a place of deep and unrelenting sorrow where there was no room for laughter or song, taking her from me as the war had taken my father. Perhaps I learned how to be happy from him; perhaps I could not be truly happy unless he was near.

Soon after my father came home, I started to make him pay.

On a sunny day, my mother decided that it would be a good idea for my father to take me to a playground that was some distance away from our apartment, so that we could have some fun together, so that we could get reacquainted, and so that she could get the apartment "back to normal" and have some time to herself.

During my father's absence, when my mother and I traversed this route, it could take us half an hour, or half a day, depending upon the number of friends we bumped into on the way, upon what stoop engaged my interest enough for me to want to climb its steps so that I could inspect it, upon whether a sudden urge on my part for a piece of cheese or mortadella necessitated a stop at Fiore's. When my father was away, "going to the park" was a process that my mother and I engaged in. What happened along the way was sometimes more important than getting there. Many days, we abandoned our destination entirely, if Argie, my mother's friend down the block, invited us in for cakes and milk, if the weather was cooler than my mother imagined, if I had forgotten to go to the bathroom.

But, to my father, our going to the park, I'm sure, meant something completely different. My mother had given us our assignment, our mission, as it were. We were to a) go to the park together, b) have fun, and c) get to know one another again. The mission could not be considered a success unless we successfully accomplished each of our three subtasks. After years of executing orders so well that he returned home from war without a scratch on him, my father probably believed that this was a simple mission, that it would present him with no problems, that he would complete it successfully and be rewarded with my mother's praise and gratitude and with my love.

What my father didn't count on was that, unlike combat-ready soldiers and sailors, I wasn't used to taking orders. I was used to getting my way, doing what I wanted, when I wanted.

As I recall, the trouble started soon after we left the apartment, while we were still on our own stoop. I wanted another drink of water, something that never presented a problem to my mother, who waited downstairs while she let me toddle up the stairs by myself into my grandmother's apartment.

My father, though, thought it was a dangerous threat to our park-going mission to allow me to retrace my steps so soon. The park was our destination, and we were to get there as quickly, as efficiently, and with as few casualties as possible. He thought that it showed a serious lack of discipline on my part, and that this bad behavior had to be stopped before it undermined our mission completely.

"No," he said. "You can have a drink when we get to the park."

"But I'm thirsty now, I want a drink of water now," I responded, stating what I thought should be perfectly obvious to my father, and turned to reenter our building. It seemed impossible to me that an adult with any sense could deny me my request. Why should I wait for hours to slake my thirst when water was so close by, a few flights of stairs away.

I felt my father's hands around my waist, and, before I knew what was happening, he had picked me up as if I were a baby (an insult to my pride), and he was carrying me down the stairs.

"No," he repeated. "You can have a drink of water when we get to the park."

"But I need a drink of water now," I persisted, throwing the words over my shoulder at him, knowing that the word "need" conveyed an urgency that the word "want" did not, and that whenever the word "want" failed, you moved on to "need" before resorting to the last-ditch effort of "have to have."

"No," he repeated in my ear, as I squirmed, trying to wriggle free. "You can have a drink of water when we get to the park."

"But I have to have a drink of water now," I countered.

"No," he insisted. "You can have a drink of water when we get to the park. No means no." By now he was shouting. He is surprised at how headstrong, spoiled rotten, and needful of training and discipline I have become during his absence.

We aren't more than a few feet away from our front door, more than a few moments into our time together, when I know that I am in dangerous territory. This place with my father isn't a place I have been, isn't a place I want to be.

I stiffen, I wail, I wave my arms, I kick my feet. I want him to put me down, let me have my way, let me have my water, let me return to the soothing, comforting arms of my mother, my grandparents. I don't want to be with him. I want him to go away.

He retaliates. I have overstepped my boundaries, challenged his authority, sabotaged his mission. I have to be held accountable, reprimanded, punished.

We haven't even made it to the park, and we have already declared war, we are already enemies.

My favorite photograph from the wartime years.

I am sitting on my mother's lap as she sits in the rocking chair in our kitchen, reading to me. During the years my father is away, my mother reads to me every night before I go to bed. Before she reads to me, she washes me at the sink in the kitchen (we have no tub or shower and we share a toilet with my grandparents who live next door), heating up the hot water for my bath on the stovetop. I am still small enough to crouch in the deep sink for my bath. After, she dries me, puts on my nightie and my bathrobe, and sits me in the rocking chair to look at a book while she prepares herself for bed. At three years old, I can already pick out a few words. By four, I'll be reading.

When my mother is dressed in her bathrobe with its pattern of enormous pink and red cabbage roses on a blue ground, she takes the book that she and I have borrowed from the local library. I climb onto her lap and lean back into her. These are the best times that I have with my mother. The formality of reading allows her to interact with me without uncertainty and anxiety. Much of the time, her voice is strong and clear, changing in timbre and pitch to suit the meaning. Sometimes, though, she reads in a monotone; her thoughts are someplace else.

Because she reads to me so frequently, and because she runs her finger under the words as she reads them to me, I soon begin to associate the letters with the sounds my mother makes as she reads. When my father comes home from the war, I can read by myself, although I continue to climb onto my mother's lap for my nightly story. My favorite story is *The Little Engine That Could*, which I like so much that my mother buys me my own copy. I'm not sure whether she reads this story of the tiny female steam engine's triumph over self-doubt into a burgeoning self-assurance for her benefit or for mine. I know I profit from its pep talk of "I think I can, I think I can, I think I can," so different from my mother's chronic "Be careful."

Teaching me to read is the greatest gift my mother gives me as a very young child. (When I am older, she and my grandmother will teach me a love of handiwork—how to sew and how to knit.) Reading becomes my greatest pleasure in life; continues to be my greatest pleasure. By nine or ten o'clock each night, even now, I climb into my nightgown and crawl into my bed to read—a nightly habit that started during the war years when my mother read to me in her rocking chair. Then, as now, I am never so happy as when I am being read to, as when I am reading. Every act of reading, a journey back to my mother's arms.

My favorite sounds from the war years.

The slap of playing cards against the card table as the old men play pinochle outside in their undershirts on sweltering summer afternoons.

The flap of wet sheets hanging in the window in the breeze of a torrid summer night—a primitive form of air conditioning.

The sound of a mother singing a lullaby to her baby floating into our kitchen from across the courtyard.

My favorite memory from the war years.

My mother, framed in the kitchen window of our apartment, in the warm light of a summer evening, is singing as she takes the washing off the line. She has protected her hair from the work of the day by tying a scarf around her head.

I am in the courtyard below, still playing. I am digging in the claylike soil at the edges of the scruffy yard with an old beat-up spoon that she has given me. I am pretending that I am creating a beautiful garden. Tiny pebbles are the seeds that I am planting. When I hear my mother singing, I stop my work to look up at her. She is singing her favorite song, one that she sings to me sometimes to ease me off to sleep. It is a peculiar lullaby.

"Show me the way to go home," she sings, "I'm tired and I want to go to bed/I had a little drink about an hour ago/And it went right to my head./No matter where I roam/On land or sea or foam/You will always hear me singing this song/Show me the way to go home."

Her voice is loud, clear, strong. It echoes off the walls of the other apartment buildings. When she finishes, she pauses a minute or two before beginning the song again. In the hiatus between her songs, I can hear the clanging of pots and pans as some other mothers begin their evening's meal.

When my mother is finished with her work, she looks down at me and asks if I'm hungry. I tell her that I am. She tells me that dinner won't be ready for a while, so she'll get me something to nibble on.

She lowers a little basket down to me on a rope. In the basket, there is a treat. A cookie. Some warm lemonade to drink.

When I'm finished, I shout out a loud "Mommy." She comes back to the window, and hauls the basket back inside.

She disappears into the kitchen.

I continue with my planting.

If I listen hard enough, I can hear my mother going about her work. I have never been, will never be, happier.

Finding My Way

WHEN MY MOTHER meets someone new, she always manages to interject into the conversation the amazing fact that I started school when I was only four years old.

"Louise was only four years old when she started first grade in 1947," my mother boasts, as soon as the other mother crows about one of her child's accomplishments.

"Because she knew how to read," my mother continues. "She taught herself how to read. Before I knew what was happening, she could pick up anything at all, and read it without any help from me. And if there wasn't a book around the apartment to read, she would read the back of the cereal box. Anything. Anything at all."

My mother explains to her by-now-reluctant audience how she took me over to Sacred Heart Academy the summer before I started school, how the nuns gave me a reading test, a hard one, how they told her that, because I seemed old for my age, I was ready to start school, and they would accept me into the first grade.

The rest of her summer is taken up with making the blue serge uniforms and white cotton blouses that are required wear at Sacred Heart. Though sewing them is hard work (especially the blouses with their darts and puffy, set-in sleeves), my mother says she thinks that wearing uniforms is a very good idea because it makes everyone seem the same so that, during school hours, the rich kids and the poor kids will all look similar, and that means no one will get preferential treatment. This is what's so good about Catholic schools, she maintains, though she is no devout believer in the faith into which both she and my father have been baptized, into which they baptize my sister and me.

My mother is probably relieved that she no longer feels she needs to keep me in fashion as she did during the war years. Once I enter first grade, my mother's concern for presenting me to the world beautifully dressed subsides and soon vanishes. My sister, she dresses in my or my cousins' worn hand-me-downs. And through the years, she herself stops dressing in the latest, most sophisticated clothes; by the end of her life, it becomes a "chore" for her to enter a store to buy anything. "Too many choices," she tells us. "I get all confused."

Once there are four of us, she worries about spending money, and she tries to save as much as she can for that house in the suburbs that she and my father dream of one day buying. She will buy what's cheapest on a clothes rack, even if she doesn't much like it, even if it doesn't look all that good on her and, as my sister and I get older, she will force us to do the same. When we argue with her, she always tells us "A penny saved is a penny earned." But the truth is that she has enough money to spend; she just can't bring herself to treat herself well, and she acts as if she doesn't deserve anything beautiful, anything expensive. By the end of her life, though she always looks nice when she dresses, she wears what she calls "garbage" around the house, and she possesses only one very good and conservative suit (though in an unusual shade of pink), the suit that I choose for her burial.

My mother's story about my starting school at four is something of an exaggeration. Although it is literally true that I start school when I am four, I turn five just a few weeks later, and so it would have been more accurate if my mother had said that I was nearly five years old when I started first grade. And although I have learned to read, in my recollection, I do not learn by myself; it is my mother who teaches me. But my mother's story, her pride in describing my precocity, suggests that she had secret aspirations for me that she never openly shared. Perhaps she dreamed that I could fulfill her thwarted ambition of one day attending college, of one day becoming a writer.

My mother stands behind me while I sit on top of the telephone book at the kitchen table, "writing." I am about three, and I haven't learned how to write, really. But my mother gives me blank sheets of paper and a pencil, and I fill them with seismic shocks and waves of meaning. I am very serious. I am writing.

Years later, she tells me that when she asks me what I am doing, I reply that I am making a story.

"What's the story about?" she asks.

"I don't know," I answer, but I suspect I mean to say "I can't tell."

"When will you know?" she asks.

"When I'm finished," I answer.

"When will you be finished?" she asks.

"Yesterday," I answer.

"You mean 'tomorrow'?" she asks. I often say "yesterday" when I mean "tomorrow" and "tomorrow" when I mean "tomorrow." This confuses my mother. Time is something I haven't yet figured out. "Yesterday" and "tomorrow" are all the same to me.

* * *

That I start school when I am four years old becomes an important family story that sticks, that is told through the years, that grows true with its repetition. It means that, despite my difficult infancy, despite my difficult early childhood after my father comes home from the war, when I give my parents what seems like nothing but trouble, I have turned out all right, and I might turn out all right in the end.

The story signals that I am special. It differentiates me in my paternal grandparents' eyes from my cousins (and from my sister), none of whom, they believe, can match my intellectual accomplishments, no matter how hard they try. And my cousins will be reminded of this at every family gathering.

One Easter, my grandmother cooks a lamb's head as a special treat for the family dinner. With great ceremony, my grandfather plucks the lamb's eye out from its socket, and gives it to me to eat. I shake my head no, refusing. "You have to eat it," my father says, "it's an honor; it's for good luck." But I refuse my grandfather's offering; I can't imagine putting such an offensive thing inside my mouth, much less swallowing it. My grandfather shrugs his shoulders, pops the lamb's eye into his mouth, and pats his stomach, as if to say "Delicious," and we all laugh.

I don't know why I am singled out in this way. Nor do I know whether I would have been singled out in this way despite my accomplishments, if my father wasn't my grandparents' only son, or if I had an older brother or cousin, for, in Italian-American families, males usually get the best treatment. But in many Italian-American families, one child is often selected by family elders to carry all the hopes for success of the family. For whatever reasons, in my family, I am that child.

What this means, for me, is that my cousins treat me, not as one of a gang of eight tightly knit, rambunctious, mischievous youngsters, but as someone around whom they feel uneasy.

There I am in a family picture taken on Easter Sunday, standing off to one side, separated from the rest of them, posing like the models I have seen in magazines, one foot in front of the other, clutching at my pocketbook in front of me, looking as I always look, far too old for my years.

"Why can't the rest of you be like Louise," my grandparents harangue my cousins, in Italian.

"Louise is the smartest, she's going to go far," my grandmother says to the others, as she hands me an extra five dollars for making the honor roll.

As the years pass, and I grow older, I become my paternal grandfather's favorite companion at the Brooklyn Dodger games he frequents and the Metropolitan Opera's performances he attends regularly. He never takes my grandmother or my sister or my cousins to either.

At the Met, he can afford only standing room, but he implores an usher to find me an empty seat, I am too young to stand for so long a time. During intermission, he asks me what I think of the performance, reminisces, with his cronies, about Caruso, for my benefit. At the ballgames, he buys me hot dogs, and loves that I remember the batting averages, the RBIs of my favorite players, and that I can predict, more accurately than he can, whether a player will bunt.

When I am fifteen, in a wildly romantic phase, he takes me to the Met to see Samuel Barber's Pulitzer prize–winning opera, *Vanessa*. My grandfather and I disagree vehemently about its merits to the amusement of the standing room regulars. He doesn't like any opera but Italian opera. Thinks you have to be Italian to compose opera, to conduct opera, to sing opera, even to appreciate opera. But I have found the music of the American opera *Vanessa* deeply haunting. To my grandfather's chagrin, I try to hum the aria "Do Not Utter a Word" on the bus ride back to New Jersey. I think he thinks I am a traitor. *Vanessa* is the last opera I remember seeing with him.

When I start school in September 1947, when I am nearly five years old, emotionally I am not ready for school, though the nuns think I am. In public, I put on a good show; alone, I am afraid, I am always afraid, but I don't share my fears with my mother, who herself seems as afraid as I often feel.

During the first few days at school, at lunch, which is taken at long tables in the school basement, its frosted windows letting in a weak light, I sit underneath the table with my lunchbox open between my knees, trying to swallow my food through huge sobs I try to stifle in hopes that no one will hear me. No one does. No one notices I am there.

That my mother packs me off for a full day when I am so little suggests to me now that, raised in the absence of my father, and lavished with her attention and that of my grandparents, I have grown to be a very demanding child and so she wants some time away from me as soon as she can manage it. That, and she is having a hard time raising both my sister (born the previous February) and me and that she wants me out of the cramped apartment for the better part of the day.

Our tiny apartment, it is true, is barely suited for two people, and certainly not for four. There is absolutely no privacy. No doors separating the kitchen from the bedroom, or the bedroom from the parlor.

We all wash up, standing in front of the kitchen sink, in full view of everyone else. There is no bathtub, no shower.

Five of us share the toilet that is in a cubicle between two apartments, and, unless you remember to lock both doors, someone inevitably opens one when you are inside, and, when you do remember, someone knocks on the door, urgently needing their

VERTIGO

turn. No matter how fastidiously my mother or my grandmother cleans, the room always smells of someone's shit.

I am too short to reach the chain to flush. I am humiliated that I have to fetch a grown-up to pull the cord to dispose of my waste, but I get yelled at if I don't or if I forget. And I won't, I won't balance on the edges of the toilet seat so I can do it myself. Once, I had managed this. But the fear of falling into the toilet stops me from trying it a second time.

My parents, my sister, and I sleep in the same bedroom. My sister's crib, my parents' double bed, and my cot are shoved so close together that there is no room at all between my cot and my parents' bed, and barely enough room between my sister's crib and my parents' bed for them to squeeze by when it is time for them to go to sleep.

When my sister awakens in the night, she wakes us all. When I awaken in the night with a nightmare, which happens frequently, I wake everyone else.

And there is the sound of my parents' lovemaking going on so close to me, too close.

When I am awakened by their stifled moans, or by the movement of their bed, I turn my back to them, feigning a profound but restless sleep, and, to distract myself, I concentrate on the holy picture of the Sacred Heart of Jesus tucked into the corner of my mother's mirror, illuminated by the dim glow of the nightlight at the foot of my cot.

Jesus is holding his bleeding heart out in front of him on an outstretched gold plate. The sounds and smells and movements of my parents' sex, and the sight of the Sacred Heart of Jesus, bleeding on a plate, commingle.

I know that my parents' nearness upsets me because, one night, in the middle of the night, long after I am toilet-trained, I shit in my cot, which perplexes my mother and my father as they tend to me and the stinking mess I have expelled.

I remember the delight I take in the attention I am getting, and in interrupting them. And the need for some kind of release, any kind of release, as if there is too much inside me. Too much that I have seen, too much that I have heard, too much that I have felt, and too too much that has happened.

Though I grow to love school in time, initially, I hate it because I think that my mother is trying to get rid of me. I am jealous that she and my sister will be alone all day, and I wait impatiently for the day to end, so I can see my mother again.

I imagine that, while I am at school, my mother and sister are spending the day going to the playground, playing peek-a-boo, and visiting other kids on the block, as my mother and I did during the war years. But I know now that this wasn't happening. My mother has far too much work to do to play games with my sister, to give her much attention at all.

She rises early to prepare breakfast. She dresses me and my sister and walks me to school. The walk to my school and back takes her over an hour. Then she starts her day's work. The washing alone takes her hours and hours. She does it all—my sister's diapers and clothes, my father's work clothes, which he changes daily, my blouse, socks, and underclothes—each day, by hand, on a washboard, in the kitchen sink. She heats the water on the stove. Leans out the window to hang the clothes to dry. Heats the iron on the stove. Starches and presses the clothes. Then, there is the cooking and cleaning. Everything she buys for us to eat, she has to cart up four flights of stairs; she has to shop every day, for our tiny kitchen has no pantry.

My mother now works hard. Too hard to enjoy my sister, too hard to be very much of a mother to her. My sister doesn't smile very much. She spends much of her day in the crib, trying to amuse herself with the toys my mother provides, so that my mother can get her day's work done before she picks me up from school.

"When Jill was a baby," my mother will later say, "she never smiled at all." And the proof is there, in the pictures of her in infancy. Eyes downcast; baby lips pulled into a frown; dull, vacant stare. I had gotten the best, the most my mother could give. My mother didn't have enough left over to give my sister.

What I like about school is being away from my mother and grandmother's battles, the vicious shouting matches between them that now erupt frequently when my father and grandfather are not there. For, by now, my mother and grandmother are enemies; they are fighting all the time. My grandmother insists that my mother shows her no respect, that she wants her dead; my mother insists that my grandmother has never loved her, never treated her as kin. When they fight, their eyes lock, their backs arch, like birds who have been trained to peck one another to death. When my mother and grandmother fight, they pay no attention to me, to Jill. We could hurt ourselves, or disappear, they wouldn't notice. Often, my mother breaks things, or hurts herself as they argue. She picks up the iron the wrong way and burns her hand. Pours the water for the washing, carelessly, and scalds herself. When this happens, she bursts into agonized cries. When, at last, one of their fights ends, it is impossible to get my mother's attention. A question, a request, provokes either no response or an angry one.

However many problems might face me in school, there are times, like when all the children are bent over their work, that it is blessedly peaceful and quiet, nothing like the maelstrom I've left behind at home. The maelstrom against which my sister grows to be a toddler.

In time, because it is such a safe, quiet place for me, I grow to love the order, the rhythm, the regularity, and predictability of the school day, its hours demarcated into periods of time devoted to penmanship, reading, spelling, arithmetic, catechism, geography. Even now, I like to plan my day in blocks of time devoted to different subjects and tasks, replicating, for comfort, this pattern that I found such a soothing respite from the whirlwind of my mother and grandmother's fights that leave my mother red in the face and in tears and unable to care for me and my sister, my grandmother, angry and distant, me, confused, because my grandmother is always kind to me when my parents are not, and my sister, withdrawn. And, during the early, hard times of my marriage, before I am able to snip away the worst things from my past, when my husband and I fight as viciously as my mother and grandmother had, I retreat then, too, to the sanctity and order of my work day.

In the Catholic grammar school that I attended, the first and second graders were taught by the same nun and were schooled in the same room. The first graders were ranged alphabetically in rows to the teacher's right; the second graders, to the teacher's left. While the first graders were receiving instruction (in spelling, math, geography, reading, or catechism), the second graders did work in their workbooks. While the second graders received instruction, the first graders did work in their workbooks. The nun who taught us (whose name I have by now forgotten but whom I will refer to by the name Sister Mary) made it a habit to write on the board directly in front of the first graders when she instructed them, and to move to the other side of the blackboard to write on the board directly in front of the second graders when she instructed them.

But because my last name began with an "S," my assigned desk was all the way in the back of the room, and right next to the first row of second graders. This meant that I couldn't see the first-grade work on the board because I was the shortest child in the class, also because we were required to "sit up straight" (no leaning to the right or left even if it was the only way we could see what was being written on the blackboard). But I could see the second-grade work on the board. Because the first graders were learning how to read and write, and I already knew how to read and write, I could com-

plete the assignments in my workbooks quickly. Which gave me
time to attend to Sister Mary teaching the second grade and learn
their lessons as well.

On the first day of school, after Sister Mary settled us into our assigned places, she asked a red-headed girl in the second grade with
the strange name of Miranda Panda to come up to the front of the
classroom for a demonstration to which we should all pay careful
attention. Miranda Panda was going to show us something that, if
we were good pupils, we would be able to do by the end of the first
grade.

I hated Miranda immediately. I hated her because I was petri-
fied and because she looked so cocky and sure of herself, as she
flounced to the front of the class. I hated her because she was in the
second grade and I was in the first. I hated her because she wore
long red banana curls and a big bow in her hair. I hated her because
she was rich and lived in a big brownstone up near Stevens Institute
of Technology. I hated her because she had such a stupid name and
yet no one dared make fun of her. Miranda Panda was someone
special, someone not to be trifled with.

I had already been laughed at for my long, unpronounceable
Italian last name (which contained twelve letters in all, seven conso-
nants and five vowels) both in the school yard when kids asked me
who I was, and in the classroom when Sister Mary called the roll. I
had already heard the insults that would become standard fare
throughout my years of schooling.

"Hey, what kind of name is that?" from the non-Italians.

"Your name is bigger than you are" from the bigger kids.

Or the far more commonplace, "That's gotta be a Wop name;
who else but a Wop would have a name like that."

I had defended my name to a slovenly boy I instantly despised
with a series of remarks uttered with all the disdain that a nearly

five-year-old girl can muster when she wants to be dismissive, contemptuous, and superior.

"I already know how to spell my last name," I told him, my nose pointed high in the air. "My mother says that if I can learn how to spell my last name, there isn't anything I can't learn. I already know how to read and write. And I know all the names of the states in the United States and their capitals. What do you know? You don't look like you know anything."

As the dirty little boy backed off, I knew that I had won. I had used the weapon of words, the only ones in my arsenal, but they were already considerable, and I had already used them in dizzying volleys against my father, who wasn't ever as quick-witted in that regard as I was. I was a girl, too young for school, very small for my age, and working-class, and Italian. In the eyes of the world, I wasn't worth much, and wouldn't amount to anything. But my father had already told me that I had a "big mouth," a penchant for "back talk," and that, whenever we argued (which was often), I needed to have the last word. He said it in a way that was critical, but also admiring. I did have a big mouth; I expressed my opinions whether they were wanted or not; I always talked back if someone said something that I regarded as wrong, or stupid, despite the consequences; I never started talking unless I was sure I had something to say, and I never stopped talking until I had proven my point and gotten the other person to agree with me, or to give up in despair.

I had refined these skills in the ongoing conversations I had with my mother, her women friends, and my friends' mothers during the war. With no men to talk to, with no one but us children to talk to, these women conversed with us as if we were their equals. They answered our "why" questions without interruption whenever we asked them. And they asked us for our opinions. My mother asked me which dress I preferred to wear, and what I wanted for dinner, and when I wanted to eat, and which book I wanted to hear read, and if I wanted to go to Long Island to visit our relatives. My mother and my friends' mothers asked us what we had been doing outside in the courtyard while we were playing, and they listened to us as we told them our very long-winded stories. With the men away at war, and no television to entertain or distract them, these women regarded their children as a source of companionship and entertainment, and engaging conversation became a high priority.

By the time Miranda Panda made it to the front of the room to show the class the special thing she had learned the year before on that first day of school, I had declared her the enemy. What I felt as she stood there, waiting for further instructions from Sister Mary, was a moment of envy. Within seconds, though, I felt a keen competition. Miranda Panda had what I wanted: everyone's attention. I decided that it was very important that I beat her.

"Now, boys and girls in the first grade," Sister Mary intoned, "Miranda Panda will demonstrate for you the wonderful kinds of things you will be learning this year. How many of you know your alphabet?"

A flurry of hands from the more eager, more intelligent first graders. I kept my hands folded on my desk. Take the enemy by surprise. Don't let them know what you know.

"Boys and girls," Sister Mary gushed, with much pride in her voice, "Miranda Panda will now recite the alphabet for you, but she will recite it *backwards*."

Sister Mary stepped aside. Miranda Panda stepped forward, made a sign of the cross, took a deep breath, and began.

"Z, Y, X, W, V, U, T, S . . ."

When Miranda Panda got to the letter "R," I stopped listening. My mother had told me that I was going to learn wonderful and important and interesting things in the first grade. Sister Mary had told me that I was going to learn wonderful and important and interesting things in the first grade. And here was a display of the wonderful and important and interesting things I was slated to learn.

After Miranda was finished, Sister Mary beamed at the class. "Now, class," she asked, "what have you learned?" And then, answering her own question, she said, "When you reach second grade, you'll know the alphabet so well, you'll be able to recite it *backwards*, just like Miranda Panda."

Miranda Panda, very pleased with herself, flounced back to her seat. I noticed that she wore ruffled socks in defiance of the Academy's strict orders that we wear only socks that were white and plain and without adornment. Yet Sister Mary had singled Miranda out as special though she broke the rules. I hated her. Whatever else Sister Mary wanted us to learn from Miranda Panda, when she settled herself smugly into her seat on the second-grade side of the classroom, I had already learned that there were insiders and there were outsiders and that it was all right for some people to break the rules.

"Now, class," Sister Mary said, "are there any questions?"

I waited a few moments, sure that every child in the first grade wanted to ask the same question I wanted to ask, but although some children moved about in their seats, no one raised a hand. I did not yet know that in certain circumstances the question "Are there any questions?" uttered by a nun or a teacher standing in front of a room did not mean "Are there any questions?" but "How can there be any questions?"

I waited a bit longer, but when it seemed that no one was going to ask my question, I shot up my hand.

Sister Mary, of course, could not yet remember my name, and so she acknowledged me with a little nod of her head.

"Sister Mary, Sister Mary," I began, having been instructed in the niceties of addressing nuns by my mother. ("You must always be very polite to the nuns. You must always use the word 'Sister' before their names.") "But *why* is it important to know the letters of the alphabet backwards as well as forward?"

I had asked the obvious, forbidden, but important question to which I wanted an honest answer, but it seemed to mock and deride what had come before.

Sister Mary paused to consider her response. And, of course, there was no legitimate answer that she could make to this question and I knew it.

I wasn't easily fooled. When I asked my question, I had already decided that reciting the alphabet backwards wasn't anything important, wasn't anything you could use, wasn't anything you had to know. It was simply a bravura display of useless knowledge. My father, a working-class utilitarian if ever there was one, repeatedly asked me, "But what good will it do you to know that? But what good will it do you to do that?" It was not just enough to know something or do something; you had to do something worthwhile with what you learned, with what you knew. His pragmatic attitude toward learning was something I had already come to share.

The truth was, I already knew the response I wanted from Sister Mary. I wanted her to admit that knowing the alphabet backwards wasn't important at all. In my mind, it was the only truly honest answer to my question. And Sister Mary couldn't answer in that way without surrendering her authority, which, of course, she wasn't prepared to do.

I do not now remember the answer that Sister Mary made to my question, if she answered it at all. But I do remember not being allowed to go to the bathroom later the same day when the need to pee was so urgent that I felt sure I would wet my pants. And I remember that Sister Mary, later in the day, after lunch, took a giant piece of Scotch tape and taped my mouth shut when she caught me asking the boy seated next to me to tell me what had been written on the blackboard because I was too short to see over the head of the tall boy seated in front of me. And Sister Mary telling me that the Scotch tape would remind me, if I could not remind myself, that, in her classroom, there was to be no whispering at any time, and no talking unless you were called upon to answer a question.

As I sat in my seat, tape over my mouth, eyes stinging with tears, staring at the birthmark on the thumb of my left hand to steady myself, I vowed that whatever else I might learn in the first grade, no matter what the cost, I would never, ever, learn how to say the letters of the alphabet backwards. I had decided that if that's what it took to gain recognition from Sister Mary, then I would forgo it. But I also decided that I would beat Miranda Panda at the game of knowledge, but that I wouldn't do it her way. And, by the end of my first year at Sacred Heart Academy, I had beaten her. I had been selected to crown the Blessed Virgin Mary during the school's May pageant.

The nuns told us that many factors were considered in selecting the person who would crown the Virgin. First, she had to have earned good grades; second, she had to have been a model student. I had been selected, Sister Mary told the class, because I had taken it upon myself to complete the work for the second grade while I was still in the first grade; also because I was the shortest girl in the first grade and it would look very nice if I led the procession.

Before the crowning, the girls in both classes spent days decorating the classroom with blue and white crepe paper streamers, preparing the shrine of the Blessed Virgin Mary in the small garden in back of the school, decking the statue with flowers, and learning to sing "O Mary we crown thee with blossoms today/Queen of the Angels, Queen of the May." My mother sewed me a baby-blue eyelet gown with puffed sleeves and a bow that tied in front.

On the day of the crowning, the nuns gave all of us girls crowns of flowers to wear in our hair. And I was given a special tiger lily to hold for the procession. My father, very proud of me, took off a day's work, and put on his best suit to come see me.

In the picture that my father has taken of us girls standing in front of the statue of the Blessed Virgin, I am in the center, in front of the statue. Miranda Panda stands to my right, wearing a store-bought dress, her hair arranged in perfect ringlets. And though the picture is in black and white, you can see that she is wearing a trace of lipstick. She is richer than I, and older and taller, but I am smarter than she is and I know it, and I have proven it, and you can see the satisfaction on my face. And it has taken me less than a year to get what I want—Sister Mary singling me out for special merit, as she had singled out Miranda Panda on my first day at school.

In the years that I attend Catholic grammar school, in Hoboken and, later, in Ridgefield, New Jersey, after we move there, the lessons that I learn from the nuns are prodigious. They go beyond book learning. They will stay with me for a lifetime, long after I renounce my faith. They will inform my intellectual work.

I learn to see life as a titanic moral struggle between good and evil; I learn that we are all God's children; I learn the importance of neatness, order, discipline, rigor, practice, and routine in learning. The virtue of work. The spiritual, soulful nature of work. That work is another form of prayer. That you must teach others what you have learned. That you teach, too, by example. That there is beauty in the structure of a well-balanced sentence. That language must be used carefully, correctly, and precisely. I learn about the beauty of austerity and renunciation. That you are important, not for what you have, but for what you are, and for what you make of yourself. That human beings can perfect themselves but that they must constantly fight the allure of evil. That you should treat others as you wish to be treated. That generosity is a greater good than selfishness. I learn the value of intuition as a way of knowing. I learn the importance of pageantry and ceremony; I learn that having flowers nearby enriches the spirit and the soul. And that taking care of your spirit and your soul is as important as taking care of your body.

And as one nun after another after another rewarded us by reading to us after a hard day in the first and second grades, and throughout the rest of my grammar school years, I learned to listen to stories and to respect them. Although I do not now remember the names of any of these books that were read to me throughout the years, I remember that they were grown-up books, gargantuan books, that these nuns read, filled with action, with the pulse of history, or with love and passion (though never with any sex as I recall). I learn to see reading as a privilege and pleasure, and to glean the lessons to be learned from those who had taken the time to write beautifully, powerfully, and well.

But, at first, school isn't such a welcome part of my life, as it becomes in time, and, at first, I can't wait for the school day to be over.

I sit anxiously outside school on the stone steps that lead up to the huge wooden front door, waiting for my mother to pick me up, balancing, on my knees, all my books (as usual, I have much homework), and my empty lunch pail (as usual, the milk from my leaky thermos has befouled the yellow cheese sandwich, which I detest and wouldn't have eaten anyway, and I have thrown the soppy mess away). I keep my possessions close to me because I am afraid that the bigger children will snatch at them and take them from me.

I guard my blue loose-leaf binder most carefully; in it is all my homework, neatly separated by tab inserts into subjects. If you do excellent work, you get a gold star. If you do very good work, you get a red star. If you do good work, you get a blue star. If you do average work or poor work or unacceptable work (work that isn't done according to the rules), you get no star at all. Everything you do is judged and ranked and marked. And you never get a star for making an effort. (One boy, transferred from public school, asks this question.) Making an effort is expected, not rewarded.

There is a concrete statue of the Sacred Heart of Jesus (Jesus, his hand on his heart, which is circled with a crown of thorns) in the front of the school. As I await my mother, I count the times that a pigeon lands on Jesus' head. It's something that amuses me, though I know it shouldn't. When Sister Mary has heard some boys laughing at this, she has said, "Even pigeons are God's children; Jesus welcomes them to him, just as he welcomes you." Welcome or not, they make a mess, and at the beginning of the year, I watched a younger nun, sleeves rolled above her elbows, scrubbing down the statue of Jesus, making sure that he is clean. I wait to catch a glimpse of my mother coming down Washington Street, pushing my sister in her sand-colored wicker stroller. I wait to see, by the look on my mother's face, whether it has been a good or a bad day.

If my mother is a few minutes late, I become panicky, sure that she has forgotten me, sure that she has died on the way, or been captured and taken somewhere, sure that I will never see her again.

Once, when she is very late, I decide that she isn't coming, that something has happened to her, and so, dizzy and disoriented, I run all the way home. Across Washington Street, and down and left and right and down and across many, many blocks. I stop, along the way, to pick up the books and belongings that I keep dropping in my haste. Once, my looseleaf opens, and I have to put all the pages back.

It is a very long distance for a very little girl to travel, even if she has a mother beside her. And I have no mother beside me.

When I arrive at our apartment, and buzz and buzz and buzz and no one answers, I buzz my grandparents to be let in and then run up the stairs and knock and knock on my grandmother's door, only to be told that my mother has left to pick me up.

And out the door and down the stairs I fly in a panic before my grandmother can stop me, to find my mother, who, by now, has arrived at my school to find me not there. Suspecting that I have tried to walk home by myself, not believing I can find my way home alone, but not knowing what else to do, she is returning home, as quickly as she can push my sister along, but by a way different from our usual way home. She is afraid I've been kidnapped, gotten lost, been taken to the hospital. She was late. It's all her fault.

And so, we miss each other again.

When my mother finally finds me around the corner from where we live, in front of Our Lady of Grace Church, she is exhausted. She kneels down and gathers me to her, sobbing and shaking in her terror at what might have happened to me.

But I am strangely calm. My earlier fear has dissipated. A bond between us has snapped, and, though I am tired and tearful, I feel good.

"What did you learn today?" my mother asks me, after she composes herself, trying to impress upon me a lesson she believes I must understand.

She expects, I think, that I will say that I have learned to wait for her patiently on the school steps even if she is late, that she will always come to get me, and that I should never again leave school until she has come for me.

"I learned that I can find my way home," I reply, which is the right answer for me, but the wrong answer for her, and I know this because she frowns at me. Still, I mean it, and I don't take the words back or change them.

She looks at me as if I am a very strange child. For, just as much as she needs me to be gone for the day, so, too, she needs to come and get me at school, needs me to wait for her there, needs to walk me back home just as I need to face the fear of losing my mother, need to make my way home without her even if it scares me, even if I have to scare myself to do it.

I have found my own way home. And I have learned that I can find my way again, anytime I need to, anytime I want to.

But my mother? What has she learned?

She has learned that she doesn't like this in me, this new bold and intrepid spirit that I have shown her on this day despite the fearfulness she knows I share with her. It is this that shall separate us. Her fear will keep her where she is. Mine will propel me, sometimes with no apparent direction, but, sometimes, with a homing instinct as sure and true as the pigeons who live in coops on the roof of our tenement display when they spiral their way down from the sky to find home.

Once I learn that I don't need my mother to make my way home, I am ready for school, truly ready, no matter how little or how afraid I am. I am ready for the lessons that I will learn.

Safe Houses

IN 1949, WE move from Hoboken to Ridgefield when I am seven, after my grandfather dies. Ridgefield, New Jersey, is in the suburbs. The suburbs are where all self respecting, upwardly mobile and aspiring first- and second-generation Italian-Americans and most GIs are grappling their way toward in the late forties and early fifties. The houses in the suburbs have wonderful amenities, unlike the overcrowded tenements of places like Hoboken. They have private bathrooms and hot water and fireplaces and lots of bedrooms and even formal dining rooms and picture windows, and garages and space enough for gardens and for workshops and sewing rooms. Though new houses are being built at a terrific rate, you also can buy an old house and fix it.

For my parents, Ridgefield is the promised land. Moving there signifies that the hell of the war years is finally behind us, that nothing can now tear this family apart, and that, suddenly, unexpectedly, inexplicably, we can be solidly, and respectably, middle class.

Harry S Truman is president; all's right with the world; everything's going to be fine for us from now on.

Ridgefield is where children can be properly raised in a private house with a backyard to play in safely (instead of the dangerous stoops and streets and tiny courtyards of the city), and trees, and light, and fresh air. Where we can have some privacy, but where we can gather together as a family at meals and in the evenings.

My parents have saved enough money during the war to afford a house that has been advertised in the newspaper as a "handyman special," which means that it needs fixing, which poses no problem, because my father is a handyman, and what he doesn't know about rehabilitating a house, he can learn by reading, by asking his friends, or by trial and error. My parents jokingly call the house "the old barn" when they first see it, and tell friends that it looks haunted, and that it has been owned by some really strange people. But it captures their imagination, and they want to buy it. And besides, it is a house they can afford.

They take us to see it one weekend after they have pretty much decided to buy. They ask me what I think in the way they have when they don't much care what I think.

I shrug my shoulders. I think we should stay in Hoboken, but I realize that it is a losing proposition.

I have gotten used to Sacred Heart. I have even made friends with Miranda Panda.

I hate change. Have had enough of it in my young life. Don't want any more of it. Don't want to move.

But my parents walk around the house, imagining what the dark green clapboard will look like painted light gray with dark gray trim. How some nice wallpaper (maybe with a Chinese pattern) could vastly improve the living room. How deep rose wall-to-wall carpeting could cover the floors that need too much work, my father thinks, to make them look respectable. How the sleeping porch upstairs can be converted into a study for me. How there are three bedrooms—one for them; one for my sister and me to share; one for my grandmother in case she decides to come and live with us instead of staying in Hoboken. "She'll come," my father promises. "She doesn't have anything left in Hoboken." And she does come. And hates it, for here she has no friends, here no one speaks her language, here there is no Italian priest to hear her confession, so she lives in a perpetual state of sin.

My father thinks that the coal-burning furnace in the basement poses no real problem. In winter, he can bank the fire at night before going to bed, and stoke it early in the morning, before we awaken, so the house will be nice and warm for us. During the day, when he is away at work, my mother can feed the fire with coal. And besides they can eventually convert to gas or oil. And they'll convert the bathroom too, modernize it, get rid of that old claw-foot bathtub. (They never do; years later, it comes back into style, and my father is amazed that people pay "good money" for tubs like the one my mother always wanted him to replace.)

My mother is thrilled that the house has close to forty windows, which can let in light and air, thirty-six more than in our apartment, if you don't count the clerestory on the air-shaft side. After we move, though, my mother covers them over as quickly as she can with shades and homemade curtains that she runs up on my grandmother's pedal-powered Singer sewing machine. At night, when my mother is working fast, sewing up a long straight seam, the sound of the old Singer is unnerving, like the ra-ta-ta-ta-tat of enemy machine-gun fire.

For months, on weekends, on the days when we don't go to the cemetery to tend my grandfather's grave, we go to "our new house," so that my father and mother can make it habitable. Their efforts inevitably end in arguments—the more work my parents undertake, the more high-strung they become.

I have to take care of my sister, who is three, and always getting in the way. It is my job to keep her out of danger (and there is much of it in this place, what with the saws and awls and nails and splintery boards), as my parents cut and saw and paint and paper and hammer the house into respectability. I don't do a very good job of it. It is a job that far exceeds my capabilities, then and later.

There is a picture of me from about this time, tending to my sister as she rides the tricycle that used to be mine. She has on a sensible outfit for playing—overalls and a sweater. I am absurdly dressed for the job, in trousers, good coat (I have no jacket for play), and bonnet.

I stand behind her as I try, unsuccessfully, to help her up and over the uneven pavement. The sidewalk outside our new house isn't smooth. It's hard for her to get anywhere on my tricycle.

I am trying to protect her, to keep her from falling forward, or from falling off the tricycle she can't manage by herself. I am also trying not to get my good coat dirty. I am eight years old. Too young to take care of my sister, yet this responsibility comes to me early, and rules my life for too long.

Hoboken is the place of my heart, though I have lived there but seven years, and, after we move, I miss it terribly. My parents have worked hard, made sacrifices, to get us out of there, I know, and they think they are doing themselves and us a great favor. (They were right. It was best for me because it was far easier for an Italian-American girl to find her way to college from Ridgefield than it would have been in Hoboken, where there was enormous pressure for working-class Italian-American girls to be anti-intellectual.)

Yet, in moving, our family loses much and it suffers, as all city people do who move to the suburbs. My mother loses her close friends, with whom she spends part of every day. She loses the community of women who hand their children back and forth so that each can have some free time. In Ridgefield, she has even more work and less fun. Now, my father has a tiring job, a long commute, and a house to rehabilitate besides.

After we move to Ridgefield, my mother's grief for her father takes her away from us. She mourns him for years. When she takes a break from her work, she sits at the mahogany kitchen table, stirs her coffee, looks down into her cup, as if it can give her something we can't. When she remembers to drink her coffee, it's too cold but she doesn't have the energy to reheat it, and, besides, she has too much work to do. Now she is an orphan and my father, my sister, and I are her only kin. But it is her first family she craves.

Our house feels empty to her, to me, even though we four inhabit it.

When we move, I feel like a person who has committed a capital crime, one who has been forced to go into hiding, like a very distant relative I hear stories about, who has been sent, against his will, to a hideout in the remote reaches of some state like Montana or Idaho for his own good, to lie low until things on the street cool off.

At first, I hate Ridgefield because I am lonely there, because I can't get used to not trotting up or down the stairs to see someone, to get out of my apartment, away from my parents. Here, my parents are always busy, my mother, sorrowing, and I have no friends and nothing (except for schoolwork) to do.

I hate it because there is no pulse, no energy, no razzmatazz, no quick escape into my grandparents' apartment if I get into trouble. There is no iceman, no vegetable man, no tripe man to make fun of, trilling "A trrrripe, a trrrripe" until all the housewives come running. No Fiore's across the street selling Italian delicacies, no honorary aunts or uncles or cousins (not real relatives, but people we treat like relatives) living close by, no fake uncle's saloon cum pastry shop (a weird and wonderful agglomeration that could only exist in a place like Hoboken)—it is around the block and I can get a free Italian pastry, a cannoli, my favorite, anytime I want, no Albini's Drugstore on the corner (where my wounds are bandaged, my eyes checked out). No old men sitting on chairs backwards in their undershirts in the summertime, no fireplug showers to cool you. No sidewalk roller skating contests, no movie theater a few blocks away, no merry-go-round truck that always comes when you need something to cheer you up, no beat-up garbage cans out front that you and your friends can bong on with sticks until someone leans out a window to tell you to shut up, no other people's laundry flapping outside your kitchen window so you can laugh at the kind of underpants Mr. Agiato wears, no nighttime hopscotch marathons lit by streetlamps.

The shock of being torn away from Hoboken, a place that had started to feel safe and familiar to me, and moving to Ridgefield, which feels like alien territory, I experience as a permanent and complete rupture from home, a home that felt, by turns, impermanent and dangerous, permanent and safe, but like home.

In my midforties, when I am beginning to write about Virginia Woolf and incest, when the work is not going very well, when I am thinking of abandoning it, and when I almost yield to despair, I feel I need to see where I grew up, and where I spent my summers as a child. As I am trying to recreate Virginia Woolf's childhood, I become impelled to remember mine. Perhaps I am having a hard time with this book because there are more congruencies between her life and mine than I am willing to acknowledge. I believe that it is only by turning the lighthouse beam of scrutiny on my past that I can understand hers; and that by trying to understand hers, I can, perhaps, come to understand mine.

At this time, one childhood memory recurs, recurs, and disturbs me: I am in Long Island during the summer and I am looking up at the patterned wallpaper in the bedroom where I sleep and I see the lights of cars coming through the slits of the blinds that cover the windows. This memory is prompted, I think, by reading of one of

Virginia Woolf's earliest memories—of "lying half asleep, half awake in bed" at the family's summer house in St. Ives, Cornwall, where she was sexually molested when she was six years old; of hearing "the waves breaking"; of the sound of the wind blowing the yellow blind of her bedroom. I begin, too, to have terrifying dreams about fires that rage out of control and consume me.

Though I say I want to, I cannot bring myself to go to that village on Long Island where I spent my summers, but I jump into my car and drive down to Hoboken often, as to a lover, and pace the streets where I have been a little girl. I go alone, without telling anyone. I go to try to find there the secret of what happened to me, of what happened to my soul, to find the thread that will take me back to my past.

I go to see if Hoboken has changed, and it hasn't, much. Finding where I lived makes me cry. Albini's is still on the corner, Fiore's, across the street; and there is Argie's house, set back from the street, the only private house on a block of apartment buildings, just as it was when my mother had to go there during the war to have a good cry in the arms of a friend who could understand how afraid she was that my father would never come home, while I pretended to occupy myself with warm milk and cookies.

Hoboken is where my memory has found a place to live. And even now, at fifty-two, when someone asks me where I grew up, I say "Hoboken," not "Ridgefield," and, despite my mother's efforts to get me to speak more eloquently, despite my graduate degrees, my diction stays resolutely and defiantly Hudson County, New Jersey. It says "street," not "avenue"; it says "tough," not "refined," and "street kid," not "suburban girl." It says "working class," not "middle class," and "Whaddaya want?" not "What can I do for you?" It says "Stay out of my way," and "Don't mess with me." It swears like the gangs of boys who hung out on street corners then (and still do), whom we listened to as children as others listened to the radio. It talks about sex as they did, and it uses the word "cock" or "prick" or "dick" and certainly not the word "penis"—a word that should never be used because it bears no relationship to the organ it purportedly represents, and people from places like Hoboken know this. It says "I'm from the old neighborhood, and if you're from the old neighborhood too, then we can be friends right here, right now, and if you're not, there's a lot of shit we need to get through before that can happen." It says "Fuck that" not "Oh dear me." It doesn't say "I'm fine where I am, thank you very much." It says "You better step aside, baby, because this girl's comin' through, whether you like it or not."

The street where I used to live hasn't changed much, though there are more men in their twenties and thirties around than I remember. But the old women who put pillows on the window sills to rest their beefy arms and lean out the window to watch what's happening on the block are still there. As are the housewives who pop out of their apartments wearing aprons to pick up a thing or two from Fiore's for supper while their sauce cooks down on the stove. A mother still stands in the street, craning her neck backwards, to talk to her friend at an open window five flights up, and she does not move when a car pulls up and blows the horn because, after all, this is her street, not his, and she's entitled to do anything she wants here. A little kid in a Catholic school uniform still hops up and down the steps of a stoop on one foot. An old guy wearing a beat-up hat with a crushed brim still sits, backwards, on a folding chair, in the street, very close to the curb; an outsider might wonder whether he is crazy and what he is doing there, but I know that he is saving a parking space in front of his apartment for his son-in-law, who is coming to visit him all the way from Brooklyn. He will sit there as long as he must, for hours, if necessary, because doing this is important.

Our old apartment house, thank God, is still standing, though its clapboard facade has been covered over with ugly imitation-brick siding, and its wrought-iron fence has been replaced with barbed wire. Still, it was ugly then, and it's ugly now, and so there hasn't been all that much of a change in forty-five years. And I can still stand on Fourth Street and see laundry that hangs in the courtyard, still see the window that faces the courtyard. The window through which my mother sang her songs to me. And I can still stand on Adams and see the stoop upon which my father and I fought, still see the door through which he came when he returned from war. And though this place, and other places where I have stayed, and where I have lived, have never felt completely safe to me, in my imagination I have made this apartment in Hoboken the safe house that is in my heart.

I wear the wound of this rupture from Hoboken as a pearl, for ornamentation. I live in Ridgefield in a permanent state of dread. I become what people call a high-strung child, a child with what my father likes to call "an active imagination."

I am prone to tempers and outbursts and fits of fainting when I become terrified, or when everything becomes too much for me, which is often. During grammar school, I faint every time we have an air raid drill. The bell rings. We leave our classrooms, assemble in hallways, assume the proper position.

I imagine bombers strafing our school, imagine myself being hit in a vital organ. I watch myself bleed, hear myself moan. I am too terrified to bear it, and I pass out. I make myself disappear.

The more I try to control my panic, the worse it becomes. The next thing I remember is a nun leaning over me with smelling salts, telling me to come to, that everything will be all right. I scare everyone else as much as I scare myself. After this happens three or four times, I sit out air raid drills in the principal's office.

During those early years in Ridgefield, the best friend I had was a small person I invented to keep me company who lived inside my right pocket, where I kept her, for safety's sake, so she wouldn't get into trouble, so nothing bad would happen to her, so no one would bother her. I hid her existence from the world as carefully and surely as I hid my own true nature. It was my responsibility to take care of this tiny person, to make sure that nothing bad happened to her, and I did a very good job of it.

I would take her out of my pocket when we were two houses away from my house, and stand her upright in the middle of my palm, and ask her things and tell her things as I walked to school alone. What the neighbors would see, if they bothered to look out their window at me as I walked along, was a little girl, somewhat small and slim for her age, looking very serious, very troubled, talking to herself, with her palm upturned to the sky, in what looked like a gesture of supplication or of benediction. (I see such disembodied children on my daily walks around my neighborhood, trudging to or from school, alone, staring at the ground or at some point in the far distance, eyes glazed over, performing some ritual act, and I have wanted to stop them, and tell them that I remember what it felt like to be so small and so helpless and so miserable, and to ask them what is wrong, and if I can help, but of course I don't do that for them, no one does that for them, just as no one did that for me.)

This little girl the neighbors see would be dressed inappropriately for the weather. In winter or in the rain, she wouldn't be wearing boots, and so her feet would be cold and wet, but she is used to it. She never wears a raincoat or carries an umbrella when it rains, and she rarely wears gloves or a sweater and so she is cold, always cold, but she is used to it. Her mother doesn't believe you should go out when it's cold, when it's too hot, when it rains, when it snows, or if it might be cold, or too hot, or if it might rain, or snow, and so appropriate clothing to be worn in inclement weather is seen as unnecessary extravagance.

Sometimes she seems to explode out of the house (running away from whom or what, who can tell, who can say), clasping her books to her chest, for protection, or so she won't drop them. She's always afraid she'll drop them, lose something, misplace her homework. Sometimes she runs all the way to school for no reason that anyone can guess. Sometimes she barely has the energy to trudge down the stairs, down the block, down the long flight of stairs to her school yard. Sometimes she has no idea what happens in school that day; she stares at her thumbs, or her fingernails, lost in what seems like thought. Sometimes she's bright and gets the answer before the teacher has even asked the question. She used to be very, very smart when she first started school, but it seems, as time goes by, that she's not as smart as she used to be.

And there are some things she can't do at all. She has no memory, for instance. Can't remember lists of things that countries are famous for producing. Can't remember dates. She forgets people's names. She cannot add or subtract or multiply or divide even the simplest numbers in her head. She counts on her fingers, like a baby.

She reads, though, constantly, and goes to the library often. It is quiet and peaceful, and that is why she spends so much time there. (Signs all over the place say SILENCE, and NO TALKING.)

When she goes to the library, before she chooses her books, she sits, first, on what used to be the sunporch when the library was someone's home. There, she reads the newspaper, which hangs suspended from a rack by a bamboo rod. She likes the way people look at her because she is reading the newspaper. Reading the newspaper is always a mistake; it scares her, but she does it anyway.

She reads about what is happening in the world, and what is happening in the world is always, always terrifying. She learns about how there are Communists just about everywhere and how you have to be afraid of them; she learns about how there is a war in a place called Korea and how the United States has declared a state of emergency (she wonders if her father will have to go to fight this war); she learns about the arms race (race?), and how just

97

about every country is exploding nuclear bombs in the Pacific (she peers at pictures of mushroom clouds, wonders if there are any people living near these places, wonders, too, whether one day, as she looks out her bedroom window, she'll see one ballooning over the meadowlands to the west); she reads about how people wonder whether nuclear fallout is dangerous; about how some people try to assassinate President Truman; she learns about the Ku Klux Klan and about how they burn crosses on people's lawns and what that means; she learns about Alger Hiss and about Julius and Ethel Rosenberg; she learns about what happened in Hitler's death camps

What she reads terrifies her. Will there be a day, she wonders, when no one is fighting, when nothing is wrong, when no one is killing anybody, when no one is threatening anybody? Will there be a day when she cannot worry? When she can relax? Completely.

Next, she selects her books. Once, she chooses ten extremely serious books, and the librarian looks at her as she checks them out and says, "I think you're reading too much. Do you have any friends? Any hobbies? Anything else that you do besides reading? Do you ever read fluff?" She answers no, no, no, and no to each question, but she is not offended. She thinks about what the librarian is trying to tell her. Still, to her, reading is very serious business. Reading is how she finds out about the world. The people she reads about in books are more real to her than the people in her life, who seem unfathomable. She can understand the people she reads about in books.

She writes, too, as often as she can. In a diary in which she writes everything but the truth. And in letters. Not to friends, but to pen pals. She has a pen pal in Peru, and another in Ecuador. Both Catholics. Both, she has gotten through her school's participation in a global effort to put Catholic children in touch with one another. To these girls, whose pictures she carries in her wallet, she writes very long letters, in which she lies about the life she is leading. She makes it seem happy, exciting, American.

When she's finished writing a letter, she posts it. It makes her feel very grown-up to walk to the post office and to buy airmail stamps. She does this often. She writes to these girls long after they stop writing to her.

My early years in Ridgefield come back to me in disconnected fragments. The drunken teacher who taught us ballroom dancing in grammar school (we waited, expectantly, for her to tumble to the floor, but she never did, though she staggered wonderfully). That I took more dancing lessons outside school, and that I was no good at it, and that I disgraced my teacher during an unfortunate performance of the Mexican hat dance. The five teachers we went through in one year when I was in fourth grade. The games I invented for my sister and me to play on the front lawn, and that I wasn't happy unless I got to make up the rules. The fact that sharing a double bed with my sister made me uncomfortable. I remember that I liked ice skating on the flooded baseball field in winter. That I liked walking down the hill to the park in summer for the arts and crafts program, but that I hated dragging my sister with me. That I tried to find other houses where I could spend time because I hated hearing my mother and stepgrandmother's constant fighting. That my grandmother taught me how to knit and that I loved it, particularly because I imagined that, in an emergency, knitting needles could be used as weapons. That my mother found pleasure in a rock garden that she created on the side of our house, where she planted mountain pinks and marigolds and weeded and watered all spring and summer long. That my grandmother spent her unhappy, lonely life with us, huddled in a chair in a corner of the dining room, close to the radiator in winter, because she was cold, bent over a tablecloth she was crocheting, because she had nothing else to do, the white of the cotton thread in stark contrast to the black of her widow's weeds.

I remember these things, but when I think about those years, it seems as if I have died inside, although there are some photographs to testify that I was still alive, that I still dressed up appropriately for Christmas, for Easter, in the clothes my mother continued to make for me. (Often, though, the hem of the skirt was longer on one side than the other, or the underlining showed, or the set-in sleeves were too tight, making it difficult to move freely. And whatever the style, whatever the color, it wasn't what the other girls were wearing.)

I know that I took First Communion, that I was a twirler in some community marching band, that we went on summer holidays, that we went to church on Easter Sundays, that I made my Confirmation, sponsored by my Auntie Vinnie, who appears, with her naked beefy arms, standing next to me, in my church robes. I know I did these things, not because I remember them, but because there are photos that testify that the body that I inhabited participated in these events. But where am I? Where am I?

There is a strange and upsetting home movie my father has made of my sister and me when we still lived in Hoboken that captures a moment that signifies what was wrong with me, that seems an abortive attempt, on my part, at communicating to my parents what was going wrong.

We are in a park somewhere, maybe the park on Fourth Street, around the corner from our apartment. My sister toddles up to the water fountain, climbs up its small step, and takes a drink of water all by herself. My father captures all this on film.

I am about six. I get between my father and my sister, I turn around, I bend over, I lift up my dress, I show my underpants, then I waggle my ass at the camera, back and forth, back and forth, as I look back toward the camera and smile a wanton smile.

My parents are furious. I'm getting in the way. What possesses me to do this?

"You were jealous of your sister," my mother says, by way of explanation, when we view this film years later. I know this isn't the reason.

My mother tries to shoo me out of the picture. I cover my ass with my dress, turn around, smile, and pretend that I am dancing, and I soft-shoe backwards, waving my arms back and forth, out of the picture, out of the camera's eye.

All this, my father films.

Years later, as I watch these images jitter their meaning onto the screen, I am horrified at the latent meaning in my childhood exhibitionism.

The look in my eyes is too seductive for a six-year-old. I have never seen this look in my eyes in any childhood photographs. The home movie captures a self I have submerged. Who is this child? Where did she come from? What happened to her?

One summer day in 1985 or 1986, I am sitting in my driveway (I like sitting there because it's shaded by an enormous oak tree), taking notes on Virginia Woolf's terrifying childhood story, "In the House of the Paterfamilias." I am doing research for my book on Virginia Woolf's childhood, and I am coming to believe the story covertly describes how she has been sexually abused as a child. My work goes well.

I note the phantasmagoric scene of a dining table, laden with food, that collapses to the ground, almost harming the central character, leaving her standing on a chair, her dress soiled and torn, unable to move. I note that this scene recalls how Woolf was molested on a ledge in the dining room when she was a girl of six, and I am thinking that she is using fiction to explain something of what had happened to her, that her story is like a symbolic retelling.

I copy the words Woolf penned at ten years old into my notebook: "I now look upon the nursery as a cage where I am made to perform compulsory tricks."

The next thing I remember is my husband pulling into the driveway hours later, blowing the horn, getting out of the car, coming up to me, asking me what's wrong. I am still in my chair, my pen poised. I haven't moved for hours.

I have had my first flashback. I remember the summer in Long Island, the light coming through the venetian blinds, the bathtub. I am back there, I am back there, I am nine or ten or six or five or four, and I am so afraid that I am hardly breathing, I am so afraid that I dare not move, and as time stands still, I circle down, circle down, toward that dark still point at the center of the spinning vortex of memory.

The story I never told my parents, couldn't tell my parents, because I didn't remember what happened, or didn't have the language to describe what happened, or because there isn't a language to describe what happened, or because I was too angry or stunned or blunted to describe what happened, came back to me in bits and pieces, in scraps and fragments, throughout my life. A moment here, a moment there, disconnected in time, removed from place. Jump cuts of memory without cause and effect, event and consequence, incident and emotion. A place that language can't describe, but a place that my body remembered. Where an intake of breath is not necessarily followed by an exhalation. Where the back of one's neck is permanently stiffened and arched. Where your body does things you don't have a name for, and that you don't even want it to do.

I push myself to get closer to what happened. So I can exorcise it with the scalpel of language. But my powers of expression fail me. I cannot organize the experience the way I organize my arguments, foregrounding certain details, glossing others. Whenever I try, the sentences run together, and the language I use is not what I recognize as my own. It sounds like a cross between the language of a child and the language of a woman. I want to write it in the present tense. I know that's the way it should be. The way to convey what I actually felt, if I knew what I felt, if I felt anything. Which I'm not sure about. But I can't do that yet. The closest I can come, the language I manage to find, is like some lunatic version of those papers we wrote at the beginning of each school year. "What I Did on My Summer Vacation." Do you remember?

My mother and father drove me to Long Island to stay with my Auntie Vinnie because my mother needed time to be away from me because she wasn't feeling too good and it took us a long time to get there and we went in my father's car and we stopped halfway to get ice cream and my Auntie Vinnie's mother used to be a prostitute and her real aunt had taken her away from her mother when she was about eight or nine years old to raise her because all kinds of bad things were happening to my Auntie Vinnie but it was too late because by then the damage was already done because by then her mother and her mother's johns had already done God knows what all to Auntie Vinnie which is probably why when Auntie Vinnie took care of me during the summer she would grab at me and grab at me in the bathtub and she would squeeze me and tell me about the titties I was going to have someday right there and right there and how the boys were going to love them and squeeze them and how much fun that would be and then she would take off her top (it had gotten all wet) and show me hers and they were ENORMOUS especially the nipples and she would lean into the tub and they would flap down very close to me and then she would grab at me and grab at me and I would move back until I couldn't move back anymore and she would grab at me under the water because she wanted to wash my be-be (it was very important to keep it clean) but I told her I was big enough to wash it by myself only she didn't care and wouldn't let me and then she'd dry me off and powder me up and put me in bed in the room with the venetian blinds (we didn't have them at home because my mother thought they were too expensive and besides they were hard to clean, old-fashioned shades were good enough for us, my mother said), but Auntie Vinnie never closed the blinds all the way so you could see the light from the streetlamp shining through the slits and if you looked at the wall beside the bed you could see how the blind sliced the light into fifty, maybe sixty pieces and I couldn't get to sleep in that house because of the stuff that went on at night after I was supposed to be asleep and because I was so homesick I thought I would die and because that's when Great-Uncle ZoZo would fall down when he tried to go to the bathroom, he had a stroke and couldn't walk too good and couldn't talk except for grunting and he would wet himself because he never knew when he had to go to the bathroom and he would sit in the screened-in porch all day long doing nothing and my job was to sit there and watch him and shout for Auntie Vinnie and Great-Auntie ZaZa if he so much as blinked an eye and sometimes my cousin Lynnie sat with me and then it wasn't so bad.

And Auntie Vinnie was a really good cook and Uncle Ronnie (her husband) would take us berrying and sometimes he would take me clamming and once I got a tick in my neck and they had to pull it out with pliers and once I cut the bottom of my foot real bad on the broken end of a clam, it was sharp as a razor, and when we got home Auntie Vinnie would make dozens and dozens of berry muffins and clam fritters and there was always SO MUCH FOOD there, I had never seen so much food, and once me and my cousin Lynnie ate a dozen muffins all by ourselves hiding in the barn (we stole them from the kitchen) and Auntie Vinnie got SO MAD she came after us with a rake and told us she was going to beat the piss out of us and they grew corn and beans and peas in the backyard and they had chickens and I didn't like it when they killed the chickens but I liked it when we picked the corn though sometimes there were these worms in them and sometimes I took baths with cousin Lynnie and I didn't like that much either because then Auntie Vinnie would do it to the two of us and there would be much splashing and water would always wind up on the floor and she probably did it to her sons too, because they were always disgusting good-for-nothing big fat slobs who never left the house, who never did anything, never pitched in and helped with the work like my cousin Lynnie and me, and they still are disgusting good-for-nothing big fat slobs, just like their mother, and they will always be, and I hated one of them more than I hated the other one, he shoveled his food into his mouth so fast it was disgusting and he ate everything in sight, he ate ENORMOUS plates of food, and I couldn't wait for the summer to end, though I liked the ocean and the waves and the clamming and the berrying and hiding in the hayloft where no one could find me and bother me and picking the corn and shelling the peas and my uncle Ronnie who was nice to me and the food and all, and if Auntie Vinnie wasn't there it wouldn't be a bad place to go. And that's what I did on my summer vacation.

Language, I have learned, by writing about this, gives birth to feeling, not the other way around.

Soon after we move to Ridgefield, my father becomes a fireman in the Ridgefield Volunteer Fire Department. Which keeps my mother, my sister, and me in a chronic state of fear. When there is a fire, we are terrified. When the fire is over, we are temporarily relieved. But then we start to wait for the inevitable next fire. Every time my father goes to fight a fire, it feels as if he were going away to war again. And we wonder, each time: Will he come back to us alive?

My mother, a fearful woman under the best of circumstances, is forced to reexperience, frequently, the terror she felt when my father was away during the war. And her terror is infectious, for during the times when my father is fighting a fire, my mother walks around the house like a zombie, worrying, worrying that this is the fire that will finally kill her husband, or burn him so badly that he will need to be hospitalized. But what can she do? He won't listen to reason. Nothing can stop him. He has a mind of his own.

We know that these are no idle fears on my mother's part. My father has a streak of heroism in him that I admire, but that verges on foolhardiness. Call it machismo, if you want. He wants to be the chief (and he is Ridgefield's fire chief, for years), the guy who leads the cavalry charge. The one who is first into the burning building. The one who figures out whether the roof is safe enough to support a few men, or whether it is in danger of collapsing. The one who will never stay behind, no matter how exhausted he is. The guy who always wants to be where the action is, even if the action is happening inside a huge conflagration, inside a building sending sheets of fire up into the sky.

As a teenager, I am tempted to emulate my father's bravery, which I come to admire, though I never tell him. And I rebel against my mother's fearfulness, which I despise, both because I don't understand its origin, and because I see the same trait in myself. But, because I am a girl, and am not encouraged to take on physical challenges, which could have channeled these impulses into constructive pursuits, what could have become bravery in me becomes merely foolish bravado: I drive too fast, drink too much, swear too much, and I pick fights and taunt people too often—once, I get myself beaten up badly after I mock a tough girl's father because he wears a cowboy hat and cowboy boots in a skit I write and put on for a high school assembly.

Though my father's heroic streak threatens his life often, once it nearly kills him.

I think that civilian life was too boring for my father, that he needed to juice things up, stir things up, subject himself to the kind of danger he had faced during the war. But I also think that his being a fireman was a cruel thing to do to my mother, and a cruel thing to do to us. Still, the smell of smoke inevitably triggers an asthma attack.

*　*　*

In the middle of the night, the fire alarm sounds, and we awaken. My father climbs into his clothes, and my mother, my sister, and I (if we can rouse ourselves from bed) show him to the door, and we all hold our breath, unable to sleep until a few hours later when we hear his car pull back into the driveway. He is back. He is safe. Nothing has happened this time.

Sometimes, my mother calls the firehouse and gets someone at the other end who tells her what is happening and not to worry. Sometimes we can figure out where the fire is by listening to the sirens on the fire engine. Sometimes, even, we can step out the front door and smell the smoke, see the flames.

My father fights many, many fires as I grow up. Most are not life-threatening; some are not dangerous at all. A roasting pan filled with grease that goes up in flames in someone's oven. A wastebasket filled with paper that someone has tossed a cigar into, unthinkingly. A few cases of spontaneous combustion.

But my father fights four spectacular, terrible, nearly lethal and lethal fires in his career, which irrevocably changes the way I look at the world, which proves to me, irrefutably, that safety is an illusion, that there is no habitation on this planet that can be kept immune from danger, and that death by fire is the cruelest death.

When I grow up, I know ten people who die by fire. In my dreams, there are burning buildings with fiery roofs tumbling inward, firemen with their helmets dripping icicles fighting fires in the dead of winter, walls weakened by fire collapsing onto the beds of sleeping children, people encircled by fingers of fire fleeing for a safety that will elude them, explosions, implosions, and flashbacks (the most terrifying).

Once, the Somers' house at the end of the next block goes up in flames. We race down the street to watch the firemen fight the fire. Lots of people from the neighborhood assemble in the street, across the way, to watch.

The people who live there are lucky. They have come home, parked their car in the garage, gone into the house, gone about their business.

The daughter (a friend of mine) accidentally touches a wall, feels that it's very hot. She has learned about what to do in school. Has learned that if a wall is hot to the touch, you are in grave danger, that you must evacuate the house immediately. She calls her parents, tells them. They leave the house, turn in the alarm.

The fire has started in their car, and has traveled through the walls of the house. Had she not touched the wall, had they waited, they might have been overcome by smoke, they might have died. Had they fallen asleep, the firemen say, not one of them would have survived. For days, every time you step outside, you can still smell the smoke from this fire. For months, the charred remains of the house stand as testimony to what might happen to you in your sleep if you do not protect your home from fire, which is, my father admits, a very difficult thing to do, no matter how hard you try. For years, before I go to sleep, I touch the wall behind my bed. Make sure it's cool. Make sure there's no fire climbing up from the basement to my bedroom through the walls of our house.

(My father reminds us. Throw away old paint cans. Safely dispose of rags soaked with oil. Keep the stairs free from clutter. Plan emergency escapes from bedrooms. If you smell smoke, hit the floor, and crawl to the nearest exit. If you find that you are on fire, fall and roll; do not run, running fans the flames, running makes things worse. If you happen to see someone on fire, grab a blanket to smother the fire; do not go near them without protection or your clothing might burst into flames.)

The Somers' house is jinxed, we all believe, as the years pass. This house is lethal, we all say. Living there can kill you. Four families' lives are disrupted by tragedy while they live in this house. First, there is the fire, after which my friend and her family move, not wanting to stay in this house that almost kills them. Then, there is the boy who dies of measles while he lives in this house. Then, the son of another family who lives there is killed on a motorcycle.

And finally, and most terribly, a car carrying five members of the same family who live in this house explodes upon impact with the car of a drunken driver. The car bursts into flames. Everyone inside—the father and mother, their two young girls, and their grandfather—is killed instantly. There are pictures of the wreck in the local newspaper. You can make out the shape of the bodies, still sitting as they had the moment before the explosion. You can distinguish the bodies of the girls from those of the grown-ups.

My father goes to the wake. The caskets are closed. I sing in the choir at the funeral service for the family. There are three children who are left behind; my friend Susan's family takes them in and raises them. This accident irrevocably changes Susan's life. These children require much care after this tragedy; one seems in great difficulty. Susan has to grow up fast. She has to help her mother because there is so much work to be done.

Another time, the school on the next block goes up in flames on a summer evening. It is being renovated; the firemen speculate that it was a case of spontaneous combustion; perhaps the workmen hadn't disposed of their oil-soaked rags properly.

The whole town, it seems, turns out to watch my father and his cohorts fight this fire. I go, too, against my mother's wishes. "The school is burning, the school is burning" is a clarion call too enticing not to heed.

At the scene of the fire, it's almost festive, like a carnival. The air is balmy. The smell of fire makes it seem like summer camp.

I stand on a lawn across the street, watching the fuchsia flames licking the sky. I see the firemen battling the fire, their hatchets at the ready, their hoses snaking along the ground, their ladders climbing to the sky. I hear the men shouting, about water pressure, about hoses, about spraying down the house next door, about getting the spectators to move back, move back.

I know my father is over there with them, in there, on the roof—who can tell? I can just barely make out the forms of the firefighters through the thick smoke. I see the ambulance standing by, its red emergency light strafing the dark; the ambulance is there in case one of the firemen becomes overcome by smoke, or injured, or worse.

On this night, I'm sure that my father will die. On this night, I wait for my father to die. This is no ordinary fire. This is a gigantic fire. This fire devours an entire school.

And what do I feel on this night? Fear, surely. But pride in him, too. In his fearlessness. Pride that I am related to him, that I am a member of a fireman's family. We are treated with respect and concern that night. Envy because I want to be a hero like him, because I know that a life that is entirely safe is a dead life, a life not worth living; I know that without risk, there will be no adventure, no experience, no happiness. But I know, too, that I am angry. Angry that I have to witness this, as exciting as it seems. Angry that he is in danger, again. Angry that he is making us worry again. Angry that he is bringing death and the smell of fire into our house. Wondering what we will do if he dies, how we will manage. Upset that he's making my mother purse her lips in the way she has when she's so frozen with fear she can't act, she doesn't know what to do.

And this night, he comes close to getting seriously injured. He gets hit on the head with a piece of debris that comes down off the school.

"Lucky I had my helmet on" is all my father says.

"Lucky you're still alive," a fellow firefighter remarks. My father, as always, has minimized the danger.

"When it's your time to go, it's your time to go," my father responds. And he really believes it. I believe that you shouldn't invite danger to come your way. My mother believes that you should stay home where it's safe, where nothing bad can happen to you. My sister doesn't know what she believes.

Years later, when I tell people that my father was a fireman, I tell them about this fire, and I tell them that I was so angry with him in those days that I wanted him to die. I tell them that I stood on the lawn opposite the fire, hoping, praying, that he would go up in flames.

This isn't true. I tell the story this way to get attention. I tell it to disguise the paralyzing fear I felt, to get some control over it. For if I had wanted my father to die, and he did, then I would have been the cause, and not something that happened to him, not fate or chance or something he invited because he refused to stay safe at home. If he had died, and I had wished it, then I wouldn't have to face how much I loved him, needed him.

Whenever my father and I fight, and we fight often, I get so angry with him so quickly I feel sure that he will harm me. Whenever we fight, I want him to die.

Fortunately, on that night, though the fire is extremely difficult to fight, and spectacular to witness, nothing terrible happens to my father or to anybody.

But then there was the fire that nearly did kill my father. The bowling alley fire in a neighboring town that killed five firemen when my father was deputy fire chief.

Many of the men had been at a community function and arrived at the firehouse dressed in tuxedos, joking about fighting the fire just as they were. When they arrived at the fire, there were no flames visible, just puffs of smoke. The chief who had been put in charge of the fire ordered men from my father's company to break open a door and to direct the water inside. My father, who was sup-posed to be with his men, had left them momentarily because he saw someone far too near the fire, and he was yelling at this guy to move back, get out of the way, it wasn't safe there.

Then the firemen broke down the door. And then, as my father tells it, "All hell broke loose."

Air rushed in, suddenly providing the smoldering fire with an enormous amount of fuel. Instantly, there was a tremendous explo-sion. The roof blew into the air. The walls blew out and collapsed. One wall, just two feet away from my father, came down, crushing the men who had broken down the door, the five men he had been with until he turned away from them for what couldn't have been more than fifteen, twenty seconds at the most.

My father was in the alleyway, the fire raging, the building coming down around him, his men, underneath a pile of rubble, obeying an order that someone else had given, that he probably wouldn't have given.

After, it was my father's duty to tell the men's wives that they had died. It was terrible for him. The worst thing he ever had to do.

My father told the story of what had happened at this fire very matter-of-factly, when someone asked him about it. Described where he was. Where they were. How he could see them. How he was about to move up to their position when the wall came down. How he saw it happen. How it almost happened to him. How lucky he was. How he nearly got killed.

It was the closest my father came to dying. Closer, even, than he had come to dying in his years in the war. Whenever he told the story of how he was ready to move up to where the other men were, of how he saw the wall fall onto his buddies, I was there with him. I could see it happening. I felt it was happening to me.

The bowling alley fire brought hordes of reporters to our small town, made the headlines in newspapers throughout the country, was seen on television on the evening news.

There was a solemn funeral attended by dignitaries from throughout the country. My father attended in his dress uniform. The town was stunned by the immensity of its loss. I never knew how my father felt about having five of his friends die at the same time. I never appreciated the loss he sustained. I never knew whether he believed they had died a senseless death; whether he was obeying orders he knew to be dangerous; whether he would have given the same order.

Quite young, while I am still in grammar school, I win an essay contest, sponsored by the American Legion. We are told to write a five-hundred-word essay on the subject "Safety in the Home, Street, and School." The nun who teaches our class gives us time during the school day to begin.

Most of the boys and girls snicker at the topic. Most of them doodle on the pieces of paper they are given. They think it's stupid. They have nothing to say.

I take the topic seriously. I have a lot I can say, a lot I want to say, on the subject. This is something I know about, something I understand. This is something about which I have an opinion.

I know what you have to do to make a home safe; I also know what it feels like to be in danger. No house I have ever been in has felt entirely safe to me. Most feel like the Fun House in Palisades Amusement Park, with shocks as you step around each corner, screaming voices that shatter the silence when you least expect it, leering faces looking over your shoulder as you look at yourself in distorting mirrors, groping hands from which there is no escape waiting in the dark to reach out at you.

Each night, I wait until everyone in my house is asleep before I can relax enough to fall asleep. I put myself to sleep each night by imagining that I am in grave danger. I wonder how my parents will behave if I die before they do. Will their lives be ruined? Will they go on as before, as if nothing has happened? In my nighttime imaginings, sometimes help comes for me just in time. Often, though, I see my broken body on the side of the road, in a bedroom in an abandoned house, down a cellar. I have died and no one has been there to save me.

I tell myself not to think these thoughts, that they're dangerous. Sometimes, before I doze off, I practice getting out of difficult situations. Scanning a crowded auditorium for the nearest exit in case of fire. Hiding under a seat in a movie theater that has come under attack by a crazed gunman. Pretending to be asleep while a burglar invades my bedroom. I'm sure that doing this will come in handy someday, sure I'll find myself in situations like these sooner or later.

A friend in school tells me that if you dream you're dead, you die in real life. Every night, when I go to sleep, I tell myself that, no matter how violent my dreams, I can't let myself dream of dying, that if I'm about to die in my dreams, I must, I must, I must wake myself. Sometimes I can. Sometimes I can't.

I write my essay on "Safety in the Home, Street, and School" in the evenings, after my schoolwork for the day is done. My father has made me a special triangular desk out of plywood to fit into a space at the top of the stairs when I begin carting library books home at a furious rate, when it seems clear I am interested in becoming a good student. There is a drawer with a special, expensive, brass drawer pull he has purchased from a hardware store for decoration. My mother has found a desk lamp at a rummage sale, cheap. I have asked for, and gotten, a Parker pen for Christmas. Though it leaks, and my fingers are black with ink, I always use it. I fancy myself a famous writer.

My essay wins a big prize. I see my name in the newspaper. This is the first time I face down my fears by writing about them. This is the first time I use the terror I so often feel in my work.

My parents and grandparents are proud of me. My mother, especially. She takes me into her room, opens her jewelry box, and shows me the medal she won as a girl for her writing. She tells me that when I get older, she'll let me wear it. She tells me that someday the medal will be mine.

Colored Paper

DOWN THE STREET from our house in Ridgefield, there lived an elderly childless couple who spoke almost no English. Their house was tiny and dark, a cottage, really, and it was set way back from the street, in a thicket of spruce trees, the remnants, my father told me, of the pine forest that had once covered this ridge. Often, on my way to grammar school, I would stop and try to pry a piece of the rough furrowed bark off one of those towering trees to carry with me as a talisman. Winter, summer, spring, or fall, the Vanyas' house received no direct sunlight. It was bathed in perpetual gloom, and, on the north-facing side of the roof, a coating of green moss had long since established itself.

No one in our neighborhood was friendly with the Vanyas, although my mother nodded to them when she was outside early in the mornings in summers doing her gardening as they passed our house on their way to a paper factory where we knew they worked. No one knew where they came from, or what language they spoke, or what they did for a living at the factory. And no one seemed to want to find out.

"Eastern Europe," was my father's best guess, when the subject came up at our dinner table. I didn't know where that was.

"Refugees?" my mother suggested. I didn't know what the word meant, but I would learn, soon enough, through the newspapers I read during my frequent trips to the local library.

From my parents' tone, the subject of the Vanyas seemed not one that they would eagerly discuss in front of me, and so I began to make up stories about these two sad people, who seemed to do nothing but work. I gave them a wild and fantastic history, which included disapproving parents who tried to thwart their love, a nighttime escape from their small village in Eastern Europe (dominated by a castle) timed to coincide with a full moon, a dangerous overland journey to a port city, the sale of jewels (hers) to provide passage money, a landing in New York City at the dock from which I had seen my grandfather depart for Italy, a taxi ride to the Port Authority in mid-Manhattan, and, finally, a bus ride to Ridgefield (which they choose from a list of possible destinations because they like the sound of the name and imagine they can live there happily), where they would make their home and a life together, but not without tremendous emotional cost.

One Saturday morning, in the dead of winter, when I was about eleven years old, on my usual desultory walk to the end of our block and back, which I took no matter how cold it was, to get out of the house, and because I had nothing better to do, the front door of the Vanyas' house opened, and Mrs. Vanya motioned for me to come inside, and I followed her command. I took these walks past their house and not in the opposite direction primarily to see if I could catch a glimpse of them because their aloofness was provocative and I was curious. But I never imagined I would be invited in. Usually, I stopped for a few moments outside their house, trying to crack into the air bubbles caught beneath the ice on the pavement with the tip of my shoe, casting surreptitious glances at their house, which seemed a forbidden, magic place, more like the places in the fairy tales my mother read me when my father was away at war than a place for habitation.

In the years since we had moved to Ridgefield and I had first learned of the Vanyas, I had refined their history to include a donkey cart ride through a great valley overhung with ferns, a furious near-successful pursuit by their parents, and a storm-tossed ocean voyage. The Vanyas had become the living symbol to me of an idea I toyed with then but later abandoned, that one should make great sacrifices for romantic love, and that love conquers all. In these prepubescent days, I maintained this view despite all the evidence to the contrary that I observed, both in the marriages of my parents and my friends' parents, which seemed overly burdened by the realities of daily life—making ends meet, finding good work and keeping it, wondering whether Eisenhower would make a good president, being exhausted by a day's work at a difficult job where you weren't appreciated, staving off a consuming disabling sorrow, and worrying whether nuclear war would come during our lifetime. I gave up my romantic ideal of love halfway through high school, when I saw a few of my girlfriends, who became pregnant, abandoned by boys who had proclaimed eternal love. If it could happen to them, unless I was careful, it could happen to me. What clinched it, though, was reading Flaubert's *Madame Bovary* and seeing Alfred Hitchcock's *Vertigo* in high school. I couldn't shake the image of Emma Bovary, a fool for love, if ever there was one, on her deathbed, or that of Jimmy Stewart, in the mental hospital, pining for a phantom woman, who had betrayed his trust. I didn't want to wind up like either of them.

There was no foyer in the Vanyas' tiny house. You walked right into the living room, and it was spooky. Overstuffed armchairs and a sofa too big for the room. Thick, lush velvet drapes covering the single window. Big, round wooden end tables with tops that looked like piecrusts. I felt uncomfortable being there, wondered why I had been invited to enter, though I wasn't afraid and didn't think I would come to harm.

Mrs. Vanya turned on a weak light, and motioned for me to sit. She turned, and disappeared from the room.

In the time that I had to myself, I started adding to my story about the Vanyas, based upon these new pieces of evidence provided by the appearance of their living room. I decided that they used to be very, very rich, maybe even royalty (you could tell from the drapes on their windows), and that they were so sad because now they were poor and had to work and they weren't used to it.

Mrs. Vanya came back in just a few moments, carrying a very large white cardboard box. I could see Mr. Vanya standing in the doorway to what seemed like the kitchen at the back of the house, and when he saw me looking at him, he waved to me, but stayed where he was. Inside the house, he didn't look as sad as he looked when he was outside.

Mrs. Vanya motioned for me to open the cover of the box, which I did. Inside were what seemed like hundreds of pieces of colored paper. They came in many shapes, sizes, and colors. The best were gold and silver, which glinted and gleamed in the light from the lamp. I wondered if they were made from real silver and real gold and imagined they must be, for what else could produce such opulent papers? There were squares, oblongs, and triangles of crimson, vermilion, chartreuse, ocher, magenta, and canary. All the colors of the rainbow, really. More colors than in the biggest box of Crayola crayons, which I deeply coveted but couldn't afford.

I was transported by the sight of such richness, such splendor, such extravagance, and I wondered why the Vanyas had singled me out to receive this gift, but, though I looked up at her inquiringly, Mrs. Vanya couldn't tell me. She simply put the lid back on the box, took a giant rubber band out of the pocket of her apron and wound it around the box to ensure I wouldn't lose its contents on the way home, and handed it back to me. Then she walked to the front door, opened it, smiled, and motioned that I should take my present home.

I took my cue to go, and left without a backward glance or wave. In the next few years, Mrs. Vanya repeated this gesture many more times, and always just as I was running out of my store of colored paper. She seemed to know when I needed more.

I never learned why the Vanyas singled me out to receive this gift. Perhaps they had watched me from their window, walking up and down the street by myself. Perhaps they imagined that I was lonely and unhappy and thought that I needed some color in my life, something to cheer me, and they could provide it, though their life seemed sad too. Perhaps they were simply generous. I never found out why. Nor did I ever find out the Vanyas' real history, though I can imagine it more realistically now.

Still, I remember their gift as the greatest and most important one I received in those dismal years, prompted by the most significant act of generosity that ever came my way. For when I got home, the quality of the day had changed for me. No longer was it dark and gloomy. No longer was I miserable. All I had to do was open my box of colored paper, and I felt better, happy, really.

That day, I began to imagine what I could do with all this stuff I had been given, and I made a list in my head. I could use my paper for school projects, yes, but I could use it for fun, too. I could decorate clothes for my paper dolls; cut the pieces up and make mosaics like the ones I had seen in *National Geographic*; paste them on Quaker Oats boxes to give as presents; fashion them into greeting cards. The possibilities seemed endless. I was very excited.

In time, as I created each of these things with my colored paper, and more, I changed my vision of the Vanyas' lives, and I imagined myself at its center.

I saw them at the paper factory working together, side by side, day by day. I saw them passing enormous sheets of colored paper and cardboard through the sharp blade of humming, dangerous machinery. I saw them amid showers of the brilliant, multicolored dust that was thrown into the air. And I saw them finding pieces of paper and cardboard on the floor to save and give me as presents.

"Here's one," Mr. Vanya says to Mrs. Vanya in his native tongue.

"For Louise," she replies. She tucks it into her handbag to take home to put in the cardboard box that sits in the bottom of her bedroom closet. Especially for me.

The Vanyas' gift was gratifying because, when we first moved to Ridgefield, we lived a very frugal, austere life, a life without extravagance. My parents had decided they would try to subsist on my father's modest salary so my mother could stay home and raise us and tend house. In the years to come, my mother's forays into the workforce were brief and unpleasant. She was a clerk in a shop, for a time. And she worked at a local bank. When she worked at the bank, she would come home flustered, telling stories about how she wasn't getting along with the other workers, and my father said that, if working was giving her so much trouble and making her so unhappy, she might as well stay home.

Staying home suited her when she was cheerful, though she often became entrapped by the rituals of homemaking, by her exacting standards of cleanliness, and by her frugality. She washed all forty windows of the house, inside and out, several times a year, sitting precariously on the ledge of each window so she could wash the outside. "Your mother's floors are so clean," a neighbor once told me, "that you could eat off them." They were so clean because she washed them daily. And though, in time, she bought an automatic washing machine, she never let it do the whole job for her; instead, she ran up and down the cellar stairs to lift the clothes out of the machine to wring them out by hand because it saved water.

Through the years, my mother left the house alone less and less, though my father sometimes managed to pry her out on weekends and for short holidays.

For Christmas, for birthdays, my mother would buy us what we needed, not what we wanted—some underwear, socks, a cummerbund belt. These sacrifices were necessary for my parents to afford the house and its upkeep. When we lived in Hoboken, though, I had been used to my mother's buying me expensive clothing, and I missed our excursions into Manhattan to Macy's or Gimbel's to shop for something special.

When I complained, by way of explanation my mother would pronounce an aphorism, one of many she used to teach us acceptable behavior as we grew up. Her favorite had become "A penny saved is a penny earned." Another, "A stitch in time saves nine." Or "If you don't want very much, you'll never be disappointed." "Waste not, want not." Or, the one I hated most, "Patience is a virtue."

Though I often made fun of my mother's sayings, and though I believe they grew out of her resignation and passivity ("If you don't want very much, you'll never be disappointed"), she practiced what she preached, and she was a strongly principled, kind, and ethical woman. "People in glass houses shouldn't throw stones," she would say to me, when I started to make fun of a classmate. "Let he who is without sin cast the first stone," when I started to tell her about how awful I thought it was that the father of one of my classmates was a drunk. "Do unto others as you would have them do unto you," when I was mean to my sister. "It is better to give than receive," when I started listing all the things I wanted for Christmas.

I remember a birthday when I began quizzing my mother about my presents at least a month before the actual day. When my birthday finally arrived, I had probably asked her no less than a hundred times to respond to questions I posed as clues so I could guess what she was giving me.

"Is it warm?" I asked.

"Yes, it's warm," she responded.

The possibilities presented themselves: a sweater, gloves, a hat.

"Is it soft?" I asked.

"Well, maybe," she answered.

"That doesn't help," I insisted. "Is it soft or isn't it?" If it was soft, I would have to rule out gloves, though a sweater and a hat were possibilities if they were made from fluffy or furry fabric.

My mother, in response to my badgering, admitted that, well, yes, she guessed you could say the present was soft.

During other question-and-answer sessions, I had nailed down that whatever it was was cuddly. Then, I moved on to color. Determining its color was very important.

"Is it yellow?" I asked.

"Not really," my mother answered.

"What do you mean 'not really'?" I insisted.

"I guess you could say it's 'yellowish,' " my mother admitted.

I went to my closet, hauled out my box of colored paper, and riffled through it to present my mother with a few possibilities.

"This one." She had picked a paper that was light mustard. Not my favorite color. Baby shit yellow.

Late at night, after I had gone to bed, I heard my mother at work on the old Singer, and I began to imagine that she was sewing something for my birthday. But what could it be if it was warm and cuddly and baby shit yellow? A special bathrobe, made out of some plush fabric? A vest of fake fur like the one she had made for Jill when she was small?

I was afraid I wasn't going to like this present and I vowed not to get my hopes up so I wouldn't be disappointed again.

I had reached the age where I didn't especially like my mother sewing for me, even if she sewed something in a color that I liked. Lately, everything I wore that she made for me, apart from my grammar school uniform, seemed frumpy and old-fashioned.

When I could bear the suspense no longer, I posed the final, and most significant question to her. One that I almost didn't want her to answer.

"Can you wear it?"

"No, you can't wear it," she answered.

I was relieved, but this made guessing more difficult.

One day, about a week before my birthday, on my way to school, I had a sudden, wonderful realization.

My birthday present was a puppy. I knew it. It had to be. It was the only thing I could think of that could be soft, warm, cuddly, and baby shit yellow. There were plenty of dogs that color. Golden retrievers. Boxers. Even collies, the dog of my dreams. But could I be so lucky? And where was my mother hiding it?

I couldn't figure out how my mother had overcome my father's resistance to household pets. To him, they were filthy, noisy, expensive to keep, and served no purpose that he could think of. But I felt sure she had.

The week before my birthday was the happiest week of my life. I gave my parents no trouble. Didn't talk back or complain or act restless or obnoxious. I even took my sister to the library without being asked.

I imagined the ribbon of my life happily unfurling before me. With a dog at my side, my life could become the life I imagined for myself.

But it was not to be.

On the morning of my birthday, when I insisted and insisted that I could wait no longer, my mother descended into the basement to get my present.

Every night when we sat down to what passed for dinner, I didn't complain because I convinced myself I could hear little yelps and barks coming from the coal cellar at the back of the basement.

My mother reappeared with a giant box, big enough to hold a puppy, and she held it out to me eagerly, expectantly, anticipating my pleasure.

No puppy sounds were coming from inside the box. Still, I held on to my hope.

It faded as soon as I took the box into my arms and rattled it back and forth. There was, I could tell, no living thing within it. I wasn't getting a puppy for my birthday. What would I tell the kids at school? Especially the ones who thought I was lying, who knew that I could never receive such a magnificent present.

I opened the box, and looked within. I was puzzled. My present seemed to be yards and yards and yards of baby shit colored fabric. I was convinced my mother had completely lost her mind.

"What is it?" I asked.

"Drapes," my mother told me. She seemed prideful. But I had reverted to my ordinary, grumpy, perennially dissatisfied self. My brief prelapsarian paradise had ended. "I made you drapes for your bedroom, just like you wanted," my mother told me.

I reached back in memory, because it seemed impossible that a kid my age would ask her mother for drapes for her room for her birthday. And then I recalled a conversation I had had with my mother months and months before after I came home from visiting the Vanyas.

My mother had asked me what the Vanyas' house was like. In response, I told her that they had drapes on their living room windows, not curtains like us. "I wish we could have drapes," I said, in a tone that showed my dissatisfaction with the window coverings my mother had sewn.

Drapes, to me, were classy. Drapes were what rich people, or formerly rich people, or the refugee descendents of royalty (as I imagined the Vanyas to be), had on their windows. Not simple sheer see-through curtains and ordinary white pull-down light-blocking shades.

My mother had taken the drapes out of the box. She was holding them up for our appreciation. Her face was flushed red, the way it was when she was happy, excited, or pleased with herself, which wasn't often.

I knew I couldn't pretend to be happy with my present. And I knew that if I didn't pretend to be happy I would hurt my mother immeasurably, as I so often did. Doing "the right thing" where my mother was concerned seemed impossible to me then. A subterranean river of spite and defiance, whose source I could not determine, ran inside me. In times like this, I could feel its destructive potential surface.

My mother is standing in the kitchen holding the drapes she has made me.

"How do you like them?" She looks to me for the approval she surely deserves after making these lined, pinch-pleated drapes late at night for her daughter's pleasure, so her daughter can pretend to be something she isn't, so her room can have lavish, costly hangings, like the Vanyas, the foreigners down the street, who have given her difficult, querulous daughter something to smile about for a change, something she can never seem to manage.

"I hate them." The lethal fusillade of words explodes into my mother's flushed face. I don't stay around to see the damage I cause.

I run out of the kitchen. Out the front door. The screen door slams behind me. I run down the block. Past the house that still smells of fire. To the library. Where I grab a newspaper on a bamboo pole and slump into a chair and hold it in front of my face and pretend to read about hydrogen bombs and fallout and nuclear waste while I sob and sob and sob. For the puppy I will never have.

For a happy life I can only imagine. For the stupid present my dumb mother has given me.

I tell myself this is the worst birthday I have ever had. This is the worst day of my life.

When my mother realizes how much I hate getting the drapes she has made me for a birthday present, and because she sees how much I love my colored paper projects, she and my father begin to buy me presents to stimulate what my father calls my "hyperactive imagination." Now, every year, until I am too old for them, they give me a pencil box as a present to mark the beginning of the school year. It contains a couple of yellow number-two lead pencils, a combination red and blue pencil, a small plastic pencil sharpener, a pink eraser, a small plastic ruler (inaccurately marked in inches and millimeters), a small box of Crayola crayons, a cheap protractor and compass. The box, itself, is a treasure because it has a hinged lid and a very small drawer. Even after I have used, or lost, all the stuff that comes in the pencil box, I hide it in the back of the closet I share with my sister, or in the attic, which is reached by a steep set of stairs. When I'm older, I dig out these boxes and use them to store my keepsakes: Valentine's Day cards I get from boys, ticket stubs from my trips to the Park Lane Movie Theatre, pebbles from the stream in the park where I meet one or another of my boyfriends, beer caps from parties—an agglomeration of mementos that remind me of events I consider important in my life.

A paint-by-numbers set, with tiny little premixed pots of oils, brushes, varnish, and paint remover. To create a "work of art," you dip the brush in the paint and fill the appropriate spaces on the canvas. I complete this first project quickly, and move on to others. Sacré-Coeur seen from a street in Montmartre; a Venetian canal; a seascape; a Mexican village. I fancy myself a great artist; my father tells me about Leonardo Da Vinci and Michelangelo and the Italian Renaissance, about which I begin reading. My mother has my father frame my pictures, and she hangs them on a wall in the television room they have recently converted from our glass-enclosed front porch. These "paintings" hang there until after my mother's death, until my father sells the house. In adulthood, I study painting (many of my paintings are of faceless women); in graduate school, the history of art. My mother, who finds it impossible to do such things for herself, seems to know that, for me, creative play is a cure for a despair that seems to come on me periodically. When she is able, she provides me with the raw materials I need to distract myself.

My mother helps me in many ways, but she holds me back in others. She realizes that, though I fear it as she does, I am as drawn to danger as my father. She doesn't encourage me to pursue the physical challenges to which I am drawn as a girl: ice skating, softball, basketball, which I practice constantly and enthusiastically, hiking, climbing. Rather, because she prefers me to stay home so that she won't have to worry about me, she encourages me to be bold and energetic, and to use my imagination to create excitement for myself, in the kinds of projects I can undertake at home, like reading and art. When I am a Girl Scout, and tell her I want to earn a merit badge in Hiking and Climbing, she tells me I can't, and she won't sign the parent consent forms. So, instead of emulating my father's bravery, I earn merit badges in things I'm good at anyway—Public Speaking, Reading.

But she suggests that I stop rereading the Bobsey Twins and that I read the Nancy Drew mystery series instead.

"You'll find them exciting," she says. She buys me one, through the mail. And I am hooked.

How I love Nancy's cleverness, boldness, and ingenuity! How I want to be like her! To find crimes and solve them. To see clues that others have overlooked, to face danger and overcome fear.

The drama of the detective life is alluring to me. When I announce, to my mother, that I love Nancy Drew so much I am thinking of becoming a detective, she says, "Over my dead body." And, although I do not become a woman detective in my maturity, my intellectual life feels as exciting to me as detective work—it *is* detective work. Like Nancy Drew, I track down clues, try to figure things out, look carefully at evidence, examine motives. Being a biographer is like being a detective.

After the Vanyas and my parents gave me these things that stimulated my imagination, I learned, in time, to find the materials myself. Newsprint, flour and water for papier-mâché. Oil paints and watercolors. Wool. The ingredients for a soup, or a homemade pizza, or a Thai specialty. Bits of information about a writer's life. Simple things that can be transformed through work into something that brings pleasure and satisfaction.

Spin the Bottle

I SPEND MOST of my time as a teenager during the years 1955 through 1958 reading the *New York Times* for our killer weekly "current events" quizzes in history, and trying to figure out how to get out of the house to see one or another of my boyfriends.

Once I begin going to public school when I'm in ninth grade, my interest in what is going on in other parts of the United States, and in the world, is encouraged by my history teachers. Each week, we are asked to identify the names of places and people in the news and briefly state their significance, which I find difficult, and to discuss a current issue. (State your views on United States policy to renew aid to Israel in the wake of the Israeli withdrawal from the Sinai Peninsula; on desegregation; on the Soviet Union's invasion of Hungary; on Fidel Castro's war against Batista in Cuba; on the "Eisenhower Doctrine"; on how the vaccine against polio will improve our lives.)

My looseleaf fills with lists of names and places I believe are important, and their significance. George Meany (elected president of the AFL-CIO). Montgomery, Alabama (place where Negroes boycott segregated city buses). Sinai Peninsula (invaded by Israeli troops). Pakistan (declares itself an Islamic Republic). Suez Canal (taken by Nasser). Hungary (invaded by Soviet troops). Richard M. Nixon (elected vice president of the United States). Martin Luther King (leader of desegregation movement). Franco (Spanish dictator). Jimmy Hoffa (head of the Teamsters Union, "a crook," my father calls him). Joseph M. McCarthy (U.S. senator, led the "McCarthy" hearings, dead, "and not a moment too soon," my mother says). Orval Faubus (turns Little Rock schools into private schools to defy Supreme Court ruling on desegregation in public schools). Rocky Marciano (retires undefeated from boxing, and my father is proud because Marciano's Italian, but my mother says boxing's not a sport, it's "barbaric," and so there's nothing to be proud of). The Brooklyn Dodgers, better known as "The Bums" (1955 WINNERS OF THE WORLD SERIES OVER THE NEW YORK YANKEES, and a cause for personal celebration, since I have been a fan since I was a little girl).

Though I have long since gotten used to Ridgefield, and don't miss Hoboken very much anymore, our family life has settled into a pattern that makes me want to escape it as often as I can. First, there is my sister, who glooms about the house almost as much as my mother does. She is probably severely depressed, though I can't know this at the time. All I know is that I want to escape what I perceive as her endless demands.

"How about a game of Monopoly?" Jill's entreaty. I'm thirteen; she's nine. I think I'm too old to play with her.

"I hate Monopoly," I tell her. "I hate playing games. Don't you have any friends?"

Then, there is my stepgrandmother, who protects me when my father gets angry. She gives me money when I run short, crumpled five-dollar bills that she keeps safety-pinned up inside the lining of her winter coat so that my mother won't find them. My mother runs our family's finances, and, though she worries about running out of money all the time, she does a good job of "stretching a dollar," as she puts it, and manages to save some money each week "for a rainy day." Still, my grandmother tells me that, after my grandfather's death, my mother has taken money that rightfully belonged to her. Because I really can't understand her Italian, I can't put together the pieces of the story she tells me, but I think it's about my grandfather's pension. My grandmother deals with this by arguing with my mother whenever she gets the chance, and by hiding her money from the Social Security checks, which she endorses with an "X" and which she cashes for herself at the bank. As she retrieves a bill, she puts a finger to her whiskered lips, warning me not to reveal her secret hiding place. I never betray her.

But she always wears black dresses, sometimes several at a time, and she smells because she takes sponge baths like we're still living in Hoboken. She is afraid of the bathtub and has never mastered the art of taking a shower. She uses rags instead of toilet paper, which drives my father nuts. Even the few friends I trust enough to take home make fun of her, which hurts my feelings because I care about her though I can no longer communicate with her because I have lost whatever meager Italian I could speak as a little girl. (Years later, when I have children, she sits in front of *Sesame Street* with them, trying to sound out English words.) My friends think my grandmother looks like a witch. They tell me I don't need to buy a costume for Halloween, I can just borrow her clothes instead.

My father, I don't even want to talk about. My father and I still don't see eye to eye on anything. When I was little, I was difficult; now, he tells me, I am impossible. He's right. I am impossible to control. I have a mind of my own. No punishment he inflicts on me can change that.

Then, there is my mother, who would prefer that I stay home to play with my sister. But I am too old to play with my sister. I have discovered a special kind of friendship with a girl. And I have discovered boys. During my high school years, these relationships will make my rupture from my family complete. My obsession with sex will make me an outsider. And an outsider is what I want to be.

It isn't that I want to be a boy. I have never wanted to be a boy because, though I have always liked boys, I have always believed that boys are somehow inferior to girls, that they are "hormonally challenged," as I now put it. I have never met a boy to whom I felt inferior. I have always loved being a girl. I just want to be a girl who does whatever she wants, who doesn't follow the rules of how a girl is supposed to behave.

What I have noticed even at age thirteen is that doing what you're supposed to do if you're a woman doesn't necessarily bring rewards. We live across the street from Mrs. Neil, an English teacher, a terrific woman, who becomes very important to me. She tries very hard to please her husband. She works a full-time job, she cooks, she gardens, she mows the lawn, she does the laundry, she shovels the snow, she changes her flat tires, she's caring, she's an interesting conversationalist, and her husband leaves her anyway. When I ask my mother why, she tells me something true, something I remember: "There is no justice in this world."

I learn about the pleasures of kissing when I'm in the ninth grade with a girl by the name of Happy Klein and with a boy by the name of Donny Lowell. By the middle of the ninth grade, I learn about the pleasures of necking and petting with a boy by the name of Carmine Carrero. And soon after, by the end of the ninth grade, when I am still thirteen, I learn about the pleasures of fucking with a boy by the name of Roy Harrigan.

Donny Lowell is in the eighth grade, though he looks like he should be in the tenth, and I see him almost every day as he walks past my house to the parochial school I attended before moving on to the public junior high. On weekdays, he looks perfectly ordinary, like the rest of the parochial school boys, in his poorly ironed white shirt, all spider web creases where they shouldn't be (sure evidence of maternal neglect) and a well-worn, too-short pair of rumpled navy blue uniform pants (evidence of either poverty or a lack of pride).

But after school and on weekends, he transforms himself and I can't help noticing him. Boys have never interested me in this way before, and I find my interest in Donny Lowell strange, yet compelling. If I ever get married (and I'm not sure I ever will because my parents have told me that there aren't many men who would put up with my headstrong ways), I know it won't be to someone like Donny Lowell. He's not like anyone I would want to marry. For one thing, I think he's too sexy to make good marriage material. For another, he's not a good student and I know he'll never become a success, that he'll work at poorly paying jobs after he graduates high school. I might fool around with someone like Donny Lowell, but I won't marry someone like him. I'm going to choose someone who will make a good husband, not necessarily someone with whom I'm madly in love. Being madly in love, though it sounds good to some of my friends, doesn't sound good to me. It's the word "madly" that bothers me. Like a character in a book I've read, who says that the best long-term marriages are made when the partners love, not madly and passionately, but wisely and well, I have decided that if or when I marry, I will marry wisely and well. I'm going to marry someone with a profession, someone who will respect my independence, someone who will make a good partner. I'm going to marry with my head, and not necessarily with my heart.

But I'm only thirteen, and marriage, if it comes at all, is a long way off, and for now Donny Lowell is on my mind. He wears his black hair slicked back in a D.A., clenches his cigarette between his teeth, puffs on it without taking it out of his mouth. I notice his mouth, its wide, wide grin when he laughs and the way he squints his eyes when the sun gets into them. I watch the smoke as it floats up into his nostrils and think that that's a trick I'd like to try. I think Donny Lowell is gorgeous, and sexy, and he looks great in the tightest jeans anyone has ever had the courage to wear in Ridge-field, New Jersey. Susan says that with jeans that tight, you can't wear underpants, you have to lie down on your bed to zip them up, and that boys have to be careful not to catch their dicks in their zip-pers (or their pubic hair if they happen to have any), which can really hurt.

How Susan has come by this arcane knowledge, I don't ask. But I take her at her word. She is experienced. She reads magazines I can't afford, like *Seventeen*, for tips on boys and dating. When she talks about boys, she gets this dreamy look in her eyes. She warns me never to gargle with Listerine before a date. "Boys," she tells me, "are turned off by its medicinal taste." And she reminds me to always blot my lipstick carefully. "You don't want it to come off all over his face, and just think of what you would do to his dick." I laugh, though I don't quite know what she's talking about. I'll learn soon enough.

I'm the youngest kid in the ninth grade, and I've started wearing makeup, because all my friends wear makeup. My father disap-proves. Too much makeup, he tells me, makes me look like a whore. Too much makeup will give the boys the wrong idea. When I tell Susan this, she tells me he's wrong. Too much makeup will give boys the *right* idea, that you're not a girl anymore, that you're a woman, and that you're ready.

"Ready for what?" I ask her.

"For having some fun," she replies, without specifying. And I'm beginning to understand what Susan means.

When I look at Donny Lowell when he's standing on the corner outside the Sweet Shoppe Saturday afternoons, I feel dizzy, my breathing changes, and I think I'm going to faint. But this is a nice kind of dizzy, not a scary kind of dizzy. I decide I want to see what being with a boy is all about, although I'm not sure I want a boyfriend. Donny Lowell seems as good a boy as any to start with.

When I'm alone, I think of what it would be like to kiss Donny Lowell, to taste his smoky lips, to pull his body close. Soon, I find I'm always thinking about him and that thinking about him sure beats thinking about the other shit I always think about, like how angry I am at my mother and my father, and how afraid I always am.

Donny Lowell's jeans are so tight, the back seam travels down into his crack like a highway I want to take to someplace else, and, from the front, I can see his bulge, and it's big, and he doesn't seem to mind if I stare at it, or at him, which I do, on my way into the Sweet Shoppe. Most of the girls stare at him, though they do it when they're in gangs of five or six, and it's safe. Many of them have a crush on him, though he seems unapproachable, and has never dated anyone we know. I stare at him when I'm alone. He stares right back. He usually hangs out with older kids, outside town, up the hill in Cliffside Park. This is why he seems experienced. This past summer, he worked at Palisades Amusement Park, hanging off the back of the bumper cars, making sure that kids didn't bang into one another too roughly, and he hung out there after work.

Susan and I have seen him a few times at Palisades Amusement Park during the summer when we walk to the park with our siblings in tow. We do this against our wishes, because they cramp our style, but neither of us is allowed to go there without them. My sister, particularly, needs watching. Summers are difficult for her; she doesn't do much. Sometimes she sits in a lounge chair on the back porch and stares off into space. Sometimes she picks at her fingers. My mother urges me to include her in my plans. I rebel. My father steps in and tells me that, unless I take Jill where I'm going, I can't go myself.

I don't want to take Jill. I want to be alone with my friends. This is my last free summer. Next summer, before I enter the tenth grade, I will start working to earn spending money, and to save for college.

Once, Susan and I see Donny Lowell climb onto the Cyclone alone, and we watch as he smiles and shouts his way through the ride, arms waving above his head (defying the rule to keep both hands on the safety bar), sunglasses gleaming in the afternoon sun, pitch black hair blowing back from his face on the ride's steep and dangerous curving downslope, making him look young, vulnerable, delicious. This is when I start paying attention to Donny Lowell.

I hope he makes it through the ride without showing off for us, without trying to stand up, without dying. Stupid kids die on the Cyclone at Palisades Amusement Park with alarming frequency. Stupid kids get killed falling off the Palisades trying to sneak into the park through a hole in the Cyclone fence. My mother tells me never to do that, it's too dangerous.

We are forbidden to ride the Cyclone, though I break the rule, and ride it, but rarely. I need to summon my courage for its wild, exhilarating, heart-stopping ride. My favorite moment is when the cars pause at the top of a long incline, before careening down and around and up again. At the top, you are well above the summit of the Palisades, above the Hudson River, across from New York City, and the view from way up there is splendid, though very few riders enjoy it because they are afraid of heights and hold their eyes tightly closed. I don't. I look around. I breathe in the air. I am surprised that I don't faint, but, after I overcome my fear of climbing onto the ride, I find that I enjoy it.

My sister, though, surprises me. At home, she can barely move. But at Palisades Amusement Park, she wants to climb onto the most dangerous and forbidden rides, like the Whip and the Tilt-a-Whirl, which I have ridden only once because it is too terrifying. The ride in which a wire cage is spun so quickly that the riders are pinned to its sides by centrifugal force while the bottom of the cage drops out, and it tilts and whirls, tilts and whirls, for far longer than anyone can tolerate without shrieking. We know some kids who go on these rides all the time. Sensation junkies, we call them now. Donny Lowell is one of them. I'm afraid my sister will become one of these kids too.

More than the Cyclone, the Tilt-a-Whirl has become a test of manhood for boys who live nearby. Boys who need to show that they can overcome their fear or that they have none. They bet their weekly allowances on how often they can ride the Tilt-a-Whirl without vomiting. Parkgoers draw perverse amusement from watching its victims stagger about in a state of vertiginous disorientation, after just one ride. On my single ride, I am trapped within its wire cage, spinning and spinning, forced against the side, unable to move, too terrified, too paralyzed to scream in protest. I know that nothing can stop this ride until it is over; I only hope that I can make it to the end without dying.

Once, despite the age requirement, my sister charms her way onto this ride while my back is turned. I am furious with her, and I watch her, helplessly, sure that, this time, the principle of centrifugal force will not operate, sure that, this time, the ride will claim one victim and that it will be my sister. If my sister dies, I tell myself, my father will kill me for sure.

She staggers off though she is nowhere near as afraid as I believe she should be. I threaten that I'll tell on her.

"Don't tell Mommy," she says. "I won't do it again." I don't tell my mother, but I do say, "That's it. It's over. I'm never taking that kid to Palisades Amusement Park again."

In the autumn, on my way to school, I see Donny Lowell coming down the block in my direction. He's headed for his school; I'm headed for mine. I stare at him directly. He stares back, though there is nothing but mild amusement in his glance. There's something about his squinty blue eyes and his dark hair and how he's so comfortable with his body and how he shows it off that suggests possibilities I want to explore. I just want to sample what I think he has to offer.

There are rumors around town about Donny Lowell, that he screws married women. "They probably beg him for it," Susan surmises. This I can understand, though I don't see myself as the begging kind. Susan tells me she knows a way we can find out who he's screwing. During the school year, he's a delivery boy for the local drugstore, and she thinks he probably fucks some customers when he's out making deliveries.

"Perfect setup," she tells me. This I can't even imagine, but according to Susan, there are many housewives who are dissatisfied with their husbands who don't have the guts to go out and get it for themselves, but who wouldn't turn it down if it rode up to them on an old, rusty bicycle looking as cute as Donny Lowell.

All we have to do, she says, is walk up and down the streets after school (we don't have anything better to do), and look for Donny's bike tied up to a tree. If we find it, and if it's there a long time, and if he comes out of the house and his hair's all messed up, then we'll know he's screwing the woman who lives inside.

Susan is often full of crazy plans like this, and she makes fun of me and calls me a deadbeat, unless I help her carry them out. I think she's right, though, about Ridgefield being one of the most boring places on earth, and about needing to stir things up. Once, she gets me to ride the number 166 bus all the way into New York City. I enjoy the ride there, though I feel I'm choking to death when our bus gets stuck in a traffic jam deep inside the Lincoln Tunnel. The exhaust fumes from the cars and buses pour in through the open windows of our bus. I am near panic.

"Relax," Susan tells me. "Did you ever hear of anyone dying down here?"

"I haven't, but that doesn't mean it hasn't happened," I

counter. But the pleasure has drained out of the day for me, and I refuse to accompany Susan as she walks up and down Forty-second Street, looking at the advertisements for the pornographic movies that play there. Instead, I sit in the seedy café in the Port Authority, drinking lukewarm tea, watching the hookers, hoping we won't hit another traffic jam on our way home.

For a couple of weeks, we walk around town, looking for Donny Lowell, looking for his bicycle. We don't see him; we don't see it. Susan refuses to give up her story about Donny. I stop caring whether it's true or not.

When it's Donny's birthday, he decides to give himself a party. Starts inviting a bunch of girls. No boys. It seems a curious arrangement, but when he asks me to attend, I'm excited, and I decide I'll go, though he hasn't invited Susan. ("You'll tell me everything that happens," she says.)

When I arrive at Donny's house, he greets me at the door, and tells me to come inside. I'm the first person there, as usual, not wanting to miss anything. He smells of cologne. I notice that his parents aren't there. I see that somehow he's gotten his hands on a couple of six-packs of beer. They sit, neck down, in a cooler, with bottles of soft drinks, including cream soda, my favorite.

Almost immediately, the rest of the girls arrive. In all, there are six of us. Barbara, now at Catholic high school in Teaneck. Lynette, Deborah, and Doreen, all in eighth grade in public school. Patrice, a girl in Donny's class. I'm the only one at the party who's in the ninth grade.

Donny offers us each a beer. "To loosen things up," he says. Each of us takes a turn with the bottle opener. Donny opens Patrice's for her. I'm jealous. I've never had a beer before, and I watch the way Donny swills it from the bottle before I swill mine. I learn how to open my throat to down the malty yeasty brew. In no time, I'm light-headed, ready for whatever the evening will bring. I know what I want from Donny; I wonder if he wants anything from me. I wonder if Patrice will get in the way of my plans.

As soon as Donny finishes his beer, he says, "C'mon, girls, let's play a game of spin the bottle." We agree. We've played the game before. We've been playing it since about sixth grade, and we are not at all abashed at the likelihood that girls will wind up kissing girls. That's always been part of the fun of this game.

The best kiss I've had thus far has come earlier this year soon after school starts at Kevin Vesay's party with a girl named Happy Klein who takes her duty in kissing me very seriously.

Her lips are soft and her kiss is long and her breath is warm and tastes like the peanuts she has been eating. Every time Happy spins the bottle, that night, it points to me, and our friends enjoy the spectacle of our kisses, which become more ardent as the evening progresses.

After, Happy and I walk to my home, and she asks me if I want to "go friendship." I say yes. The next weekend, we go on the bus into Hackensack to a jewelry store. We buy matching silver rings encircled with hearts, and we exchange pictures, and sign them "All my love, forever," on the back, and pledge ourselves to an eternal devotion.

For the next month, we spend all our free time together. We walk down the block with our arms locked around each other's waist or we hold hands. As soon as we part, we wait a bit, and then call each other on the telephone. Bolder than I, Happy has emblazoned "Happy and Louise, together, forever" in an enormous heart on the cover of her looseleaf. Not so many people mock us. A few boys ask, "What are you, a couple of lezzies?" I don't know what they mean, don't care. This kind of thing I have with Happy is commonplace in our town among girls our age.

But the hugging and kissing that we have enjoyed doing in public, I can't bring myself to do in private, and so Happy and I part, in an agony of unsatisfied longing, and amid tears and recriminations.

My relationship with Happy isn't unusual. In the early months of ninth grade, there are more girl/girl couples than boy/girl couples, though this will change by the next year. Lust is beginning to find us, and girls are the earliest objects of our affection.

What I liked best about Happy was that she had no father. Her apartment, which she shared with her hard-working, hard-smoking mother, was an ebullient, festive place, with magazines and makeup and clothing and take-out cartons of food and pizza boxes strewn all over the kitchen table. I couldn't imagine our house ever being so chaotic, or so filled with life.

Happy had been well named, and, until our breakup, she was always laughing. I connected her happiness with her mother's being a widow who had only herself and her daughter to please, though my mother regarded the fact of Mrs. Klein's widowhood as an unspeakable tragedy. I never realized, until later, that being with me made Happy happy, and that she continued to love me for a long time after we parted.

Sometimes I glance out my bedroom window and see Happy standing across the street, staring at my house, trying to look inconspicuous. I can't figure out why. I have made myself stop caring about her; I assume she has stopped caring about me. I don't know yet that one of the tragedies of love is that, although two people might fall in love simultaneously, as Happy and I did when we kissed one another, often one person falls out of love sooner than the other.

Through loving Happy I have learned, though, that loving someone outside my house distracts me, takes my mind off things, permits me to see how other families behave, makes me feel better than I'd ever felt before, more real, somehow, more connected to the world, and I want to repeat the experience soon, and often.

Something, though, held me back from loving Happy the way

that I knew Happy loved me, and she remained my only same-sex relationship. Maybe it is because of what had happened with my Aunt Vinnie. My feeling for boys seemed safer, more predictable, more controllable. With boys, I believed I had the upper hand. They interested me, but I didn't care that much about them.

In honor of his birthday, Donny Lowell tells us he's going to change the rules for playing spin the bottle. If it's all right with us, he says, with a roguish glint in his steely blue eyes, he's the only one who'll get to spin the bottle. We agree. It seems that he's prepared to do a lot of kissing.

We sit in a circle in anxious anticipation. Waiting. Hoping for the neck of the beer bottle he's spinning to point in our direction.

First, it's Deborah's turn.

Then Doreen's.

Then Patrice's. I'm jealous.

This is less fun than I thought. I decide that if chance doesn't choose me soon, I'll leave. Walk home the long way. Go past the school. See what's doing at the gym where the kids hang out Friday nights. See what boys are free. Find one. Make him walk me home. I'm not one to waste my time.

When it finally is my turn, I'm ready for Donny Lowell. Ready to see what he's all about. Ready to see if he was worth waiting for.

I don't bend over and give him a quick kiss on the lips like Patrice, like the other girls. I stand. Donny stands. I take a step into the center of the circle. He takes a step into the center of the circle. I look straight into his eyes without blinking, without looking away. And he looks straight into mine. I take a deep breath, to get ready, and I smell his smell, and I suck it deep inside. I know I'm going to like this.

I pull Donny Lowell to me and we kiss and now I know why there's so much fuss in town about how sexy Donny Lowell is. His lips tease mine, then mine tease his. Whatever we've started, I think, will take a long, long time to finish. When we stop kissing, I take a deep breath, look at the others, and say, "Hey, girls, I think it's just about time for you to go home."

That night, though I had told my parents that I was going to a "school function," and that I'd be home by about ten, I stayed at Donny Lowell's until well past eleven. During the two hours that we spent together, I didn't worry that the roof of his porch would cave in, I didn't think about my family, didn't think of the trouble I'd be in for coming home late, didn't think of all the homework I had to do, of all the names and dates I had to memorize for my next week's current events quiz.

When I left Donny Lowell's at about eleven-thirty, he asked me if I wanted him to walk me home. I told him that wasn't necessary, that I didn't have far to walk, that I wasn't afraid of going home alone. The truth was that I had had enough for one night and that I wanted to spend the time walking home alone savoring what had happened to me, thinking about whether I would tell Susan everything that happened, or whether I would keep it all to myself. And, though I knew that Donny Lowell and I would never be boyfriend and girlfriend, I had taken what he was willing to give me. I had learned that kissing was a powerful narcotic. But I had also learned that sexual excitement, when it occurs between equal, willing partners, can be exhilarating, and not at all frightening, and so I started to come alive.

Boy Crazy

"BOY CRAZY, THAT'S what you are, and it's going to get you into trouble if you don't watch out," my mother calls to me as I scramble out the door to meet this boy or that one at the Sweet Shoppe.

"Being boy crazy is better than being crazy crazy, like you," I tell myself, as I race down the steps, pulling on my jacket.

My mother does things I don't understand, and I tell my friends she's nuts. They don't believe me. But I don't understand the forces that drive my mother to do what she does, to not do what she can't. Like leave the house alone very often. Or drive (which she learns to do, eventually, though she never in her life has the gas tank filled; this is something my father has to do for her). She sets the breakfast table at night and turns our cereal bowls upside down so dust won't get into them. She reverses the direction of every other hanger in our closets so if thieves break into our house, they can't grab all our stuff at once; they will have to take our clothes out item by item.

"It's a deterrent," she tells me. "It'll take them more time to rob you than they want to spend."

But we almost never go any place, I tell her, and someone is usually home.

"They can enter a house when you're sleeping." She tells me that if you wake up, and see a burglar in your room, you should pretend you are sleeping. That's the safest thing to do. You might get robbed, but you probably won't get murdered. She reads about this in the *Bergen Evening Record*. I tell her our stuff isn't worth stealing. She says, "You never know what someone else needs." She's right about that. But who would want to steal the dress she made me from two different leftover pieces of yellow curtain material? I wear it once, to some fake relatives' house in Brooklyn. I don't care about these people, so it doesn't matter what I wear when we visit them. I never wear it in Ridgefield. But they look at me in a funny way, as if they have seen this fabric before on the windows of our kitchen and dining room, on their only trip to visit us.

As it turns out, they have lots of money and no taste. Their pink plush wraparound sofa is sheathed in plastic, and they have plastic runners on their white shag carpet so it won't get dirty and my mother can't hide her disdain.

"Mafia," my mother spits at my father, after we leave. "You can tell by the crystal chandeliers." According to my mother, any Italian who owns a crystal chandelier has gotten it with Mafia money. Such luxury is way out of my parents' reach.

"We may be poor," she says, "but at least we're honest." And then she launches into one of her little set speeches about how you should never do anything that will compromise your integrity, that will prevent you from sleeping at night. During these moments, my mother is the wisest person I know. If everyone lived according to her standards, the world would be a wonderful place.

Years later, when she hears that the daughter of this family has become a junkie, she is not surprised, and she has no sympathy for the family. The sins of the fathers, according to her moral code, are inevitably visited upon the children.

"What did they expect?" she tells me. "That they could push dope in the ghettos and ruin entire neighborhoods and get rich from it, and that it would never affect them?"

My mother is right about my being boy crazy and I'm wrong about her being crazy crazy. What she is, though I do not know it at the time, is severely depressed. She has an illness that comes and goes, and I don't understand it, and neither does she. She thinks that if she tries hard enough, works hard enough, it will go away. She tries to control her moods; tries to cheer herself up; tries to hide the pain she feels, but it doesn't work.

My sister, too, shows early signs of depression. One summer, when I am still a teenager, she sits in a lounge chair on our back porch day after day, day after day. Nothing interests her. Nothing can rouse her. No one can get her to move. When she's older, she refers to this period, laughingly, as "the summer I sat in the chair." But it is no laughing matter.

No one gives this illness a name. I'm sure my mother did not know what afflicted her, and what threatened my sister. Depression is not something anyone talks about as I'm growing up in Ridgefield.

Why I am boy crazy is no mystery to me. I like thinking about boys. I find that obsessing about kissing and, eventually, about necking, petting, and having sex, though it surely creates problems, keeps your mind off all the other problems you have. Like how worried you are about your sister, who always seems so unhappy, and how you have to always take care of her. Like how tired you are of your mother and grandmother fighting. How afraid you are of your father. How you hate being shipped off to Long Island for weeks on end during the summer. How worried you are that you worry about everything. How you wonder what you're going to do with your life, and how you know that whatever that is, it isn't going to be anything like what your mother is doing with her life.

As soon as I discover the pleasure of kissing with Donny Lowell, I try to find ways to indulge in it as often as I can, and with as many boys as possible.

Over the next few years, there are many boys in my life. So many boys that, when I graduate high school, I get voted "Class Flirt." This means that everyone thinks I'm the most sexually active girl in my class. This isn't exactly true. At one point in high school, my major claim to fame is that I have, in quick succession, "dated" the entire starting lineup of my high school's basketball team. I also "date" many of its football players, all the baseball infielders, and a few wrestlers. I am partial to guys with good bodies. They have to be nice and smart, too, though I am willing to make exceptions about their being smart if they are gorgeous, nice, and have great bodies. It amazes me that there are so many boys who meet my very exacting standards.

There is Donald Zavier, who is good in math, who tastes like vanilla; he doesn't like sex as much as I do, and we are a couple for a very short time. John Corwin. I remember nothing about him except that he is a baseball-playing boy, and he can never get his cowlick to lie flat; this, and not me, is his primary preoccupation; he leaves me for someone who is very proper (we all know she kisses with her lips closed) who wouldn't dream of having any kind of sex before marriage. Lou Zariga, who plays basketball in a disconnected, lanky, half-assed kind of way, which turns me off, because it means he lacks the will to win, no drive, no ambition; it also happens to be how he makes love; we are a couple longer than we should be. There is a group of boys I call "the car boys"; they work in gas stations, and strip down their cars, then rebuild them, then strip them down again; I date them primarily because they drive my parents crazy; I drop each of them quickly, though I learn about differentials, detailing, carburetors, downshifting, butterfly valves (this impresses my husband, many years later when I diagnose a problem with one of our cars that has eluded our mechanic); I drop "the car boys" because they would rather be under their cars than under me.

Actually, though I've had all these boyfriends, and though I've done a hell of a lot of necking and petting throughout high school, I only fuck one boy, Roy Harrigan, with whom I have an on-again, off-again, clandestine sexual relationship. I have sex with him for years, and tell myself, if I can have my way, I'll sleep with him forever.

I use sex to separate myself from my family. To establish my freedom. To establish that I'm different—a girl to whom the standard rules of behavior don't apply. And besides, being boy crazy sure as hell makes life in Ridgefield, New Jersey, the most boring place on this planet, a hell of a lot more interesting.

I'm no athlete, though I love playing basketball, and I am a ferocious guard. I don't play a musical instrument; my family can't afford one. I have taken dance lessons, but I can't force my body into the contortions required by classical ballet. I have no real hobby, though I read a lot. My interest in crafts has temporarily faded. I have nothing I feel I can excel at. Except attracting boys.

I perfect the art of seductive banter. Unlike many girls I know, I am willing to follow through with what I've started. I'm not "all talk and no action" like some girls. I'm "all talk and some action." Necking, petting, become gratifying enough pastimes and I am lucky with the boys in my life. They give me far more pleasure than pain. They never pressure me to do more than what I'm willing to do. If there's any pressure, it usually comes from me.

Sometimes, though, I tell myself that if I spent as much time thinking about schoolwork as I spend thinking about boys, I could become a rocket scientist, but I don't want to become a rocket scientist. The truth is that I'm not sure what I want to become. So I fill the time with thinking about boys, with thinking about sex.

Sex is the one thing in my life (besides reading) that feels good, and can usually be counted upon to please. It lets me forget how miserable my life is. It doesn't cost anything. And, though I have been working at odd jobs since I turned eleven, I don't have very much money to spend. I've been saving it all for college.

"The trouble with sex," Susan says, "is that although it's cheap, it's also dangerous."

Over the next few years, I discover that, while all my friends are interested in finding true love, in entering steady relationships (an astonishing number of which will end in marriage), I relish experience and variety. This means that many girls don't like me or don't trust me. They see me as a threat because I am the kind of girl who, if given the chance, will go after their boyfriends. If I take a fancy to someone, I don't wait for him to take a fancy to me. I put the make on him, and I usually succeed in attracting him, though the relationship doesn't usually last very long.

This behavior singles me out, means that I'm different, not like the other girls. Susan, though, is like me, and she remains my friend because we're no threat to each other, because we're sure we have different tastes in boys.

Neither Susan nor I are members of the "in" crowd, though I float on its fringes. I never make the cheerleading squad, though I try every year. During tryouts, I do a terrific cartwheel, a great back jump—I even touch my toes to my head. Yet I am never voted in by the other cheerleaders, probably because I've messed around with most of their boyfriends.

I see myself as a loner. Someone who can see through people, who can figure them out (though I can't figure myself out), and I don't like what I see. Often, the girls of the "in" crowd snub me and mock me. There's a lot to ridicule. How I'm rarely without my sister in tow. How, at parties, I drink too much and disappear into a back room with one boy or another. How uncool my homemade clothes are. How my grandmother always wears black and ties scarves under her chin when she goes to church. How she sits in the window and menaces anyone who passes by our house. How she shines the flashlight out the window at me when a boy walks me home.

But no matter how boy crazy I am, I am not involved in the biggest scandal that hits Ridgefield in my adolescence.

One day, after school, the police raid a local house and break up a sex ring. Some of my girlfriends and ex-boyfriends are involved, I learn, through gossip, because the newspaper can't print the names of the kids involved because they're juveniles. Lurid pictures of soiled mattresses, girls' underpants and bras, sex magazines, and empty liquor bottles are published in the local newspapers. I wonder if the guy who owns the house films what goes on there with hidden cameras. My mother can't believe this kind of thing is happening in our town. I'm not surprised; I know all my friends have sex. But, though I'm glad I'm not involved, I can't figure out why, given my reputation, I haven't been invited to join them. Can it be that I'm not as bad as I think I am?

My mother says the girls' good reputations are tarnished forever. I tell her not to worry; none of these girls had a good reputation to begin with.

The first important boy in my life is Carmine Carrero, whose parents own a garden shop. He is a football player, a wrestler, and a bodybuilder, and he is almost as wide as he is tall, and he has a beautiful body and the biggest biceps in the school and he flexes them for me whenever we take off our clothes. All the petting we do is prefaced by me being treated to a personal display of his sculptured body, of his amazing triceps, his "traps" and "lats," and I wait patiently through the posing, although it is his cock that interests me the most. Unlike his other muscles, his cock does not necessarily obey its owner's commands. I seem to exert more control over it than he does.

Carmine's mother spends her whole day out in the garden shop and she smells of manure and mulch and she wears rubber hip boots because the ground is cold and damp. Her red hair frizzes over her forehead. She never wears makeup and her hands and nails are filthy, but I think she is the most beautiful woman I have ever seen because she can pick up a hundred-pound bag of mulch and fling it over her shoulder and take it out to the customer's car as if it were as light and easy to carry as a newborn baby. Carmine's father is shorter than she, and not as strong, and he smokes a pipe that he holds between his teeth, and tends the cash register and the phone, while she does the lifting and carrying.

I hang out at the garden shop even when Carmine isn't there, as if I am an anthropologist who has discovered a new and very interesting tribe, whose mores and manners are far superior to those of the rest of the humans I have encountered. Mr. and Mrs. Carrero work together, without complaint, side by side, day after day, throughout the seasons, and, though they rarely speak, they are always nice to one another when they do, and they are polite and helpful to their customers. During the winter, they huddle together in the shed, warmed only by a small space heater and the steaming mugs of milky coffee they pour from matching thermoses that Mrs. Carrero refills several times a day in their tiny kitchen in their house next door. All this rubs off on Carmine, and, in spite of his size and strength, he is a polite and gentle giant, a tender, solicitous lover. The perfect boy to have for a first boyfriend. (Every girl should be so lucky.)

I work with the Carreros one Christmas, selling Christmas trees. Carmine and I move in synchrony as we tie up the trees, hoist them to the tops of cars, secure them with heavy twine. We make a good team, and I can imagine what a lifetime with him would be like.

It is from Carmine that I receive my first bought present from someone outside the family, but he hasn't selected it himself. His mother has. He tells me he has asked her for help and she buys me a lemon yellow Banlon sweater set for my fourteenth birthday because she thinks I should wear more cheerful clothing. "She's so pretty," she tells Carmine, who tells me what she says, after he gives me my present, "but she always dresses like she's on her way to the morgue to identify a body."

(Years later, when I pack my meager wardrobe for college, I take the sweater set with me; it is still like new because I have worn it only for important occasions, and I think it will be perfect for college. I wear it to a college mixer with a circle pin, trying to be collegiate. Some rich girls who live in my dorm make fun of me because it's Banlon.

"She thinks she's so cool, but how can she be cool when she's wearing an oil slick?" one chuckles to another, making sure I'm within earshot.

"Leave her alone," the other one says, "she doesn't know any better."

When I get a chance, I ask my father, who knows about such things, about how Banlon is made. He tells me about how polymers are made from petroleum products. Though I have concluded these girls are assholes—one brags about how she keeps little note cards to keep track of the outfits she wears so that she won't wear the same thing twice with the same boy—I never wear the sweater set again.)

Mrs. Carrero ignores that Carmine and I spend the time he is supposed to be working on Saturdays up in his very small airless room, our mouths locked together, our fingers touching and probing. She always rings the doorbell loudly before she comes into her home because I'm sure she knows what we are doing and she wants to give us some warning so that she doesn't embarrass us and so I feel safe with Carmine in his room.

Carmine is my first real boyfriend, and we meet after school in the nonfiction section of the library, which is way in the back, to continue our sexual adventures.

Through the dirty window of the library, I watch him running toward the library, toward me. He can't seem to get to me fast enough. I am excited, but I pretend to be engrossed in a book about Hannibal I need to take out for an oral report in Latin.

I feel someone come up behind me. I turn around. Carmine's standing there, smelling loamy, like the earth. It's nice. He tucks my hair behind my ears and kisses me, lightly, on the cheek. So lightly, it's barely a kiss at all. It feels more like a whisper.

As always, I pull him to me, turn him around, push him back against the books so I can enjoy myself while he watches out for the librarian. I kiss Carmine hard, unzip the fly of his school pants, and reach in through the opening in his jockey shorts to find his cock.

He's uneasy about doing this in the library. I'm not.

I wrap my fingers around his cock. Hold him. He starts to move. I keep touching him, stroking him. He looks over my shoulder to make sure that no one is coming, not quite enjoying himself, and he can never understand how I can take such risks, how I seem not to care about getting caught. I lick the sweat on Carmine's neck, kiss his ear, tell him I want more.

"Not here," he says. "Come to my house after I finish work."

"But I can't wait," I tell him. I don't tell him that it would be impossible for me to get out of the house after supper on a school night.

Carmine drops to his knees, lifts up my skirt, pulls down my underpants. He can't wait either.

When I am in my thirties, I find out, through a high school friend, that Carmine is dead from an incurable disease whose name she can't remember. He was a phys ed teacher, and happily married, with two young daughters.

When I am dating him, whenever my mother tells me I shouldn't be getting so serious with Carmine so young, I tell her how nice he is to me. Although she likes him because he helps her choose flowers for her rock garden, she continues to admonish me with what I then think is a crazy warning, "Only the good die young," but, in Carmine's case, my mother was right.

My relationship with Carmine ends when I betray him when I go on my class trip to Washington, D.C., without him. I can't resist necking on the bus with Sam Lawler, all the way there, and all the way back, and the news gets back to Sam's girlfriend, who threatens to beat me up, and to Carmine. Despite my entreaties, and my telling Carmine that I have made a gigantic mistake (which I know I have), Carmine has too much self-respect to take me back. He tells me that my big problem is that I have to learn how to control myself, and he's right, and I know it.

I wish I could say I learned an important lesson from Carmine, but I didn't. But while I was away from Carmine, I wanted to be with Sam, even though I knew I was betraying him. My impulses, not my sense of right and wrong, or of what it was good for me to do to protect myself, were driving my behavior. I had begun to enact the cycle of loving, loss, grief, and mourning that I would repeat often throughout high school and college. It was a cycle I was familiar with because it dated back to when my father went to war. It was a cycle, too, that I now suspect had its roots in what happened to me with Aunt Vinnie. Maybe I betrayed Carmine because I wanted to feel in control of the cycle that had made me so unhappy as a child, though I surely did not realize this at the time. And maybe I betrayed him, too, because being part of a couple so young threatened my freedom to come and go from school as I pleased, to explore relationships with other boys, to do whatever I wanted to do without having to answer to anybody.

* * *

My high school career is getting off to a good enough start. I am a high average student; in time, I become a very good student, in college, an excellent student, in graduate school, a superior student. I am doing hours of homework at the special desk my father has made for me. At my mother's urging, and despite the school's counselor (who has suggested I take secretarial courses because I look like the type of girl who would make a good secretary, and, besides, I'm Italian, and he hasn't in all his years of counseling, met an Italian who was serious about going to college), I enroll in the college preparatory curriculum.

I'm not sure what I want to study at college. Anthropology, maybe. I have taken home books from the library about some tribes in the Pacific. I have read about the Mayans and the Aztecs. But I don't know whether I have the courage I suspect is required to do this kind of work, to go to far-off places, to camp out under the stars, to eat strange foods. My mother suggests that I should be practical and perhaps think about teaching; my father thinks I'd make a great lawyer because I'm so argumentative.

English and history are fine, though our only readings come from textbooks, and I find them boring; I'm used to reading "real" books, not snippets from books, not textbooks that are deadly dull and nearly impossible to read without falling asleep. The mysteries of Latin are eluding me; this dead language has too many endings for me to learn before I can read it, which is what I want to do. For some reason, I want to read accounts, in Latin, about how Hannibal crossed the Alps, about how Julius Caesar died.

All the girls are required to take home economics to make them into good homemakers, and I think it's stupid, although I like the cheery kitchen with the stoves, sinks, and well-stocked refrigerators all lined up in a row. I already know how to sew and knit, but I botch our first project, an apron trimmed with rickrack, because I'm not interested. Nor am I interested in learning the miracle of making your own mayonnaise; we use Miracle Whip at home when we have sandwiches for lunch, which isn't very often. The food this teacher makes us cook—eggs en cocotte, broccoli with hollandaise sauce—seems strange to me, and I know I will never cook it, never eat it. One of my friends, who's Syrian, says it's "fake food," though our teacher calls it "continental." I'd rather take shop, because eventually you get to work on a car, which I think would be useful; besides, it would be an easy way to meet boys.

Though I have no trouble grasping its concepts, math continues to be difficult for me; I still count on my fingers like a baby, because I've never learned to add and subtract in my head, nor do I know the times tables by heart, and I never learn them, no matter how hard I practice. (Years later, when I learn that Virginia Woolf counted on her fingers, too, I am delighted.) My teacher can't figure out why this should be, and she thinks I'm lying when I say I have no memory, that I can't remember numbers or formulas. This makes math hard, but I am determined to stick it out because the teacher had told us that girls don't have the kind of logical mind you need to do math, and so she has seated all the boys across the front of the class, so she can give them the attention they deserve, and all girls across the back, so she can ignore them. These are the days before such blatant sex discrimination raises eyebrows, and I take it, without complaint, though I am determined to prove her wrong. In my imaginings, though, I toss her onto the top of the Christmas bonfire so she can burn to death, or I stab her with the pointy end of my protractor. Thinking these thoughts gets in the way of my learning about sines and cosines.

I don't get how my teacher can be so unfair. This bullshit of hers about girls not being logical, I don't buy. I'm the most logical person I know. I'm so logical, I drive my father crazy because he can never win an argument with me, and he has to walk away or threaten to beat the shit out of me to make me withdraw from a fight. I'm logical enough to figure out that what my teacher says about how girls can't learn math, given that she is a woman and has learned math well enough to teach it, is completely illogical.

My not remembering numbers not only makes math hard, it makes life hard. I carry around folded and dusty pieces of paper in my pockets upon which I write the numbers I need to remember but can't. Telephone numbers of my friends, whom I call from the Sweet Shoppe, so that my parents can't hear my conversations, which are invariably about boys, kissing, and sex. Telephone numbers of boys I'm interested in or might become interested in (there are lots of these). Locker combinations (gym, hall locker, bicycle lock, combination lock for the lock box in which I keep my valuables so my mother can't riffle through them). Important dates in history. The square root of pi. The number of the bus you take to get to Hackensack, to get to Palisades Park, to get to New York City. My parents' and sister's birth dates.

"Why do you bother carrying all that stuff around?" Susan asks me one day when an avalanche of papers overflows my jean's pocket as I root around for the number at Carmine's garden shop. "It would drive me nuts."

I don't tell her that, if I don't carry these numbers with me, I worry that someday I'll find myself somewhere I don't want to be, and I won't remember my telephone number, my home address, or the telephone number of anyone who can help me, and I won't find my way home, though home isn't really a place I want to be.

If I am ever stopped and searched by policemen, they will be sure they have nabbed a kingpin numbers runner for a famous Brooklyn Mafia family trying to extend its operations into suburban New Jersey; that I have an Italian last name will clinch it. I worry about this occasionally. It takes my mind off worrying about getting pregnant. I worry about getting pregnant even before it's possible for me to get pregnant. I worry that, as I'm kissing this boy or that boy, some tiny, very active spermlet will swim through the boy's jockey shorts, through his jeans, through my jeans, through my white, little-girl underpants, up through my vagina, into my birth canal, and find its way to the egg I know is waiting there to be fertilized, just like the diagram in the booklet about the facts of life my doctor has given me when I am thirteen years old and start menstruating.

After I stop seeing Carmine, I have a lot of free time. So I start reading a series of books about sexual entanglements—*The Scarlet Letter, Madame Bovary, Anna Karenina*—that scare me. They show me how illusory romantic love is, how dangerous sex can be, and how, if you have it with the wrong person, it can ruin your life forever. Yet these tales of great passion also attract me. Hester Prynne, Emma Bovary, Anna Karenina are women who broke the rules, pushed the boundaries of the way women were allowed to behave in their society, and I like that. Yet I wonder why having illicit sex is the only way for these women to assert their independence and why they're made to suffer. Is there any other, less dangerous way to do this?

I see something of myself in these women and I worry. I start to wonder if being "boy crazy" as I am can make you "crazy crazy." I want passion in my life, but I know I don't want to go crazy because of it, I don't want to die for it. I can't figure out how to find it without taking risks and I don't know if you can have passion in your life if you marry. I think I want to marry, eventually, but I don't want a boring marriage, a stultifying, traditional marriage, like Emma Bovary, like Anna Karenina, that will limit my freedom. Yet there aren't any marriages I have seen or read about that are like the one I'd like to have for myself—a working partnership, with tenderness and respect, like I've seen in the Carreros' marriage, but with more "zing" to it, and with far more independence.

There aren't any women who are married whom I've read about or seen who are what I'd like to be when I grow up. And there aren't any women who aren't married whom I've read about or seen who are what I'd like to be when I grow up.

And though I act cocky, and have a big mouth, and my father always tells me I have all the answers, I know I don't have any of the answers about love, about being grown up. I feel as small and scared and defenseless and damaged as the small sparrow I'd pried out of the mouth of a neighborhood cat and bandaged up and fed, for days, with an eyedropper, before taking it down to the park and releasing it, after my father convinced me that it was wrong to keep it, and that eventually it would have to make it on its own or die.

Vertigo

1 9 5 8

I AM FIFTEEN years old and crazy about a boy named Roy when I become obsessed with Alfred Hitchcock's *Vertigo*.

One Saturday afternoon, my friend Susan and I walk into Palisades Park to the Park Lane Theatre to go to the movies. We have no idea what's playing; it doesn't really matter. We would go to the movies Saturdays, anyway, no matter what movie was playing.

The movie theater is only a mile away from where we live, and if we hurry, we can walk it in fifteen minutes. Today we are in no rush. We have given ourselves plenty of time to get there. We want to enjoy our time alone together. And, besides, if we're late for the movie, it doesn't matter. The show, Saturday, is continuous. If we miss the beginning, and the movie interests us, which it rarely does, we'll stay to see what we missed.

As always, Susan and I have much to talk about. Boyfriends. Sex. Our households. How much Susan hates her mother, "the witch." Their latest fight. (I get undressed next to Susan in gym and know how to slip in and out of my clothes without exposing myself, but Susan doesn't. When she takes off her sweater, I can see the bruises on her back, her arms. It's something I don't ask her about, a wordless bargain we have struck: you don't ask me; I don't ask you.)

I tell Susan how furious I am at my father. Describe our latest battle. (How I run away, don't know where to go, and spend a couple of hours in the research room at the library, pretending to be absorbed in a volume of the *Encyclopaedia Britannica*, unable to read through my tears. We fight because my father has pried the lock off the bathroom door, the only room in our house that has ever had a lock, the only place in the house I can lock him out of, that I can lock myself into. Our argument escalates rapidly after I tell him that what he's doing is nuts and he replies that it's my fault: if I didn't always lock myself in the bathroom, he wouldn't have to do this.)

Susan and I talk about how tired she is of taking care of her stepbrothers. How much my responsibility for my sister bugs me. I make jokes about how my sister stares into space. (Secretly I worry, but this is not something I can tell Susan.)

Susan and I share dreams of how different life will be for us when we're out on our own. We talk about how many more years we have to wait. We say we'll never do to our children what our parents have done to us.

Susan tells me she wants to get married soon. She can support herself and her husband by being a secretary. I plan to go to a college that is far away, and, though I'm not yet sure what I'll study, I'm thinking I might study English and become an English teacher. I've started to think about this since I've been working for Mrs. Neil, the English teacher who lives across the street. She loves her work, and she has summers free to travel.

Susan and I wonder what our lives might have been like if we had different sets of parents. All we want is to break with our past. All we want is a life with a little fun in it.

"Fun," Susan says. "What's that?" I tell her that fun is what I have when I'm with Roy. She gives me a look. She's heard too much about how unhappy I am when I see Roy with his steady girlfriend to believe this.

The truth is that neither Susan nor I have much fun. We both work harder after school, during summers, on weekends, than other kids we know. You name it, I've done it. I've worked in a bakery, baby-sat, run errands, been a clerk, done odd jobs, raked lawns, organized people's closets, polished furniture, tutored, shopped for shut-ins.

Susan and I are usually so serious, so cheerless that the kids have started calling us "the little old ladies." I hate the nickname, but see the truth in it.

It is no coincidence that, as a child of three or four, when we were still living in Hoboken, and my father was away at war, on Halloween, my mother would dress me up as a little old lady. I suspect that she chose this costume at first because she was trying to save money, and it cost nothing to assemble from her and my grandmother's castaways.

I have recoiled from a picture of myself in our family photograph album, all dressed up in this costume. I wear an old, gored, striped skirt of my mother's, which falls to the ground, a huge-brimmed hat with a bow tied round the crown that flopped down over my face, a large jacket, secured with a belt. Over my shoulder, I carry an enormous, extremely ugly, pocketbook.

Grouped around me are other children in more normal costumes: the girls dressed as princesses, movie actresses, or ballerinas; the boys, as cowboys or bandits. I look very satisfied with my costume, with myself, as if I welcome the garb of maturity that denies me my childhood, even in play.

For years, on Halloween, I wear a version of this outfit. I trudge along, begging for candy, next to my far more resplendent sister, whose costume is always homemade, always highly destructible, because it is constructed from a length of tulle or net or taffeta that my mother collects from our relatives in the garment industry, and always crowned by a battered headdress of sequins or seed pearls donated by a friend who owns a bridal shop. (When my sister is thirty-five years old, she still dresses up for Halloween, still trick-or-treats. The year before she dies, I can't contain my sarcasm when she calls me to ask whether I think she should dress up for a Halloween party as an Apache dancer or a pregnant bride.)

In high school, I try out for all the female leads in Oscar Wilde's *The Importance of Being Earnest*, and, though I covet either of the roles of the two young women, I am disappointed, though not surprised, when I am assigned the role of the elderly nurse, Miss Prism. The casting director tells me she has chosen me because I am the only girl in my class who would make a believable old woman. My old girlfriend Happy Klein gets a lead. Someone I barely know, Susana Wilkins, gets the other.

"If I cast Happy or Susana as Miss Prism," she tells me, "we would have the whole audience in an uproar, and that would be the end of the play. They're too immature to play Miss Prism. You have the maturity the part requires."

Instead of wearing a gorgeous pink or turquoise frock made by the sewing classes for the other female leads, I get to wear another version of my standard little old lady costume. A floor-length black taffeta skirt, made by my mother, who volunteers her services. A white ruffled blouse. A black fringed shawl. On my head, I wear a doily that my grandmother crochets. I am surprised at how easily I develop a quavering voice, a doddering walk. My pal Eddie has been cast as the elderly Reverend Chausable. At least, Eddie says, there are two of us playing "old farts."

During the week of performances, I have to spray my hair gray, and I wear it that way to school. I'm not that self-conscious. Somehow the gray hair seems to suit me.

At the cast party, on the show's last night, I overhear an out-oftowner, who hasn't seen the play, ask one of my friends what has happened to me to turn my hair prematurely gray. My friend thinks this is hilarious.

"Why don't you ask her yourself?" he says.

And he does, and I answer, "Just ordinary life." But when I realize that he asks me because he really thinks the gray hair is mine, I run out of the room, crying, crying because I never wanted to play Miss Prism, crying that I have played an old woman for so much of my young life.

I've been earning spending money, clothes money, and college money since I am eleven years old. My aim is to have $5,000 in the bank after I graduate college, when I get married. I've made a schedule, and, because of the miracle of compound interest, which I have learned about in math class, I know I can do it. It means leading an austere life, though I have more money to my name than most of my friends, but most of that money is "money to save," not "money to spend." I keep my money in a joint savings account with my mother. My grandmother tells me I'll be sorry. My mother keeps my passbook and makes deposits for me. I trust her; this is a mistake.

By now, I have saved so much money, I have even made up an unofficial will. If I die, all my money will go to Susan, but she doesn't know this. I don't tell her because I think it would freak her out. I keep my will in my jewelry box on top of my dresser. I'm sure my mother has seen it. I'm not sure she would abide by my wishes. I think she'd take it herself. My mother is always so worried about whether she has enough money, that she doesn't enjoy the money she has. Years later, when she is hospitalized, all she talks about is not having enough money to pay the bills, to pay the mortgage, to make the payments on the car. I guess having enough money was my mother's way of buying a sense of security, which she never felt she had. "Even though I have a wonderful husband, and a nice home," she tells me near the end of her life, "I've felt homeless all my life."

My most recent job is organizing the vast library of Mrs. Neil, the woman who lives across the street from us. She's an English teacher and has no children of her own to do this kind of thing for her. This is the best job I've ever had. It's clean, easy, and I'm well paid.

When she hires me, she tells me she has chosen me because she knows I love books: I am the only child she has ever seen trudge home from the library with as many books as she used to carry when she was my age. She will pay me fifteen cents an hour above minimum wage because she doesn't believe in exploiting the labor of the young; I can take as much time as I need to do the job, because she's in no rush to have me finish. After I finish, I can come back once a week to keep the library in order.

Mrs. Neil doesn't mind if I take time away from my work to sit in the inglenook of her kitchen and dip into one of her books. Sometimes, when I'm engrossed, she makes me a cup of herb tea and places it on the table near me. After the day's work, I insist on subtracting the time I take for these "intellectual breathers," as she calls them, from the hours I work. She insists on paying me for my breaks, saying it's a "fringe benefit."

Sometimes she asks if she can interrupt me, and we talk about books.

"Tell me about some of your favorite books," she says. "Tell me why you like them." I tell her about Hemingway's *Old Man and the Sea*, how I love that, though, on the surface, it looks as if the old man had been defeated, to me, he had been victorious, because he had proved something to himself.

"And what did he prove to himself?" Mrs. Neil asks, curious.

"That he had a very strong will, but that he could accept things that could happen to him that were beyond his control," I tell her. Mrs. Neil tells me she thinks I have arrived at an important insight.

She asks me if I have written it down. When I tell her I haven't, she recommends that I use some of my earnings to buy myself what she calls a "commonplace book." A commonplace book, she tells me, is more important than a diary because it is where we record our thoughts and insights about our reading, where we copy passages that are deeply meaningful.

"I could buy you a commonplace book for your next birthday, Louise, but it won't mean as much to you as if you use your money to buy it." And I do. And begin to keep a record of my reading, just as Mrs. Neil does.

I'm surprised to see that, besides books that I know to be classics, Mrs. Neil has a large selection of best-sellers. *Dr. Zhivago* by Boris Pasternak. *Exodus* by Leon Uris. I ask her why. I'm not sure these books count as literature.

She hands me *Dr. Zhivago*. "Read it," she tells me. "When you come back next week, you can tell me whether you think it's literature." And, of course I do, and I thank her for suggesting that I read it.

"Then repay me," she says. "Recommend something for me to read." Judging from the size of Mrs. Neil's library, I can't imagine I've read something she hasn't, but she insists, so I suggest Kobo Abe, *The Woman in the Dunes*.

"It's in the library," I tell her. "I'll check it out for you."

"How did you learn about it?" she asks, and, sheepishly, I tell her about my system, how I start with the letter "A," pick out the first book, read a few pages, see if I like it, take it home if I do, move on to the letter "B," and so on, through the alphabet, then back through it again.

"How long have you been doing this?" she asks.

"Since the ninth grade," I tell her. I'm afraid she'll think this is a foolish plan, but she tells me she must try it: "Having a reading plan is a wonderful thing; you must always have such a plan, though it might not be the same plan," she tells me.

Sometimes I think Mrs. Neil has hired me to do this job so I can be around her books, so I can have someone to talk to about books, so she can show me, by her example, that it's possible to make a living by doing something you love, something you'd do even if you weren't paid for it.

"Teaching," she tells me, "is the most noble profession on earth. You help shape the character of the next generation. Think about it, Louise. I think you would make a very fine teacher."

When I tell her I'm not sure what I want to do, she tells me I must do what interests me.

"What interests you, Louise?" she asks me.

"Reading," I tell her.

"Then you must follow your heart," she responds, "and you must find a way to make reading your profession."

Mr. Horton, my high school physics teacher, has told me much the same thing.

He routinely catches me reading in the back of his classroom as he tries to explain the intricacies of the inclined plain or the Archimedes principle. I am in the middle of a Russian novel's kick, and can't seem to find enough time for all the books I want to read—*The Brothers Karamozov, War and Peace*—so I read them in his class, hunched down in my seat in the back, hoping he won't notice. I am reading Russian novels because I love their epic scope and their portraits of people living in momentous times.

In Mr. Horton's class, I read my assignments, do all my homework, participate in the experiments. It's just his lectures that I ignore.

One day, when he catches me reading for the umpteenth time, he comes up to me after class, exasperated. But instead of chiding me for ignoring his lecture, again, he rubs his hands together, and asks to see what I'm reading. I usually sense in him a quiet understanding which helps me realize it's all right for me to like Russian novels, all right for me not to like physics, even though he likes it.

Today is different; I feel that I have pushed the limits of his patience.

When Mr. Horton is on hall patrol, he always witnesses one of my hallway scenes with a current boyfriend. A gentle "Break it up," "Move along now," or "Louise, you should know better," the most severe of his reprimands. I feel safe around him.

I show him my current book—Dostoyevsky's *The Possessed*—and he takes it.

"Dostoyevsky," he remarks. "Not something an average kid reads."

I wonder whether he'll give the book back to me, or whether he'll take it away. It would serve me right, I think, for ignoring him in class.

He holds the book, taps it against his hand, and says, "Instead of sending you to the vice principal's office, I'll make a deal with you."

"What kind of a deal," I ask, suspicious.

"The deal has four parts. You must agree to all of them," he tells me. "One: from now on, you pay attention to my lectures even if they don't interest you; you find something that interests you, and you cultivate self-discipline. Two: I read *The Possessed*, which I've never read, because it means so much to you that you ignore my lectures. Three: we discuss the book during the week's worth of detentions you owe me for reading in my class. Four: you read your books on your time—and you'll have plenty of time for yourself, and making something of yourself, if you don't spend so much time fighting with your boyfriend. You might even make a fine teacher one day. You already have what you must have to become a fine teacher."

"What's that?" I ask.

"A passionate interest in your subject."

He hands the book back to me, telling me to scram, that he'll start reading it when I'm finished.

As I'm leaving his room, he looks straight at me, and says, "You will notice, Louise, that I said 'a passionate interest in your subject,' not 'a passionate interest in boys.' Catch my drift? Get my meaning?"

"Catch my drift?" or "Get my meaning?" are two things Mr. Horton always says after he tells you something important, something that will be on an exam. All us kids know this.

"Yes sir," I tell him. "I catch your drift; I get your meaning." And, eventually, though not immediately, I do.

Though Susan and I could walk to the Park Lane Theatre through pretty suburban streets, we prefer the truck route. This way, we won't bump into anyone we know and we can share confidences, unimpeded.

Susan and I walk past the garden apartments, along scruffy Broad Avenue, with eighteen-wheelers rattling by and sheets of newspaper attempting flight like damaged birds along the dies of the road, past the World War I monument, the Toddle Inn Guest House (which, we joke, has never housed a guest, for who would want to come to Ridgefield, New Jersey), past undistinguished brick apartment buildings with prominent air raid shelter signs. Today, the sick sweet smell from the chemical company in the industrial part of town seems especially bad. We cross the bridge over Route 46, and walk down a few more blocks.

Susan and I buy our tickets and go into the darkened theater. We are very excited, but not at the prospect of watching the movie.

Actually, saying that we go "to see" a movie is inaccurate. We rarely watch the movie. We don't really care what's playing. When our parents ask us what the movie is about, we improvise.

We don't go to the movies to see the movie. We go to the movies to hang out, to smoke, to talk, to walk around, to see who's there, to eat hot dogs and bonbons and drink Pepsi, and, if we're very lucky, to meet the boy we like, or one we can like for the afternoon, and make out.

Susan and I have a pact that if either of us meets a boy we like or one who interests us, the other one will bug out. We'll hook up again outside the ticket booth after the double feature so we can walk back home together. We have to walk back home together so our parents won't get suspicious, so they won't suspect the real reason Susan and I go see every movie that has come to the Park Lane Theatre this year.

Susan and I are not alone in using the Park Lane Theatre for these purposes Saturday afternoons, which might be why there are never any grown-ups in the movie theater. Saturday afternoons, there are only gangs of teenagers. The darkened theater becomes one gigantic mating ground.

The management has given up trying to enforce proper movie-watching behavior. A lone, pimple-faced usher, carrying a very large flashlight, more suitable for waving away oncoming cars from a wreck on the side of a highway, patrols the aisles. He ignores the kids whose feet are propped on the backs of chairs. The ones necking and moaning. The gangs of girls, seated seven abreast, talking a mile a minute. The guys reprising last night's CYO basketball game, complete with jump shots. The kids standing on the seats to cast shadows of rabbits, donkeys, or obscene gestures up onto the gigantic screen.

The usher's primary responsibilities are to ferret out the burly manager from his office to stop fights before they become dangerous (though routine pushing and shoving are tolerated), and to make sure that no one takes off their clothes. Hands reaching through flies into jockey shorts, under blouses into bras, up under skirts into underpants, he has trained himself to ignore. (Our mothers can't figure out why we willingly pull on our skirts on movie Saturdays, and why they have to fight to get us out of our jeans and into our skirts when company comes on Sundays.)

Susan is in hot pursuit of someone I barely know, a guy by the name of Ernie DeSalvo, who goes to some Catholic high school in the Bronx.

I have seen him careening around the streets of Ridgefield on his noisy purple motorcycle with rusted wire wheels, wearing a black leather jacket and sunglasses, and I don't think very much of him. I can't imagine why Susan is so gaga about him. According to her, he's very sexy, and she says she should know. She rolls her eyes, and gets this wanton look on her face whenever she tells me how sexy he is. He has no steady girlfriend, though he's supposed to be madly in love with Helen Wall, who won't give him the time of day. So Susan has her hopes up, though he's never taken her out on a real date, though she suspects he's using her. (This boy Susan moons over I decide to marry a few years later. When I start dating him, in my junior year of college, he's given up his motorcycle, and is the only boy I've ever dated who is willing to talk about philosophy, who likes a woman with a mind of her own, who doesn't think she should stay home and raise kids. And, though every one we know thinks that Ernie and I are not likely to stay together very long, for we argue all the time, about everything, here we are, thirty-three years later, still arguing, still talking, and still married.)

I hope I will bump into Roy, but in all the times we've come to the Park Lane Theatre, Susan has never bumped into Ernie, and I've only met Roy without his steady girlfriend once. The memory of us, slumped way down in our seats in the last row of the theater, beyond the reach of the usher's prying beam of light, in near violation of the Park Lane's loose code for movie-watching behavior, has impelled me to return here repeatedly.

Roy. The first time I see him is at the Christmas bonfire, when I am in the ninth grade. I am with Carmine, and Roy is with his girl-friend, Eleanor, and the flames of the burning trees are reaching skyward, making the couples who stand arm in arm glow red, orange, fuchsia in the firelight.

When I turn away from Carmine and look over and see Roy, and he turns away from Eleanor and looks over and sees me, our eyes meet, and say, where have you been in this small town that I haven't seen you before, and when can we meet, and let's make it soon. I know, and he knows, and our eyes say, that we will be fucking as soon as we can find a time and place to indulge this lust that begins to lick our bodies on the night of the Christmas bonfire.

And so we begin to satisfy each other in the way that only children can, there being nothing else this interesting in our lives, nothing more important or significant for us to do, but to please one another. We concentrate on what we feel with our wet fingertips, as we caress, with the moonlight as witness. When we make love, we do so quietly, holding sound deep inside, for safety's sake, so that no one who passes by us might hear.

And because we don't see one another much, rarely talk, barely even glance at one another, except to signal to each other that, yes, it is time, that, yes, we are ready, there is never anything between Roy and me—no unresolved argument, no resentment, no hostility, no cause for grievance, nothing, nothing at all, to dilute the pleasure that we find with each other.

In the years that follow, either Roy calls me or I call him and we arrange to meet. We make love in the way kids do when they are making love for the first time, and can't believe their bodies can have such pleasure, that being apart can be such agony.

We make love on the sofa of his sunporch when Roy is babysitting, afraid that his sister will awaken; on the back lawn of his house, looking up at the stars; in the back room of a friend's basement, during a party, against a tree on a street not far from my house; in the woods in the middle of our town; in the bleachers in the ball field; in a shed by the ice-skating rink; in a bus on the way home from a football game; in the reference room of the local library; at one or another of the overlooks on the Palisades Interstate Parkway after Roy gets his license; in various parking lots in New York City when we are older, and venture there together.

When I am with Roy, I feel as if I have clawed my way out of the cotton wool in which I live my life, and the world comes rushing in. My passion for him spills over onto everything, everyone. When I leave him, and remember our pleasure, I see the leaves reddened by autumn, but also the sadness of my mother's eyes. That I have learned how to feel is, for me, this love's greatest danger.

If I sit in the enclosed porch outside my bedroom, and it is winter, and all the leaves are off the trees, I can look across the valley and see Roy's bedroom window and whether the light in his room is on. Sometimes, I tell myself I can see him walking around. I imagine what he is doing, and wonder whether he is thinking of me as I am thinking of him.

Sometimes, after we are on the phone together (which isn't often), Roy goes into his bedroom and blinks his light on and off, on and off, so I can see it. A beacon of hope that comes to me across the valley.

In the years after Roy and I became lovers, I put my time with him into a small box, outside the space that I inhabited with my parents, and with Jill, and I told myself that this experience with him was nobody's business but mine. I told no one but Susan what I was doing, and I only told her because I needed to use seeing her as a reason to get out of my house.

This was private. This was my body, my business, my way of getting free of it all.

Roy and I told one another repeatedly that what we shared was only about sex, and that it would stay only about sex. When we were together, over the years, in those few moments we felt we could spare from lovemaking to talk, we discovered that we liked one another, shared the same taste in books, wanted the same things from life—peace, solitude, exquisite meals, meaningful work, a comfortable family life. Unlike other boys, he didn't quiet me when I talked about my family; he listened, without commenting, never offering advice. It never occurred to me that we should become a couple—once, he suggested this as a possibility that I immediately, thoughtlessly rebuffed—that, if we did, we might have a very good time, if not forever, then at least for a while. Perhaps I did not want to risk losing this special relationship we shared; I did not want it to become something ordinary.

Although I often feel bad because of Roy, I tell myself I can handle it.

Susan and I walk into the lobby of the Park Lane, and buy our popcorn and ice cream bonbons, to which I have become addicted; I love the resistance of the cold, hard, bitter chocolate frosting, the yielding softness of the ice cream.

We slip into our favorite seats, on the aisle, in the last row. We sit here so that we won't miss seeing anyone who comes in, anyone who goes out. Also, so that no one will sit behind us. Neither of us likes to have anyone sitting behind us. It makes us feel uncomfortable. Susan is sure that anyone sitting behind her is talking about her. I'm sure that the kids sitting behind me will annoy me so much by their foolish behavior that I'll have to fight them.

We slouch down in our seats, anticipating, not the start of the movie, but the arrival of Roy or Ernie. They are the featured attractions. Susan and I each hope for hot sex on a Saturday afternoon.

Vertigo opens like no movie I've seen. Spirals of color. Swirls of red, blue, green, gold. Discordant, jarring music. Lips, in close-up on the screen. Eyes darting right, left, right, left. I am disoriented, but captivated. The eyes on the screen are like my mother's eyes, when she is agitated, which is often.

I forget Roy. I start watching the movie.

Moments after it starts, Scottie (played by Jimmy Stewart) chases a criminal across rooftops. I cover my eyes with my hands, watching through the slits between my fingers. Already, I'm afraid of what I'll see on the screen. Afraid what I'll see will make me faint.

Scottie loses his footing, falls, grasps a gutter, dangles in space, looks down, gets dizzy. I can't stand it. I'm afraid he'll fall, but he can't fall, I tell myself, because he's the star. He hangs, helplessly, sees someone else—a policeman—fall to his death.

In the next scene, Scottie tries to climb a stepladder. He has developed acrophobia, vertigo, a fear of heights, because of what happened. Slowly, slowly, he climbs. One step. Another. He tries to control his fear, but can't, and collapses into the arms of his friend Midge. Vertigo, he has been told, is something you have your whole life, unless you experience another, equally terrifying, trauma.

I know the warning signs Scottie describes. You feel dizzy, weak-kneed, light-headed, like you're falling through space, like you're in the middle of a whirling vortex. Your pulse races. You gasp for air. You feel like you're going to die.

As I sit in the Park Lane Theatre, listening to Scottie describe his symptoms, I notice my breathing becoming shallow, notice that I am starting to feel light-headed, hope that I won't faint. And realize I have vertigo too. I have never talked about it with anyone. Not my pal Eddie, not Roy, not even Susan. Nor have I read about it anywhere. Before this, I never had a name for what I suffer.

During grammar school, I fainted every time we had an air raid drill. I haven't fainted for a while, but I'm always afraid I'll faint at the slightest provocation—a violent movie, the sight of blood, a traffic accident, crossing a bridge—as I have before.

When the picture of a catastrophe appears on the front page of a newspaper, when a radio announcer describes a train wreck, when my father tells my mother how a workman almost severs his finger, I grip the edge of a table to steady myself. I can see the broken bodies, the gush of blood. I feel myself starting to fall. I have no way of protecting myself, shutting out other people's tragedies. They become mine. My father says it's my hyperactive imagination. I don't agree. I feel as if I'm living through something terrible that has happened to me, that I've lived through before but can't remember what it is.

I'm often afraid. Worried that I'll pass out, anywhere, anytime, anyplace. My friends think me fearless. It's a good act. "You're tough as nails," Susan says. She doesn't know that everyday life scares me shitless.

I have to watch this movie closely. Maybe it has something to tell me.

There is something about Scottie that reminds me of myself. The intensity of his eyes. The way he studies Madeleine Elster (played by Kim Novak) when he's hired by her husband to tail her because Elster is afraid that Madeleine will commit suicide like an ancestress. The way he hangs back, looking at everything suspiciously, trying to figure things out, trying to find the story behind the story. That's what I do. Always. At home. In school.

"Stop looking at me like that," Susan says. "You're giving me the creeps."

"Stop asking me so many questions," my mother says. "Who do you think you are, Nancy Drew?"

Sure enough, Scottie sees Madeleine leap into San Francisco Bay, and he rescues her, and takes her to his apartment. I'm happy. I knew he'd save her.

When she awakens, she tells him she doesn't know what has happened to her; she must have had a dizzy spell, fainted, fallen into the bay by accident. And sure enough, they fall in love, even though Madeleine is married.

A love triangle. I know all about this. So does Susan. Both of us turn to one another and nod, knowingly.

And then Madeleine ascends the mission bell tower. Scottie can't follow her; he has vertigo. She's going to kill herself, and he can't save her. And she plunges to her death. Or so it seems.

But after Scottie recovers from his bout of mental illness, sees someone who looks something like Madeleine on the street, and follows her, we learn that she has been Elster's accomplice, that they have set Scottie up so Elster could murder his wife, but that she has fallen in love with Scottie.

And as I watch Scottie try to turn this woman into Madeleine, I hope that everything will turn out fine. But when Scottie sees her put on a piece of Madeleine's jewelry, realizes that she has betrayed him, but doesn't tell her, I know that something terrible will happen. And it does.

He takes her back to the top of the bell tower to show her he knows, show her how it felt, and she is startled by a nun, and plunges to her death. And I wonder if Scottie, who stands on the ledge, arms upraised, at the end of the movie, will follow her.

"Oh my God," Susan says. It's what Susan always says when she doesn't know what else to say. She's as shaken as I am by the movie's ending. "What do you think?" she asks me.

It's time to leave, time to walk home, but I can't answer her question. I can't move. I want to see *Vertigo* again. Everything puzzles me. I want to stay and try to figure out some things.

Saturday, the Park Lane has continuous performances, and you can stay to see the feature again if you want to.

"I'm staying," I tell Susan.

"I can't," Susan responds, "I have to get home or I'll get in trouble." So will I, but I decide to stay anyway.

* * *

Susan leaves, and I'm left in the darkened theater to watch *Vertigo* again. This will be the first time I see a movie alone. For a few seconds, I feel afraid. Then I settle down.

After I see the movie a second time, I get up, make a phone call, tell my mother I've met some friends, that I'm staying to see the movie again, that I'm not sure when I'll be home. She protests, but I don't care. I want to see *Vertigo* again because I'm still confused.

The first time, I think the movie is all about a tragic love. The events in the movie are accidents. They just happen. Jimmy Stewart is in the wrong place at the wrong time. He gets caught up in something dangerous. It's not his fault. He's helpless. He couldn't have done anything to stop what happened.

The second time I see *Vertigo*, though, I see how Scottie drinks, how he falls in love with Madeleine without really knowing her, how he can't have her anyway, because she's married, how tormented he becomes because of his love for her. I wonder whether he loves her because he can't have her, and whether loving someone as he loves her can lead to madness, murder, suicide. This is something I connect with, something I understand. This is sometimes how I feel about Roy, like I've put myself in danger, and that I've done it deliberately. Will I drive myself crazy by loving Roy as Scottie loves Madeleine, I wonder?

The third time I see *Vertigo*, I'm sure of it. Scottie could love Midge, who loves him, but he doesn't want her. He wants to love someone he can't have, someone who will harm him. He's in pain before he even meets Madeleine, though he doesn't know why.

About a year before, I start drinking a little at parties. To loosen me up. To make me feel good. Then, I start drinking too much at parties. Later, I start drinking much too much at parties.

One night, I'm at a dance at the firehouse on the top of the hill. I go because the firehouse is close to where Roy lives, and I hope he'll come to the dance, hope we can leave together.

When Susan calls for me, I haven't heard from Roy yet. I want to wait awhile; Susan persuades me that's crazy.

"You can't change what you want to do for some guy," she tells me. I know she's right, but I tell her I'm only going to the firehouse dance because Roy might be there.

Susan and I walk down one hill, and up another. The firehouse is about a mile and a half away from my house. It's cold. As usual, I'm not dressed warmly enough and I've forgotten my gloves. I'm jumpy. Distracted. Can't tell if I'm going to see Roy or not. I want to see him. I need to. It's been a long time.

The firehouse, on this night, is filled with kids from the top of the hill, kids from Cliffside, lots of kids I really don't know. But some cheerleaders are there. And Eleanor's there. But Roy's not there. At least not yet.

A guy Susan knows comes by, and asks her to dance. She doesn't want to leave me alone, but I tell her I'm all right. He hands me his flask, inside a paper bag. I go into the bathroom, take a drink, a long one. It's Johnnie Walker Black, I can tell. This guy's got good taste.

When I return to the dance floor, I see Susan, still dancing, I see Roy dancing with Eleanor.

Oh no, I think to myself. It's going to be another one of those nights.

I decide I need some more booze. Just a little bit more to get me through this. I go back into the bathroom. Drink a little bit more.

Now, I'm getting that dizzy feeling. When I'm feeling like this, I think I can handle anything. Susan comes over. She's talking through cotton. The guy she's with is pissed. Pulls the flask out of my hand. I laugh. Susan tells me to shut up. I say, too loud, why did you think your booze'd be safe with me?

Susan pulls me by my elbow.

"Shit," she says, "let's get out of here."

"I can't leave yet," I tell her. "I might go home with Roy."

"Roy's with Eleanor," Susan tells me. "He left with Eleanor."

Outside there are lots of older kids. Lots of them have beer or booze. I want some. Susan tells me to cut it out, I'll only fuck myself up. I tell her I can't fuck myself up because I'm fucked up already. I think this is very funny.

Some guy with a Cliffside jacket asks me if I want something to drink. Yeah, I tell him, yeah, sure I want something to drink. I always want something to drink. I take the bottle of beer he has in his hand. I don't care what kind it is. I chug it. Fast. I'm a pro at this. I hand the bottle back to him. Empty.

He smiles at me. Tells me I owe him something. Asks me what I'll give him in return. His buddies laugh. Nothing, I tell him. I think this is very funny. He doesn't.

Susan starts yanking me away. I don't want to go. I think I can have some fun with this guy. This seems like a guy I can fool around with. What the fuck, I think. Roy's gone off with Eleanor. What do I have to lose? But Susan drags me toward the boulevard. She is trying to push me toward home, but I can't go home, I don't want to go home. I won't go home. We see a few more kids, on their way to the dance. Do you have any booze? I ask them. Susan tells them I'm kidding. I tell them I'm not. The kids think I'm funny. They think some more booze would make me even funnier.

"Oh Christ," Susan says. "It's going to be another one of those nights.

My legs, by now, feel like jelly. And everything starts spinning. I hate this feeling. I'm halfway across the boulevard. Try to make it across. Can't make it across. Dizzy, I'm so fucking dizzy, I tell Susan. She's pushing me. Trying to get me across the boulevard. I think all this is very funny. I try to laugh. Can't. Get weak-kneed.

And collapse in the center of the boulevard, on the double yellow line. And pass out.

And come to, with Susan standing over me, waving her arms back and forth, back and forth.

I look up at her.

"What the fuck are you doing?" I try to ask her, but I feel too sick.

Susan pays me no attention. She continues waving, waving. The boulevard is a four-lane highway with no divider. Cars whiz by on either side.

Susan is trying to wave the cars away from my body. Susan is trying to save my life.

Soon after I see *Vertigo*, I am sitting in Mrs. Purdy's sixth-period English class, a class in the history of English literature that I enjoy.

Mrs. Purdy is a very good, very hard teacher. She is very direct and doesn't play games; she controls the boys in the class with a sardonic humor that lets them know that she's the boss. They respect her. She makes sure the girls get their turn to talk.

Mrs. Purdy makes us work very hard. She makes us read a lot, and she won't tell us what she thinks about what we read, we have to tell her, and we have to defend our point of view. She has taught us how to read *Beowulf* and *The Canterbury Tales*. She tells us that, by the end of the year, we will be writing a forty-page research paper. She will take us through the process, each step of the way, but she expects perfection from us. I'm not afraid like some kids in the class. I'm looking forward to this challenge. I'm doing well in this course.

On this day, we are continuing our discussion of Shakespeare's sonnets. Most of the kids are confused, and have been, since we've begun. They complain to Mrs. Purdy that they can't figure anything out. Mrs. Purdy is frustrated. But she won't budge. She won't tell us what these enigmatic lines mean; she insists we think for ourselves.

"Don't make a mountain out of a hill," she tells us. She tells us this often. She also says that we're smarter than we think we are; that, if we relate the words on the page to our own experience, we can unlock "the miracle and the mystery of the text," and that this will give us great satisfaction.

I am in my seat, toward the back of the class, in the row by the window. I have learned from Mrs. Neil that if you have trouble figuring something out, you should copy it. It'll be easier to understand than if you simply read it.

We have puzzled our way through a love sonnet, noticing the equation between love and death, and that writing can memorialize someone. But we have hit a stumbling block at Sonnet 87. So I reread a few of the lines as I copy them into my notebook.

> *Farewell! Thou art too dear for my possessing,*
> *And like enough thou know'st thy estimate.*
> *. . . For how do I hold thee but by thy granting*
> *And for that riches where is my deserving?*
> *. . . Thyself thou gavest, thy own worth then not*
> * knowing,*
> *Or me, to whom thou gavest it, else mistaking.*
> *. . . . Thus have I had thee, as a dream doth*
> * flatter. . . .*

We think we know what the sonnet means, but Mrs. Purdy is not satisfied with our interpretation. She is pressing us to think more deeply.

She leans against the desk, holding her book open. "I'm waiting," she says. "I'm waiting for someone to tell me what 'Thyself thou gavest' and 'Thus have I had thee' mean. I can't believe there isn't a student in this room who can't figure these lines out," she says. "They're lines any normal teenager should figure out. I'm waiting, and I'm willing to wait until suppertime."

Sometimes, when we haven't performed as well as Mrs. Purdy would like, she keeps us after school. She can do this because English is our last period. We groan. We know she means what she says.

Suddenly, in writing the words out, I see what she is trying to get us to see. It's simple: it's the word "have" that holds the clue to the meaning. I raise my hand.

"It's about having sex," I say. "I think Shakespeare is using words like 'gavest' and 'have' to say something about how you feel about someone you've had sex with. You think that because you've had sex with someone, that you can 'have' them, especially if they have sex with you willingly. But it's only 'a dream,' as he puts it, and that's what's so sad about sex: that it leads you to believe you have something with a person that you can never have. He's using the word 'have' in more than one way."

I wonder if I have overstepped my bounds, talking about sex like this in English class. But I know what I'm talking about and I'm sure I'm right. I'm relieved that someone as famous as Shakespeare feels the same way about the person he's writing about as I feel about Roy.

The class snickers. They cast knowing glances at one another. Most of the kids by now have heard the rumors about Roy and me. They guess I'm talking about something I know. And they're right.

Mrs. Purdy looks over her glasses at the class. She gives them a withering look, but they don't stop. She looks directly at Anthony Damato, who snickers the loudest, and says, "Anthony, do I have to keep you after class and give you a private tutorial in the meaning of the word 'sex'? You're acting as if you've never heard the word before." Then she looks at me.

"Thank God," Mrs. Purdy says. "At last. I was beginning to think there wasn't a 'normal' teenager in this room." She praises my response effusively, remarks upon its wisdom. She looks at me, wonderingly. I suspect she's puzzled by how I have learned such things, though she has suggested that what I know is normal for a teenager.

In this moment, my hidden life of love and sex counts for something academically. It is transformed into something valuable beyond itself. Something I can draw upon to understand literature. I can understand my life and transform its meaning because of what Shakespeare says; but I can understand Shakespeare better because of my life. And this will be true of everything I read: I can use my life experiences to help me understand works of literature; but I can also use my understanding of what I read to help me transform my life.

A friend of mine named Vivian has gotten pregnant, and has had to drop out of school. I worry that what has happened to Vivian will happen to me. Knowing about sex has helped me figure out a Shakespeare sonnet; but if I don't take care of myself, I can wind up like Vivian. And I don't want that. I want to go on to college.

I have had sex with Roy with rubbers, and sex without them. I've been careful, and I've been careless. So far, I've been lucky. I've been lucky a long time. I'm afraid my luck will run out.

Every month, around period time, I am a nervous wreck, watching for the first drop of blood that signals that I've made it safely through still another month. It's exhausting. It takes its toll. It's no way to live.

While I'm in high school, three of my good friends, besides Vivian, get pregnant.

One pretends she's not pregnant, though her belly swells as the months go by; she tells us she has a strange lung condition that causes fluid to seep into her bodily cavities. I go see her before she disappears for a few months to deliver her child and give it up for adoption. Her mother serves us cookies and milk. While she's away, her boyfriend, a football hero, goes to all the high school and firehouse dances, and he dances cheek to cheek with lots of other girls. He doesn't seem to be suffering. When his girlfriend returns, he breaks up with her.

Another one of my friends tries to get her boyfriend to marry her, though they're both still teenagers. She's sure they can work it out, that they love one another enough to overcome the obvious difficulties. But he refuses, so she starts a paternity suit against him, because she can't support the baby herself. He is a basketball star and gets his friends on the team to testify that they fucked her, and she loses the case, and she has the baby, and moves out of town and lives with her sister. As her baby boy grows, it resembles his father more and more; yet his father insists the baby isn't his. He goes away to college unimpeded, unrepentant.

A third of my pregnant friends marries her boyfriend while they're still in their teens. When Susan and I visit her, we leave real fast: this is no place anyone should live in. The apartment is over a store, and you can hear the scurrying of rats, and our friend has deep, dark circles under her eyes, and her husband is always furious. He had dreams of going to college and becoming an engineer and now he's a delivery clerk and he still can't support them. She was studying to become a concert pianist. Both sets of parents have disowned them.

These are the days before the pill, before legal abortions, and, if you get pregnant, you have a few alternatives, but no real choices. If you have the baby, that's the end of high school or college for you, because you can't be pregnant and in school, nor can you hope to go back to school, because there is no such thing as a "returning woman" student. Or you can go away to some home to have the baby and give it up for adoption. Or you can go to some tenement in New York City or Newark or Trenton and have some guy who says he's a doctor do things to your insides with instruments that might or might not be sterilized and you can pay him the five hundred dollars you've collected from all your friends and then maybe you won't be pregnant or maybe you still will be pregnant (we know many of these guys are crooks and don't do the abortions they're paid to do) and maybe you'll be fine or maybe you won't be fine, maybe you'll start bleeding like some girl that Susan knows, and if you bleed from an illegal abortion you're up shit's creek because no emergency room will agree to take care of you, so then you'll probably die.

These, very definitely, are not the "good old days."

On the Saturday that I see *Vertigo* three times, I walk home alone through the dark, poorly lighted suburban streets, thinking about my favorite scenes in the movie—the kissing scene in Scottie's apartment, and in the hotel room, Madeleine's plunge into San Francisco Bay, how she stands in front of her ancestress Carlotta's tomb, and sits in front of Carlotta's portrait, how she promises to love Scottie forever, and how he promises to take care of her, banish her fears.

During the next week, I see *Vertigo* five more times. Each time, my understanding of what the movie means to me deepens. I know I don't want to wind up like Scottie, in love with death. Nor do I want to live like the "fake" Madeleine, obsessed with the past, possessed by the family's madness.

Each time I see *Vertigo*, I move closer to learning that loving someone the way Scottie loves Madeleine is dangerous. That if I want to live a contented life, and not what Susan and I call "a falling-down life," one day, and soon, I will have to give up my phantom love for Roy. I know that he cannot take away the deep sorrow that seems to circle around me everywhere I go. I know that I must study this sorrow, dissect it, understand it in myself and others, figure out where it comes from, and if I will ever be able to put it aside for even a little while, or if it will be my constant companion through life, the basso profundo of my everyday existence. Though, with Roy, I have learned the meaning of ecstasy, and though I don't want to live a life without it, I do not want to pay what seems to be its price: living in the unsatisfying realm of longing, yearning, and regret.

The Still Center of the Turning Wheel

September 1959

THE THREE OF us—my mother, my sister, and I—are standing in the dirt in the unpaved driveway in front of Woodbury Hall at Douglass College in New Brunswick, New Jersey. The dormitory is new; it has barely been completed in time for the beginning of the semester. I consider myself fortunate to be housed here, fortunate to be going to college.

My father is taking a picture of us on this very important day. I am irritated that the unpaved dirt driveway sends up clouds of dust, spoiling the shine on my new shoes, getting into my carefully shampooed, curled, and combed hair.

The picture my father takes is peculiar. We have not posed, as other families have, arms interlocked around waists, all smiles and hugs and kisses, father and mother so obviously proud of their girl, the father having shown a bystander how to take a picture with his camera so that he, too, can be included in this photographic record of the important day when his daughter leaves home for the first time. My father has, unwittingly, captured us as we really are.

My sister and I stand a foot or so apart from each other, and there is an even greater distance between my mother and me. My sister, wearing a red crewneck sweater, a pleated skirt, and red knee socks, stands in the left of the picture, looking down at the ground, away from me. She is furious. She thinks my leaving her alone with our parents is a great and unforgivable betrayal. Without me, she feels unprotected. Without me, she doesn't know what to do with herself.

My mother stands to my right, wearing a gray short-sleeved sweater, a gray skirt, flesh-colored stockings, and sensible flats. Gray is my mother's favorite color. She covers her face with her hand. She is not enjoying this, she is not smiling, and she is not looking at me. She knows that going away to college is the right thing for me to do. Yet, without me, she feels insecure, unanchored. Without me, she doesn't know what she'll do with Jill; she doesn't know what she'll do with herself.

I stand in the center of the picture, feet planted slightly apart, trying to compose myself, trying to ground myself. It isn't easy. I am terrified. I have never been away from home before, except for summertime stays with my relatives on Long Island. I don't know what to expect.

I am wearing a sensible brand-new brown and black shirtwaist dress with roll-up sleeves, sheer nylons, and black flats. The dress is made from a miracle fabric my mother convinced me will be easy to care for, but it feels like I'm wearing a plastic bag, and it makes me sweat. I hate it; I never should have let my mother talk me into buying it. Slung over my shoulder, I carry a new, very large, very ugly black handbag. An old person's handbag. I look like an imitation grown-up, far older than my sixteen years.

I look out into the distance, away from my mother, from my sister, past my father. The beginning of a smile plays at the corners of my mouth. Even so, my right hand is clenched into a fist, the only outward sign that I am afraid.

I know that, soon, I'll be unpacked and alone and free. No lying to get out of the house when I want to. No questions about where I've been and why I'm late. No discussions about why I don't want to spend more time with the family. No dinner-table rages. No talk about why I don't want to eat what's been put before me. No waiting until everyone is asleep so I can go to sleep. No lying to get out of the house when I want to.

My dormitory room, I have decided, will be my private sanctuary from the world. It will be my place of work, and thought. A place I can become quiet, go deep. This past summer, I have been reading works about Buddhism and Buddhist texts. The idea that it is possible to find stillness within the chaos of the world through various disciplines—among them, study and meditation—appeals to me. I have decided that I will devote my life to trying to find the still center of the turning wheel.

The other arriving students are outfitted very differently from me. They wear comfortable jeans or shorts, white man-tailored shirts, sneakers or loafers, ready for the work of unpacking their parents' cars, of setting up their rooms.

I have dressed in imitation of magazine pictures depicting girls on their way to college. I have worn what I imagine is suitable. But because I am the first person in my family who goes to college, I have no way of knowing what college students really wear, except for the photos I have scrutinized, and so I am, as always, inappropriately dressed.

Even before I enter Woodbury Hall for the first time, I have gathered my share of stares from the other students. I have a lot to learn, I realize, if I want to fit in. But then again, I tell myself, I might not want to fit in.

Clothes have always been a major problem for me. There is the issue of money. Our family doesn't have much of it, so, in the past, except when I was a child, I have had very few clothes, and my mother has made many of them. The clothes I wear are different from my friends', and they are never in style. They are chosen to last, to be serviceable, not to be fashionable. Then there is the issue of image. In high school, I have never really known what I want to look like. Some of my friends sport a collegiate look; others, my mother tells me, look like tramps. I have a strange assortment of clothes that don't seem to belong to the same person. A pair of ballet shoes, spike heels, a pointy bra, a skin-tight angora sweater, a short, tight skirt, in imitation of one of my sexy friends. A pair of loafers, Bermuda shorts, a sweater set, an oxford shirt or two, in imitation of my collegiate friends. Some castoffs from a rich friend that are far too big on me; my mother persuades me they are too good to be tossed out. I wear them, though the in kids laugh at me; they remember her wearing them and they know they're hand-me-downs. Nothing I have goes with anything else. Getting dressed in the morning to go out is always a nightmare. I have been complimented on my clothing just once, when I have worn a beautiful subtle teal plaid dress that fits me well—unusual, because my mother routinely persuades me to buy my clothes a size larger than I need, "so you'll grow into them," even after I'm sure I have stopped growing.

Shopping with my mother is an excruciating experience. Fortunately, it is infrequent.

After I choose what I want from the possibilities she offers, based upon what we can afford, she says, "Now, are you sure?" Suddenly, I become unsure that I like this item; often, I become paralyzed, unable to choose, and so leave the store angry, without anything. My mother and I have had public battles—over the skin-tight teal sheath that fits me beautifully, which I adore and refuse to put back on the rack until she concedes, and she lets my buy it; over a pair of navy-blue pumps with sensible heels that I detest, that she insists will serve me well throughout the years. She buys them, over my objections; I pay her back by never wearing them, which means that for over a year, I have no dressy shoes to wear.

Everything I bring to college fits into the small trunk of my father's Ford. One medium-sized baby-blue Samsonite suitcase, containing all my clothes, except the few on hangers. One matching baby-blue Samsonite hatbox, containing my shoes, portable alarm clock, and toilet articles. My baby-blue Smith-Corona portable typewriter. And—an extravagance that I have paid for myself—a ream of Corrasible Bond paper, the miracle paper that you can erase easily. I suspect I will have much writing to do, and I am ready. I suspect that I will make many mistakes, and I am ready.

Some of my clothes are new, purchased from my savings. Over the years, I have earned an enormous amount of money. During the summer before my freshman year, I have worked in New York City on Park Avenue at a job my father has helped me find through a friend. I have earned the remarkable salary of eighty-five dollars per week—more than my father earns. Lying about my age during the interview, I have been given the job of running an office during the office manager's leave of absence. My responsibilities include answering the phone, providing the prices of the valves the company sells over the telephone, typing up orders for the salesmen, filing, working a Teletype machine, and trying to get along with the crazy secretary, prone to temper tantrums. She jumps up and down when she's angry, pounds her fists on the desk, rips up my work when she really goes nuts. I learn, quickly, that the best strategy is to ignore her completely.

The job involves a long commute on the bus from New Jersey, a long walk over to Park from the Port Authority Bus Terminal on Forty-second Street (past the sleazy X-rated movie theaters, the prostitutes and their pimps, the drug dealers). When I get home, I'm so tired, I eat my dinner and fall into bed. But the job has its compensations. On the bus ride to and from work, I read *The Golden Bough*, the *Rig Veda*, books I purchase from a bookstore in New York City. A few times, the grown men on their way home from work who sit next to me want to talk about Fraser, about Buddhism, and I oblige them, finding I can hold an intellectual conversation with a grown-up.

I get to eat my breakfast at the Dunkin' Donuts coffee shop in the building where I work; I soon develop an addiction to their whole-wheat doughnuts, which I can satisfy every morning of the summer. Perched on the stool, ordering my coffee, light, and my doughnut, I feel like a grown-up, and I like it. I sit in the same place each morning, and after a few weeks, the red-headed waitress starts calling me "Dear." On my lunch break, on fine days, I wander over to Fifth Avenue, and eat my packed lunch, or a hot dog (with sauerkraut, mustard, *and* sweet relish) on a soft bun, on the steps of the New York Public Library, though I never enter. I loiter there, in the sun, wondering if the tourists take me for a native New Yorker, or if they can tell I'm a naive, rough, and unsophisticated girl from New Jersey.

I promise myself that, by the end of the summer, I will treat myself to a dress off a bargain rack from Peck & Peck, a department store on Fifth Avenue, and I do. It is the first dress I buy for myself, with my money. I find the dress of my dreams—a scooped neck, tight-waisted, flared-skirt number in cocoa-colored raw silk for fifteen dollars, reduced from seventy-five dollars. Before I buy it, I imitate my mother's practice of inspecting the garment both inside and out, to make sure its workmanship is perfect, and it is. I watch, with pleasure, as the clerk folds it neatly, packs it in tissue, and boxes it. I take the box, and hold it proudly by its string handle. Walking down Fifth Avenue with my purchase, for the first time in my life, I believe that I am normal, that I am just like everybody else. It is a heady, exhilarating feeling, and I love it.

* * *

Before I buy my wardrobe for Douglass with my savings, I check out the pages of some recent issues of *Seventeen* magazine. I discover that Black Watch plaid, knee socks, kilts (secured with giant imitation gold safety pins), crew-neck sweaters, loafers, and circle pins are "in" on college campuses. So, I buy a pair of Black Watch plaid Bermuda shorts, a Black Watch plaid kilt (with imitation gold safety pin), a navy-blue crew-neck sweater, a circle pin, and a pair of loafers. This is my first shopping spree. These clothes will fit in with the clothes that can pass for collegiate in my meager wardrobe—a pair of red plaid Bermuda shorts, the uniform for my PAL softball team, the Banlon sweater set given to me by Carmine Carrero, which I have hardly worn, a few white shirts. I have five changes of clothes, two good dresses, a couple of nightgowns, a brand-new quilted bathrobe, and fuzzy slippers. My mother has helped me shop, but this time the choices are mine. I give in only on the sensible brown shirtwaist dress that she tells me I'll wear often, especially for "casual dates."

My baby-blue portable Smith-Corona typewriter has been a gift from my parents a year before, in anticipation of my attending college. It is an expensive gift, a thoughtful gift, signaling to me, more than words, that they approve of my ambition to go to college, though they themselves haven't.

I have taught myself to touch type in the summer of the eleventh grade, using a record and a book that you send away for after the purchase. I have done this diligently, in the evenings, figuring I can use the skill in summer jobs, and that I can type my papers in senior year and in college, and that, if all else fails, I can become a secretary.

I stick to my regimen, until I master all the letters, the comma, period, slash, question mark, apostrophe, and quotation marks. I give up when I get to the upper row of keys, and never learn them. No doubt, I already know that, in the line of work I will choose, I will rarely have need of @, #, $, %, +—the symbols so important in the world of commerce.

I am the first person in our Italian-American family—the first of ten cousins—to go to college. My paternal grandparents are proud of me. To the chagrin of my older cousins and my male cousins, at family gatherings, they always say, loud enough for everyone to hear, "Louise is the smartest. We expect the most from her." I hope I won't disappoint their faith in me. As the eldest child of their only son, I hold a position of prominence in the family usually reserved for a male. My grandmother has slipped a $10 bill into my hand the last time I have seen her. She wipes the tears in her eyes with the handkerchief she keeps in the sleeve of her dress. Her tears come easily. Her life has been hard. My grandfather, though he favors me, is a very difficult husband, who often abandoned his family to return to Italy. My grandmother tells me she hopes my life will be easier than hers.

My mother has discovered, in an article in a local newspaper, that Douglass is an excellent college but that it is inexpensive be-cause it is a state school. She suggests I apply. It is close by, a short drive down the New Jersey Turnpike, which means I can come home holidays and weekends, if I want to. Because I have a boyfriend who lives in town, this is important to me.

As a working-class girl, I have had no guidance, other than my mother's suggestion, in choosing schools. Luckily, I take her advice. Something I am not in the habit of doing.

Between my savings, a couple of scholarships, some govern-ment loans, and my parents' contribution, I can afford college, al-though I will have to repay the loans myself after I graduate. In 1959, it is possible for a working-class girl to attend college full-time, to live in a dormitory, and to immerse herself in learning.

I have decided to major in English, and to become an English teacher. In my imagination, I see myself reading novels for the rest of my life. To think that I might someday be paid for doing what I would do anyway strikes me as impossible, what my mother would call "a pipe dream." In my family, the work you get paid for is hard, physical labor. I can't imagine that I will one day earn my living by using my brain, but I know that this is possible.

I am lucky, on many counts, in choosing Douglass, an all-girls school, though I don't realize this at first. An all-girls school will become a haven where I can test and sharpen my intellect, away from the distracting influence of boys, where I will learn that I have the interest and ability to do rigorous intellectual work, where I will have brilliant women professors as role models.

At first, though, the freedom of college, the separation from my family, from whom I want to break free, to whom I am tied, is traumatic. At week's end, I am back home, suffering from something—the flu, a cold, perhaps even an attack of asthma—having climbed on and off trains and buses, dragging my baby-blue Samsonite luggage (nearly stolen at Grand Central Station), heavy with its load of books.

I am sure I will fail out of college, sure that I can never read all the assignments, never write all the papers, and I know I will never, never, never learn the Russian alphabet. On my first in-class writing assignment in freshman comp, given on the first day of class as a "diagnostic exercise," the professor has scrawled in red ink, across the top of my paper, "You write primer English; you have a great deal to learn." I have not taken his words as a challenge; I have read them as a condemnation. I have tried—and obviously failed—to articulate what the challenge of reading Dostoyevksy meant to me as a high school student.

Friday evening, when I arrive at home, weepy, exhausted, barely able to breathe, my mother puts me to bed. She brings me soup and tea and tells me she knows I'll feel better in the morning.

Saturday, she tells me to call up some friends, to get out of the house, to find something to do.

Sunday, early, she comes into my room, and tells me to pack. My father will drive me back to school before breakfast. She has seen all my books and knows that I have much work to do for Monday.

I protest.

I don't want to go back. Now I want to stay here at home as much as I've wanted to get away. But my mother won't allow it.

This is a mother I haven't often seen. A decisive mother. A wise, tough mother. A mother who won't take no for an answer. A different mother from my former mother, from my sister's mother, who, when she pulls the same stunt four years later, allows her secondborn daughter to stay home.

This new mother of mine will not allow her firstborn daughter to thwart her ambition, as she had thwarted hers.

My mother, I know, had received a special award in her senior year in high school that recognized her talent as a writer, though she couldn't afford to go on to college. It is a pin, depicting a draped female figure, a soaring eagle, and an elk's head. On the back, an engraving: 1ST PRIZE, 3RD DIV., PRESENTED BY HOBOKEN LODGE B.P.O. ELKS, and my mother's name.

She wears it, proudly, throughout her life, on the lapel of her Sunday suit. When I ask to see it, she removes it from her jacket and turns it over, so I can read the engraving. When I ask her if I can have it, she says no, that, besides her wedding ring, it is the only object she owns that she values.

"You can have it when I'm dead," she laughs. "If it means so much to you, I'll leave it to you in my will." She does, and after her death I wear it around my neck, on a chain, as a lucky charm, when I write.

"I was a good writer," she tells me. "The best writer in my class. I had hoped that writing would become the center of my life.

Oh well," she continues, "I guess it wasn't meant to be. No use crying over spilt milk."

She takes the pin from me, secures it back on her lapel, and drifts off.

She walks away from me, back into her own private world, leaving me wondering what she might have done with her talent if she had gone on to college, if her battle with depression hadn't claimed so much of her energy. But even as I know her dreams were never realized, I also know that in having those dreams, and in sharing them, she has helped me—she has begun something that I can continue.

Anorexia

WHEN I FIRST went away to college, we had a dormitory meeting. To break the ice, the dorm leader asked us to tell the group what our favorite home-cooked meal was.

In my memory, we are sitting in a circle all dressed in brand-new pink or yellow bathrobes and matching slippers, specially purchased for dormitory life at college.

Around the room we go.

"Fried chicken, mashed potatoes, and peas," says a girl in a pink bathrobe. A few of the girls nod their heads; this is their favorite too; they wonder what they will say when it's their turn.

"Pot roast and vegetables—carrots, onions, parsnips—and gravy, lots of gravy," says a girl with big rollers in her hair. (I don't know what a parsnip is, but what she describes sounds like a banquet to me.)

Now the group is relaxing. All the girls are smiling, all the girls are eager to share their favorites. All but two of us. Me. And the girl sitting across from me looking as sour as I can look when I want to look sour. We exchange looks. She will become my best friend.

My turn comes.

I tell the group that I can't think of a favorite home-cooked meal, because I don't have one.

The leader laughs. She thinks I can't think of a favorite meal because I have so many. I mean I can't think of a favorite meal because I don't have a favorite home-cooked meal. I like what my friends' mothers cook, but that doesn't count in this exercise. I know my dorm leader won't believe this, but I don't like anything my mother cooks.

If it hadn't been for my grandmother's homemade pizza and bread, and for my mother's toasted cheese sandwiches (served burned side down), I am sure that, as a child, I would have starved to death. (This is somewhat of an exaggeration, but not much: I also liked, and ate, Cheerios with milk and bananas, Oreos, and Campbell's tomato soup thinned with milk.) It isn't that I was a picky eater, or that I didn't have an appetite. I was always hungry. But I lost my appetite as soon as I sat at the table to eat, as soon as I saw what my mother had tried to cook.

These are the things my mother cooked that I couldn't eat, or wouldn't eat, or that I objected to for one reason or another.

Liver and fried onions, at least once a week (my father's favorite; he smacked his lips when he ate this).

Dried salt cod (soaked in water for days, and cooked with tomatoes, too salty and too watery, and this was supposed to be special).

Heart (I would never let a bite pass my lips).

Snails (too disgusting to even contemplate; after you bought them, live, they spent time in your kitchen in a pail with sand in it to clear out their digestive systems before being cleaned and stewed with tomatoes; my grandmother and my father picked at them and ate them with open safety pins).

Soup meat (fatty, stringy, and you could even see the veins, served with mustard on the side).

Squab, a nice-sounding name for pigeon (they fly around and live on people's roofs and settle on your windowsill where you can see them; the good thing about pigeon is that you can get them free from a friend; my father calls them flying rats and sees nothing wrong in eating them; if I wouldn't eat a rat—and I wouldn't—then, I ask him, why would I eat a pigeon?).

Tongue (looking just like a tongue, and I knew where it had been, and I didn't want any part of it).

Tripe (looking just like a stomach, although my mother tried unsuccessfully to convince me that it wasn't *the* stomach, but another kind of stomach that had nothing to do with digestion).

Chicken. (When we spend the summer on Long Island, my grandmother and her sister were responsible for executing the chickens they raised out back. Any time we had chicken for dinner, the two of them would chase the chicken around, catch it, and try to wring its neck. They didn't always succeed on the first try.)

Pig's feet and pig's knuckles (not always at the same meal; not cooked, but pulled, already cooked, from jars packed with gelatin that I insisted was pig snot; you had to go out of your way to find a store that stocked them).

Brains (looking just like brains; my mother once tried to get me to eat them by claiming that they would make me smart; I told her that I was smart enough).

Ovaries (not really, but that's what I called the poached eggs in vinegar served on water-logged toast that my father seemed to like).

Kidneys (she told me the English liked them; that tells you all you need to know about the English, I said; they smelled like piss, even when she soaked them in milk—many things my mother cooked required soaking; once, to tease my sister, I make her look into the basin with the kidneys soaking and I tell her "It moved, did you see it move?" and because I'm her big sister, and she believes me, she runs from the kitchen shrieking, and she refuses to eat for the rest of the day, and the next, and the next).

Head cheese (which, so far as I could figure out, was all the stuff that came out of, or could be picked off, the animal's head; I never ask what kind of animal).

Waffles, served with links of greasy breakfast sausage on the side (which I liked, but objected to for dinner, because to my organized, everything-in-its-proper-place mind, waffles were supposed to be breakfast food).

Corned beef, very salty, very stringy, and cabbage, very watery (served with mustard on the side).

Omelet (too greasy, filled with unacceptable vegetables, like onions and zucchini, fried until they were black, and this was supposed to be dinner).

Mashed potatoes with canned gravy, no meat.

Bratwurst (a giant hot dog that looked like a swollen dick to me), served with canned sauerkraut (too watery).

Eels.

Octopi.

Blood sausage.

Even special occasions were ruined for me. The birds that we ate for Christmas, for New Year's, were fresh-killed. You went to a garage around the block (when we lived in Hoboken) or in the next town (when we lived in Ridgefield), and you selected your live bird that made gobbling or clucking noises. Then the butcher took the bird in the back room. The bird made frantic gobbling or clucking noises, which meant it knew what it was in for.

Whack, the sound of the hatchet decapitating the poor thing.

Within a few minutes, the bird, still warm, still leaking blood, would be handed over to you for your holiday dinner.

For years, my mother cooked things that I believed no one should eat, things that I certainly couldn't eat, Old World things, cheap things, low-class things, things that I was sure were bad for you, things I was ashamed to say I ate, and that I certainly couldn't invite my friends over to eat. I wanted to pass for American. I wanted a hamburger. I wanted to eat like we were middle class. I told my friends that my mother used food (or the lack of it) as a lethal weapon. They laughed. But, to me, it wasn't funny. Especially because my not eating these things that she cooked always caused arguments between my father and me.

"Eat what's put in front of you. Your mother worked hard to make this."

"I can't eat this. I don't like this."

"It's good for you."

"I don't care if it's good for you, I still can't eat it."

"If you could see what I had to eat when I was in the navy, you'd be grateful for the food you have in front of you."

"But I'm not in the navy."

"You always have to get the last word, don't you. Go to your room. Come back when you have an appetite."

"Then I'll starve to death."

The dinner table had become our favorite battleground.

Once, just once, I wanted to be served something I really liked, a decent, normal dinner like I knew my friends were eating, and I wanted to eat it without calamity. When my mother dished up a meat loaf, or a hot turkey sandwich on toast (burnt because she was either fighting with my grandmother while she was making dinner, or because she was deep within her own thoughts) with gravy, I rejoiced and ate as much as I could. I used to tell my friends that I loved TV dinners, and they never believed me, and they couldn't understand why. Especially Swanson TV turkey dinners, which I ate with relish, down to the very last pea.

Through grammar school and high school, I chose my friends carefully from among those whose mothers were good cooks. There were a few fellow-suffering exceptions: Susan, who had boiled potatoes every night of her life, and she had to make them. If she wanted to make baked or fricasseed or mashed, her mother had a fit. Larry, whose father was a bartender, whose mother was a hatcheck girl at the Copacabana, and so were never home for dinner; he seemed to subsist on gigantic bowls of cereal taken standing up, leaning against the sink.

My friends' mothers had to be generous with food. It was what we expected from mothers in the fifties, in the days when not many women worked outside the home, when women were expected to cook wonderful meals for their tired husbands, and have it on the table the moment they stepped through the door.

I couldn't see making friends with someone whose mother wasn't willing to feed me. If I came by at four o'clock, my friends' mothers had to invite me to stay for dinner, and mean it, so I could avoid going home to supper at my house.

Once, one of my good friends in high school accused me of hanging around with her because I couldn't get enough of her parents' Middle Eastern cooking. In part, she was right. Would I have liked her as much if she hadn't smelled so fragrantly of her mother's simmering saucepans of pungently spiced concoctions? I don't think so. But I learned in her house, too, that dinner could consistently be a delicious occasion. Her father also cooked—extremely rare in the fifties. And I saw the special pleasure a woman takes from eating a meal at her own table that she hasn't had to prepare.

*　*　*

"Come on, Louise. Think harder. What's your favorite home-cooked meal?"

My dormitory leader presses me to answer. She isn't satisfied by my silence. We're supposed to be sharing.

"Okay, if you insist," I say. "Pizza. Pizza is my favorite home-cooked meal."

"That's not a meal," says a girl who is wearing a dangle bracelet with her bathrobe. "That's a snack." I hate her. In my house, pizza is a meal, not a snack, but about this I'm not going to argue.

The girl across the room with whom I have exchanged glances looks at me in sympathy. She gets it. She hates the girl with the dangle bracelet too.

When her turn comes, she shrugs her shoulders, takes a deep drag on her cigarette, inexpertly, starts laughing, and says something flippant but beautifully phrased. Something about how that would depend on whether she's dieting at the time or not, on whether she's eating at the time, or not. She uses words well. I like this young woman's style.

Later that night, Rebecca and I share what we call "nearly lethal meals we have eaten" and "if food could kill, and it can" stories. We talk about how we never invite any of our friends over for dinner because we're afraid of what our mothers will cook and of what might happen at the dinner table.

Rebecca tells me about how her mother serves frozen string beans, frozen. Her father, not wanting to rock the boat, swears they're delicious this way. Tries to persuade Rebecca to eat them.

Rebecca tells me about how her mother cooks the family meals in the morning, leaving them unrefrigerated all day to "ripen the flavors."

Rebecca tells me about how her mother buys scraps of cold cuts, which are green-molded, and how she sets them out for dinner.

I tell her about all the stuff my mother cooks that I hate. How I feel my health has suffered as a result.

I tell her about the time my gums are so rotten that they have to paint them purple with Gentian Violet to cure them and that's how I have to go to school and the stuff doesn't come off my teeth for a month and how all the kids make fun of me.

"Trench mouth?" Rebecca asks. "You had trench mouth? I thought only soldiers and poor people got trench mouth."

Somewhere else on our campus, on this night, in another living room of another dormitory, sits another freshman girl who, perhaps, has been asked the same question by her dorm group leader to break the ice.

Years later, in the seventies, sitting at the breakfast table, lingering over the Sunday *New York Times*, I take up the magazine section, and pause.

On the cover, I see a face, a recognizable face. A headline, about anorexia nervosa, starving yourself to death. The woman on the cover looks like a girl I went to college with, a girl in my class, a girl who lived in my dorm, but on another floor, maybe freshman year, maybe later?

I open the magazine, scan the piece. Sure enough. One of my classmates. Dead from self-starvation. She is the first member of our class to achieve fame. She does it after she dies. She becomes famous because she's starved herself to death.

Pictures of her, of her family.

Questions. How did this happen? How did the family let this happen? Could the family have stopped it from happening? What caused this to happen?

It is the first article I read on anorexia. I haven't known this young woman well, but we inhabited the same spaces at the same time, went to the same classes, shared the same experiences. She was young, and gifted, with her future bright. Once, we shared a dormitory. A library. A dining hall. What happened to her, and why? What made her want to disappear? And why didn't what happened to her happen to me?

I feel the aftershock of this article for days. Years later, whenever I read about anorexia, I think of my classmate. Wonder what her story was. What her story really was. What made her want to die.

I think: Fainting is one way of disappearing. Anorexia is another.

During our freshman year, Rebecca and I seal our friendship over meals at the campus dining hall. We are two of the few girls in the college who rarely skip a meal. We go to the dining hall for breakfast, and Friday nights when they serve what we call "wet fish," and on the week nights when they serve what the other girls call "mystery meat"—Rebecca and I know it's lamb because they serve it with mint jelly. Here, they tell you what you're going to eat beforehand so you can decide whether you want to come, not like at home, where the latest atrocity is slipped in front of you without your knowing what it's going to be.

Some girls don't mind the "dry fish"—fried fish, served with wedges of fresh lemon and homemade tartar sauce and crispy coleslaw. But no one but us can even look at, much less eat, the "wet fish"—fish baked with tomatoes and onions—or the "mystery meat." They dine out, or they order in. We think the "wet fish" and the "mystery meat" taste wonderful.

Throughout my college years, my mother sends me occasional "CARE packages." They are loaded with canned foods she thinks I'll like. Canned beef stew. Canned hot dogs. Canned raviolis. Canned spaghetti. Canned ham. My mother encloses a note saying that if I don't like the food at the dining hall one night, I can prepare something for myself in the dormitory kitchen. But I hate the canned food. It's a waste of money. I won't eat it.

But sometimes Rebecca eats it. She eats it when she's too depressed to get dressed for dinner, or when she's decided she'd rather stay in the dorm to get some work done or pick at the pimples on her face. And because neither of us has come to college equipped with pots and pans to cook for ourselves, like some other girls, Rebecca just eats the stuff, cold, right out of the can, sitting cross-legged on her bed.

At breakfast, we are in heaven. At breakfast they serve us home-made buns. My favorites are coconut and walnut. Hers are crumb and almond. And with the buns, you can have eggs (poached, scrambled, or sunny side up) and bacon (both at the same meal).

At lunch, we are in heaven. At lunch, they serve you what we say we might get for a special dinner at home on a very good day. Lasagna. Hamburgers with french fries. Sloppy Joes. Hot turkey sandwiches with gravy and mashed potatoes (all at the same meal). And you get dessert. A piece of cake. A piece of pie. Or fruit. (And it isn't even a holiday, just lunch.)

At dinner, we are in heaven; at dinner, we get what we usually get at home on holidays. Roast beef, with baked potatoes, gravy and vegetables (sometimes two kinds). Yum. Fried chicken, with mashed potatoes and succotash. Yum. Yum. Plus dessert. And some girl are so spoiled they get irritated if they serve the same dessert for lunch and dinner. Not us.

Rebecca comes bounding back through the dining hall after checking out the dessert selections with a waitress friend.

"They have caramel custard again," she tells me. "Left over from lunch."

"Oh good," I say, "my favorite."

"Liar. I thought the apple pie was your favorite," Rebecca says.

"It was my favorite," I say. "Yesterday. Today the caramel custard is my favorite."

"They're all my favorite," Rebecca tells me. She tells me she has to go on a diet, has to starve herself.

"Wait 'til semester break," I say. "Eat here. Starve yourself at home."

We both laugh. It's true. We won't have any trouble losing weight at home.

In my first year of college, I gain twenty-five pounds, which brings me up to a normal weight of 120 pounds for a girl my age.

The dining hall, Rebecca and I have both agreed, is the best part of college, even if you have to wear skirts to eat your meals, even if you have to get up early, even if you have to walk across a wind-whipped plain to get there.

It is always bitterly cold in winter when we walk to dinner, especially when not properly dressed, which Rebecca and I never are. With her flair for the dramatic, and because she is taking Russian, and has seen Russian movies, she calls this place "the tundra," and she sings a Russian song that sounds like "Ochichonya, ochichon-ya" as we walk, arm in arm, to Nielsen Dining Hall in the dead of winter, laughing and laughing, and looking forward to what we'll be eating for dinner that night.

I don't know whether I make this up, or whether it's true, but I tell Rebecca that the chef at the dining hall is a man called Doctor Lasagna, a famous chef, who once cooked for the president.

Once, Rebecca and I are invited to our friend Sissie's for Thanksgiving. Sissie warns us we might be in for trouble, her mother drinks too much, but she wants us to come anyway. If we come, it won't be so bad for her. Rebecca and I agree to go. How bad can it be?

For a first course, there is a potato leek soup. Then a gorgeous turkey (cooked until the skin is bronze and crackly) with chestnut stuffing. There is another stuffing, served on the side, cornbread stuffing, which they call dressing, because it hasn't been used to stuff the bird. Creamed onions. Brussels sprouts in browned butter with caraway seeds. Popovers. Homemade cranberry sauce with slivers of almonds and pieces of orange peel.

Rebecca and I heap our plates. We have seconds. Thirds.

For dessert: Pecan Bourbon pie. Homemade. Hooray!

Between courses, Rebecca and I disappear into the toilet together to compare notes.

Rebecca asks me if I think all WASP Thanksgivings are like this one. I tell her I don't know.

I say, if it takes a mother who's a drunk to make a dinner like this one, then I'll take a drunken mother any day of the week.

Throughout the meal, our friend Sissie is nervous. She isn't enjoying herself. She doesn't eat much. Nothing compared to Rebecca and me.

She picks at her fingers and smokes, picks at her fingers and smokes. It's a habit of hers we hate and try to get her to stop.

After, as we wash up, Sissie apologizes.

"What for?" we ask.

Sissie tells us that her mother, who, by now, is reeling drunk, has fucked up again. The turkey was overcooked. The brussels sprouts were mushy. The gravy was lumpy. The meal was nothing like when Yolanda (the ex-maid) did the cooking. Sissie's family has come down in the world; her parents are divorced; her mother is now running the whole show.

We tell Sissie that this is the BEST Thanksgiving meal we've ever eaten, anywhere. She thinks we're being nice. We aren't being nice. We mean it.

In the years that Sissie goes to school with us, she smokes more and more, gets thinner and thinner. The last time we see her is after she transfers to another school.

She comes back to school to see us.

"Hey, you guys," she greets us, our old, familiar greeting. "What's up?"

"Nothing much," Rebecca and I chorus. But that's not true. Rebecca is in love, and will marry as soon after college as she can manage. I am in love, and will marry as soon after college as I can manage. Both of us will teach to support our husbands through graduate school. Rebecca and I have it all figured out.

Sissie tells us she doesn't know what she's going to do with her life after she graduates. She has no idea.

"Maybe bum around," she tells us.

Throughout our brief visit, Sissie displays her same nervous habits—the constant smoking, the small self-mutilations. She looks awful. All "skin and bones," as my mother would say.

When it's time for Sissie to leave, we walk her to her beat-up old car. She says, "Hey, you guys, take care. See you soon." We watch her, as her car rattles down the road.

We never see Sissie, never hear from her again. Rebecca and I are convinced we're luckier than she is.

I wasn't as thin as Sissie. Never wanted to be as thin as her. I wanted big, fleshy tits, like a friend I had in high school. I used to dream of waking up on my next birthday with breasts so big I would need a real bra, not the miserable excuses for bras called "trainer bras" I wore. But it never happened. When I was in high school, I was always very thin; I weighed less than a hundred pounds. I never had to worry about my weight, like other girls. Never binged. Never dieted. Never threw up in the bathroom as some of my friends did after they'd eaten a quart of ice cream. All I wanted was to have enough food to eat that I liked.

And I was very thin, too thin, earlier in my life. When I was seven years old, after my grandfather died. After my grandfather died, my mother got depressed (and I think I did too).

There is a picture of my sister and me, both looking very sad, standing in the cemetery, next to a tombstone. We go there every Sunday, so my mother can tend her father's grave. He is the first person to be buried in this family plot, which he has bought. Later, my stepgrandmother, my mother, and my sister will be buried there.

I am wearing overalls and a striped pullover I hate because it reminds me of the clothes men wear on chain gangs. My arms, my face, are too thin, thinner than in the pictures taken of me before my grandfather's death. I look like I'm not eating enough; I look like I'm not getting enough to eat. Maybe I got so thin because my mother was too depressed to feed me enough; maybe I got so thin because I was too depressed to eat.

Whenever I tell someone about my grandfather's death, which came as a great shock to me, I tell it in this way.

My mother and my sister and I come home from an errand, and my mother knocks on my grandparents' door, and there is no answer. My grandfather is supposed to be home, so my mother is concerned.

My mother bangs and bangs at the door and yells, "Papa, Papa," and still there is no answer. She suspects something is wrong.

So we go into our apartment, and she tells me to crawl out the kitchen window, across the fire escape, and into my grandparents' kitchen window, which I easily manage.

So this is how I am the one who finds my grandfather on the floor, dead. He has been standing on a chair, trying to change a lightbulb. The chair is on the floor, overturned. The lightbulb is still in his hand. There is a tiny stream of blood coming out of his mouth.

I stand on my tiptoes to unlatch the door to open it to get my mother. I am almost smiling when I tell her what has happened. She pushes past me and begins to scream. She leaves my sister all by herself out in the hall. I take my sister's hand and bring her in to see what has happened.

I am not afraid of my grandfather's dead body, not afraid of the blood either. I feel very important to have been the one to find him. This is the first dead body I have ever seen.

Later, when the doctor comes, we find out that my grandfather has had a heart attack. My father blames the wine my grandfather drinks. It has given my grandfather a heart condition, my father says. My grandfather has had to work hard all his life. He has worked on the railroad, laying tracks in the broiling sun of summer. The railroad gives the workers (many of them Italian) a ration of cheap red wine to have with their lunch to keep them quiet and working.

After my grandfather's death, my grandmother starts wearing black. She will wear black until the day she dies. When we move to Ridgefield, she comes with us.

After my grandfather's death, I can't remember my mother smiling for a very, very long time.

After my grandfather's death, everyone is astonished at how well I take it, at how I don't cry, though we got along so well. They think I'm a very strong child. They tell me to be good, for my mother's sake.

After my grandfather's death, my father tells the story about how, once, when my grandfather was supposed to be taking care of me, he had gotten me drunk. I was really little at the time, and when my mother bent down to pick me up, she smelled alcohol on my breath. My grandfather told her he'd given me wine to keep me quiet, to put me to sleep.

No one asks me whether I miss my grandfather. No one asks me whether I'm sad or sorry he's dead. No one wonders why I don't cry. They think I don't cry because I'm being such a good girl.

Soon after my grandfather's death, I start forcing myself to look closely at the dead bodies of squirrels and birds in the streets and in the park around the corner from where we live. I am surprised that I have never noticed them.

Soon after my grandfather dies, we move to Ridgefield.

Soon after that, I start fainting.

When I meet my future husband, in the summer of my sophomore year in college, my mother tells me to bring him home for dinner. I know she hopes my roving days are over; I know she thinks it's time for me to start looking for a husband, a man who will be a "good match." If I marry well, she tells me—someone with prospects, someone who will have a profession, someone who can support me well—all her sacrifices will have been worthwhile. I tell her not to worry, that I can take care of myself and support myself and that I don't need a man for any of these things. I say that what I want is an equal partner. Someone who wants the same things for me that I want for myself. She's not sure this is possible. But I think that I've found such a man in Ernie.

I don't want to take him home for dinner, though my mother invites him. I'm not stupid. I don't want to fuck up my chances with this guy. We get along. He knows about Sartre, Camus. We play bridge. Go to see foreign films together. He's Italian. He likes pizza. He's sexy. Spent most of his life in an Italian neighborhood in the Bronx like mine in Hoboken. He's going to be a doctor.

My mother persists.

"I'll cook him a nice meal," she tells me. I'm skeptical. I can't wait to see what this will be, what she'll manage. I tell her what not to make. I tell her not to make anything like liver or brains or kidneys or any of the other stuff I hate. She looks at me like she never makes these things, wouldn't think of making them.

"I'll come up with something," she says.

"Just make it good," I plead.

She wants the meal to be a big surprise, for me, too. She likes the sound of this guy I tell her I'm bringing home. He sounds much better to her than the other guys I've brought home, whom she hasn't liked, but whom she has welcomed.

Like the guy I told her was an auto mechanic.

He *wanted* to be an auto mechanic, but, really, he pumped gas. He drove a Ford that was rotting, which he was trying, but failing, to fix up. She told me she was afraid that one day the two of us would drop through the bottom of his car onto the roadway. I knew there was little chance of that happening. We never went anywhere, didn't want to go anywhere. We only drove as far as a deserted street by the railroad tracks in our hometown so we could make out. We had very little to say to one another. No matter. He was sexy, he turned me on, I liked his body, and that was enough.

After we broke up, when I asked my mother why she was so nice to him, though she didn't think he was suitable, she said, "I thought you read *Romeo and Juliet* in high school? If you didn't read it, read it now. If you read it, read it again." I got the message.

Coming between us would have sealed our love, turned it fatal. My mother wanted better for me. By not standing in the way of my loving this boy, my mother was standing in the way of my loving him.

On the night that I bring Ernie DeSalvo to my parents' home for the first time, my mother serves the best meal I've ever eaten in that household.

A lovely consommé for the first course. Little triangles of crisp toast on the side. (Not burnt.)

Broiled lobster tails (lobster tails!) for the main course. Sprinkled with paprika so they have a nice color. Served with double-baked potatoes (potatoes, baked, their insides taken out and mashed with butter and cream, then put back into the potato skins, and baked again) and Le Seur tender tiny peas (a premium brand my mother has never bought before).

For dessert, Indian pudding with vanilla ice cream (expensive brand). Somehow, my mother has learned it's Ernie's favorite dessert.

At first, I'm happy that my mother has tried to please my new boyfriend. But then I'm not. I'm furious. To me, this now seems an even worse betrayal than if she had served him what I call "the usual garbage."

This is a wonderful dinner, beautifully conceived, executed, and served, at the dining room table, on china, with crystal and silver, on one of my grandmother's crocheted tablecloths.

To me, this meal means that my mother knows what's good, and that she has known what's good all along. She just hasn't cooked what she knows is good for me, though she's willing to cook it for this young man who isn't even one of the family. At least not yet.

I don't know what to do. I want to make a scene. Tell my mother off. Ask her why she doesn't always cook like this. Why, for him, and not for me?

But I know better. I don't want to scare this guy off. I don't want to show him how bitter, mean, and sarcastic I can be. How I try to punish my parents with my sharp tongue. How I try to get back at them. For what? For everything.

I control myself. But clearly I am not happy and my mother, who has tried so hard to cook this excellent meal for me, can't figure out what she's done to get me so upset this time.

Now, if I could travel through time, and do this night all over, I would do it differently.

I would look across the table at my mother. I would see the tremendous effort it took her to cook this dinner. I would remember how afraid she was of knives, of fire, how she was always cutting herself, or burning herself by accident, and how that would

217

make cutting, chopping, cooking so hard for her. I would see how food was a problem.

I would remember how she got herself dressed, how she (who didn't leave the house unless she absolutely had to) got herself out of the house early this morning. How she walked to the market, chose the ingredients, so carefully. How she carried them up the big hill.

I would remember that she spent the day preparing, making sure that everything was perfect. Perfect for the young man she thought might make a suitable husband for her troublesome daughter who had a way of bringing the most unsuitable young men home, men who couldn't or wouldn't give her a good life.

If I could do this night over, I would remember these things and I would look across the table at my mother and say, Thank you. Thank you very, very much.

A Portrait of the *Puttana* as a Woman in Midlife

THE YEAR IS 1975.

I am thirty-two years old, married, the mother of two small children, a Ph.D. candidate, on a charter flight to England with a friend to do research on Virginia Woolf at the University of Sussex in Falmer. This is the first time in my whole life that I am going away by myself. I have no idea where Falmer is, except that it is near Brighton. We have no hotel reservations. We have no idea how we will get to Brighton. But we are gloriously drunk on our third sherry, free from the responsibility of our children for a while. (We have already had enough sherry so that each child can have her or his own little sherry bottle as a souvenir when we return home.) We are, at long last, grown-ups, going to do *real* research. The next generation of Woolf scholars, in incubation. We are formidable.

I come from a family, from a cultural heritage, where women don't go away to do things separately from men. That is not to say that men don't go away to do things separately from women. They do. And often. But in the land of my forebears, women sit around and wait for their men. Or they work very hard and watch their children and wait for their men. Or they make a sumptuous meal and they work very hard and watch their children and wait for their men. But they don't go anywhere without their men. Or do anything for themselves alone without their men. Except complain. To their children or to anyone else who will listen to them. About their men and about their bad luck in having been born female.

A few years before, I had decided, like everyone else, to explore my ethnic roots. It lasted a very short time. I bought a pasta machine. Learned how to combine the ingredients for pasta, to roll out the dough, and cut it. Word got out that I was a terrific pasta maker. Then I began to realize that you can tell how enslaved the women of any country are by the kind of preparation their traditional foods require. Any recipe that begins "Take a mortar and pestle" now drives me into a frenzy.

Well, pasta making is something like that. Women who really care about their families make it fresh every day. Purists insist that if the sacred pasta dough is touched by metal pasta machines (i.e., twentieth-century labor-saving devices), it becomes slightly slippery—a quality in pasta that is akin to infidelity in wives.

Oh yes, I now remember what women who do anything without their husbands are called. *Puttana*. Whores. I remember hearing stories in my childhood about how women like that were stoned to death in the old country.

Well, given a background like that, you can imagine the way I felt as we flew high above the Atlantic. There I was, a *puttana*, alone at last.

Early in my career, I thought that I would devote the rest of my life to carefully considered scholarly essays and books on every aspect of Virginia Woolf's life and art. Those were the heroine-worship days when I blanched at the sight of her manuscripts, when I did not dare to think that she had an outhouse, much less that she and her husband, Leonard, used the typescripts of her novels instead of toilet tissue, that she could be hardy enough or human enough to walk across the Downs in her beloved Sussex. I saw her as an earlier generation of critics painted her for me—frail, weak, crazy, tortured, looking out of windows, vacant, probing her troubled psyche.

I loved the sight of myself, briefcase in hand, walking up the steps of the New York Public Library, past the lions Patience and Fortitude (I would have preferred lionesses), thinking that the kid who grew up on the streets of Hoboken, New Jersey, was now striding past the painting of Milton's daughters taking down the immortal words of his verse, now walking down the third-floor corridor to the Berg Collection, now pressing the buzzer. And they were actually letting me into the sacred recess where I would soon sit next to all those famous literary scholars whose work I had read and do my own work.

My version of the American Dream.

And as I sat there, beginning my work, I thought that if only I could have the good fortune to sit over a glass of sherry at the Algonquin, or even over a cup of coffee at Tad's Steak House down the block, with someone really famous to talk about Virginia Woolf, life would be so sweet, so very sweet, and I would ask for nothing more in this universe.

I got into Woolf scholarship quite by accident. (Or so I thought at the time.) When I was in graduate school at New York University, I took a course with the Woolf scholar Mitchell Leaska. He was in the throes of his work on *The Pargiters*, his edition of the earlier draft of *The Years*. I was enthralled with his classes. I'll never forget the day he brought in his transcription of Woolf's holograph, the handwritten draft of that novel. I changed my mind about what I would be doing with my scholarly life in the moments it took him to read to us from Woolf's earlier version of *The Years*. Here was a more political, less guarded Woolf.

I hadn't known that earlier versions of literary texts were available. It hadn't occurred to me that one could study how an author created a novel and learn about the writing and revision process. It sounded like detective work. It was meticulous. It required stamina. Drive. It was exciting. I too would be working with manuscripts. I think I understood subconsciously that I required a grand consuming passion in life.

I soon decided to work with the manuscript of *The Voyage Out*, Virginia Woolf's first novel, because I wanted to catch Virginia Woolf in her beginnings where I thought she might be least guarded.

The Voyage Out is about Rachel Vinrace, a young, inexperienced woman, who accompanies her father on a trip to South America. On her father's ship, the *Euphrosyne*, she resumes a relationship with her aunt and uncle, Helen and Ridley Ambrose, and she meets Richard Dalloway, a former member of Parliament, and his wife, Clarissa. Rachel becomes involved with two parental surrogates— Helen and Clarissa—but the relationship with Clarissa is complicated because Rachel is sexually attracted to Richard. During a storm at sea, Rachel and he embrace. That night she has a dream that she is being pursued.

Later, when she is in Santa Marina, a South American port city, she meets Terence Hewet, who is spending his holiday there. They fall in love and decide to marry. But both are extremely reluctant lovers. Rachel dies of a mysterious illness before the couple can marry.

When I decided to work on *The Voyage Out*, I didn't know

that I would have great difficulty keeping the problems in my life separate from the issues in Woolf's novel.

I had reached that moment of sexual reevaluation that often occurs at thirty. Although I was married, I identified with Rachel so strongly that I believed I shared her distrust of intimacy. It was simpler for me to see myself in terms of Woolf's character than it was to look at my problems. I vacillated between thinking that Rachel and I were like all women, and thinking that her hesitations (and mine) were pathological. It took many years for me to separate myself from Rachel Vinrace. It took many years for me to understand that part of the reason for Rachel's hesitation was her submerged rage at the misogyny and brutality of the men in her life and at her mother's emotional unavailability.

While separating myself from Rachel, I learned not to make disparaging judgments about Rachel's behavior—or mine—but to look for the causes of that behavior in family and social histories. I also saw that I was letting this very close identification with Rachel hold me back, keep me in check, because my work was making me feel very powerful. And I was terrified of feeling powerful.

I wake up in the middle of the night from a dream. The dream is easy to describe, difficult to comprehend. Ishtar, the many-breasted goddess—with a face that changes from Virginia Woolf's to my mother's to that of a woman who looks familiar but whom I can't recognize—has placed her hands under my armpits and has picked me up. Her face is impassive. She does not look at me, does not recognize me, stares past me.

She begins shaking me—not violently, but powerfully and rhythmically. As she shakes me, my breasts, my vagina, fall off. They form a pile beneath my feet. As she continues to shake me, still staring beyond me, impassively and without emotion, what is left of me begins to shrivel into the baby doll, Patricia, that I remember having in childhood.

The only openings I have, now, are the hole in the middle of the little red mouth where you put the toy bottle and the one where the water runs out, between the legs. I begin saying, in the doll's voice that I remember, "Mama, mama." Ishtar stares impassively ahead. But she stops shaking me.

Working on Woolf's composition of *The Voyage Out* was my first long project. One that would take years. It terrified and thrilled me. Sometimes I would feel immensely powerful, feel that I, single-handedly, might change the course of Woolf scholarship. Or I would feel impotent, wondering how could I make any contribution to our knowledge of Woolf.

I learned what it is humanly possible to do in one day; what one cannot do; that one must trust the times when no work is getting done, because it is in those fallow periods that the unconscious mind is working. I had to change the way I thought about time. I had to scale down my expectations to a human level. All this was very hard for me to do.

Every time I worked on the project, my infantile power fantasies reared their ugly heads. I always thought that I would get more done in one day than it was possible to do. Then my feelings of potency would turn into feelings of powerlessness and despair. I slowly learned that the work could proceed only as quickly as it could proceed. (I have not entirely learned that lesson yet.)

I learned that I have the same trouble that anyone else has in working, in writing comprehensible sentences, in revising them, but that if I worked every day, the work would get done. I gradually realized what working on *The Voyage Out* for seven years must have been like for Virginia Woolf. I too was working on a project that was taking a very long time.

There was the temptation, too, to which I often succumbed, to work constantly, without interruption, to get it done more quickly. There was the temptation to work incessantly—days, nights, weekends—at the mountain of manuscripts, at the letters, diaries, and journals that Woolf had written while composing the novel.

Somehow, without my realizing it, my work has become more important to me than my life. I know, at some point, I must look back over my life to try to salvage something of myself, to try to see clearly what of my past I have tried to bury in doing my work; what of my past I have been trying to understand through my work. But I am too close to my work to do this now. I don't have the time.

When I work too hard, my husband reminds me of a moment in the days preceding our marriage. He is at work. I am at our apartment. The place is filthy. I am trying to clean it so that we can move in. All the stores in the neighborhood are closed because of some holiday.

I decide that I will clean all the tiles in the bathroom. The only thing I have that will do the job is a toothbrush. So, instead of waiting for him to come back to help me, instead of waiting for the next day to get a scrub brush that will speed the work, I take the toothbrush to the tiles.

When he comes to pick me up, I am exhausted and miserable, but also triumphant because I have finished.

At the beginning, much of my work was like that day with the toothbrush.

One day, after two years of work, I go to the Berg Collection to begin work, as usual, and discover, to my chagrin, that the manuscripts of the novel are not now in the order in which Virginia Woolf wrote them. Why I haven't noticed this before is beyond me. On the day I realize I will have to sort, sequence, and date the thousand or so pages of manuscript, I become slightly ill. I even believe that I am being punished for having been grandiose in my expectations. I know nothing about dating manuscripts.

I spend that summer taking an inventory of the manuscripts, noting the watermark on each sheet, the color of the ink, how many perforations it has—anything that might help me sort the manuscripts into drafts. Although I read about the dating of modern manuscripts and certainly learn from the experience of experts, I am also secretly grateful that I have voraciously read Nancy Drew detective books when I was a girl, that I have learned, through her, to be alert to every possible clue.

I go back and reread the thousand or so letters that I have read before, searching, now, for clues to the dating of those sheets.

One night, at four in the morning, I awaken from a dream in which I see Woolf using pages from earlier drafts of the novel in later drafts. I have overlooked this possibility. I suddenly realize that if I use the watermarks as a guide, assuming that Woolf has used different kinds of paper during the several years the novel was in progress, I can sort the manuscripts into drafts.

I also realize that there is a code to the two sets of page numbers that are on several hundred sheets, now scattered through the manuscripts. The paginated sheets might represent one draft—one set of page numbers indicating the placement of the sheet within the draft, the other, the page numbers within a given chapter.

There it is, happening to me—my very own "Ah ha!" experience. Just like in the textbooks.

I rush upstairs to my desk and in the space of an hour or so, I have figured out the order of four earlier drafts of the novel. Now I can study the stages of the novel's development, although I still have to date the drafts.

One morning, on my way to the Berg, I discover that I have forgotten my see-through ruler, the one I use to measure the sheets of the manuscript. I am passing a stationery store, hesitate, but go in and buy another one. On that day, as I am reading Woolf's letter to Violet Dickinson, searching for clues to date the manuscripts that I have already sorted, I am fiddling with the ruler. I put it beside the letter I am reading and suddenly realize that the sheet is the same size as the paper Woolf used in a draft. I quickly check the watermark. Sure enough. The letter is dated. That accident enables me to date, to my satisfaction, a major draft of the novel.

Now I am ready to do what I have always wanted to do: relate the composition of the novel to the events in Woolf's life.

I remember sitting in the Berg, surrounded by a thousand sheets of paper, while the rest of the world was swimming and sunning themselves, thinking, "This is where I belong. I am in my element."

As I record the progress of Virginia Woolf's days to figure out what she was doing as she was writing *The Voyage Out*, I start realizing that this was one hell of a woman, filled with incredible energy, so different from my original impression of her.

Reading about her life in London, her visits to the British Museum, the books she read, the jaunts down to Sussex on weekends, the trips to St. Ives, to Wells, to the Lizard, to Lelant, Cornwall, the walks, the work, the lived life, fruitful beyond my wildest imaginings, her engagement with the most important political and social issues of her day, her teaching working-class people, I begin to revise my picture of her and my hopes for myself.

I decide that it would be foolish of me to spend endless days alone inside libraries working on Woolf when the great woman of my dreams had spent no small portion of hers walking around the countryside, cultivating important relationships, particularly with women, taking tea, learning to bake bread, teaching, getting involved in politics, becoming an essayist, a novelist, integrating work and pleasure, and having what seemed to me, in contrast to my confined scholarly life, a hell of a good time.

That's when I buy my first pair of hiking boots and start walking, first around the lower reaches of New York State and then, at long last, through Woolf's beloved Sussex and Cornwall and later through, Kent, Cumbria, Northumbria, Yorkshire. I retrace the trips she took while she was writing *The Voyage Out*; visit the places she visited; read the books she read; begin having important friendships with Woolf scholars; start teaching; begin writing essays; start writing poetry; write a novel.

In 1975 I am on my way from Brighton to Sevenoaks to see Knole, Vita Sackville-West's ancestral home, delighted by the likelihood that Virginia Woolf herself, when she was writing *Orlando*, has traveled these very roads to see Vita. We have just come through a small stretch of moor that smells powerfully of damp and peat when we see a road sign that reads, simply, SEVENOAKS, the village where Knole is.

When I see that sign, I begin weeping, inexplicably, and uncontrollably, filled with a sense of myself newly born, able to work and have fun, able to enjoy my life, and my life's work. This is released somehow by a sense of the flesh-and-blood reality of the Virginia Woolf who passed, a long time ago, by that very spot to see a friend, another woman.

I think that I would like to write about these two women, about their friendship, about their love affair, about their work. I think about how the creative act has been misconstrued as a solitary, solipsistic act, and how we must correct that misapprehension; we must write about the creative act as it is nurtured by loving friendships.

1 9 7 6

I am sitting outside a speech therapy room, balancing Lyly's *Euphues: The Anatomy of Wit* on one knee and a yellow pad of paper and some note cards on the other. What I am trying to figure out as I sit here, waiting for my four-year-old son, Justin, to finish his session, is whether any part of Virginia Woolf's conception of *The Voyage Out* may have been due to her knowing this work. After all, she *did* say that *Euphues* was the germ of the English novel. Is there any evidence that *Euphues* may have been the germ of hers?

I open the book. I am delighted to find that there is a character called Lucilla in the work and that, for Euphues, she is an inconstant woman (another *puttana*). In Virginia Woolf's 1908 draft of her novel, a central character is called Lucilla, and I become convinced, as I sit here, that it was no accident.

I glance, occasionally, through the one-way mirror and watch the therapist working with Justin. Every time he sounds a letter correctly, which is virtually impossible for him to do, he gets an M&M candy.

Today, because they are working on *s*, the most difficult sound for him to produce, because he cannot hear it, he is angry because he hasn't gotten very many M&Ms and he *loves* M&Ms and this is the only time he can have them (the therapist's amazingly successful strategy). I know I am going to have my hands full when his session is over. Maybe an ice cream cone will help. Chocolate-chip mint, his favorite.

I come to the breakfast table one morning, trying to shake the effects of a night of work. My son, Jason, usually cheerful in the morning, is sitting at the table in a foul, rotten mood.

He glares at me. I ask him what is troubling him. He tells me that they had a discussion in school about the generation gap. Do I realize that he is the only child in the class who sees his mother less than he sees his father? Do I realize that my work is killing him? That he hates it? That he can't stand to have me up at my typewriter or buried in my books when he comes home from school?

That the sound of the typewriter keeps him up all night? That he needs his sleep?

I know all this, but I can't find a balance. I don't want to be just a mother, just a wife. I want the time to do my work. And to find the time I need requires that I work when my children are home. How else can I manage the hundred and one things that need to be done each day, and write, too? The cooking and cleaning and homework-checking and shopping and all the rest of it.

Learning to enjoy my work, learning to find a balance between my work and the rest of my life, and learning to play will take me many years.

Recently Jason has come into my study after school. I continue working. He looks at me and says, "Mom, do you realize that at this moment, mothers all over the world are making their children snacks?" before trudging off to his room to play his music loud.

On this morning, he begins sobbing. I want to hold him, but he won't allow it. The only time this child ever has an uncontrollable temper tantrum is on the day he overhears me talking about writing a second book. He looks at me and says, "Second book?" Then he throws himself off his chair onto the floor, begins shrieking and beating his fists against the floor. When I calm him enough so that he can talk, he tells me that he thinks when I finish what I'm working on, he will have me back.

I understand why he is so angry. My work takes me away from him far more often than he would like. I ask him if he thinks anything I have done has rubbed off on him. We often write together, in my study. I love his compositions. He writes wonderful fiction. He says no, emphatically no. Nothing about my work has ever done him any good.

He calms down quickly. Asks if I'd like to hear the latest thing he has written. I say yes. He pulls a sheet of paper out of his notebook and begins reading the story of a man called John C. Lectica. As he reads, I think, "A chip off the old block."

* * *

A while ago we have been told that Justin's hearing is severely impaired. Or rather, *I* have been told. A teacher at his nursery school has called and told me that Justin responds to commands only after he sees other kids doing something. I was too unconscious, in those days, of my needs to understand that taking your child to a specialist to find out whether he is hearing-impaired is not something you should do by yourself, even if you are a tough woman.

And so there I am, on a rainy day, in the elevator, on the way to the appointment my husband has made with the specialist, by myself, holding Justin's little hand, thinking, maybe he *is* hearing-impaired and not emotionally disturbed. I have been secretly afraid that this extraordinarily difficult child, who had been an absolute angel as a baby, who never cried, who slept all night almost from the beginning, has become the way he is because I have gone back to graduate school. I share my private fantasy with no one, partially because to share it would be to admit that something might really be terribly wrong, and in admitting that something might be terribly wrong, I might have to confront my fantasy that I have caused it.

Sitting in the doctor's office, holding Justin on my lap, I listen as the doctor says, "Yeah, we seem to have a deaf one on our hands."

I will never forget those words. I will never forgive that doctor his callousness. I will never forget choking back my tears, swallowing my vomit, as I sit holding my son on my lap, thinking, I must not let this child see me crying, not here, and not yet.

But on the way back to the car, we walk, Justin and I, through a rose garden adjacent to the hospital, and, by now, the rain has stopped, and the sun has come out, and the sun is hot, and the roses are so beautiful, and Justin tugs at my hand and looks up at me, as I touch his tangle of red curls, and I think to myself, What do I do now? What's to become of him now? And he says in his garble that only I can understand, "Mommy, mommy, so happy, the sun," and

I kneel down, and hug him, and cry and cry and cry, but I know he is going to be all right, and I know that it hasn't been my fault.

What strikes me now is the insane incongruity of my reading *Euphues*, the most esoteric and highly cultivated prose in the English language, while my son struggled to utter his first comprehensible sounds, while a Vietnam veteran, a multiple amputee, struggled, in the room next to Justin's, to speak again, while a woman who had cancer of the larynx struggled, in the room on the opposite side, to belch up her first sound. What I do know is that taking Justin there day after day and week after week, admitting that he *was* hearing-impaired, and seeing other courageous people work to express themselves, helped me. It made me understand that I had to find a way to make my literary studies congruent with Justin's struggle, and that of other people. I knew that I couldn't study works of literature as if they had no relevance to life.

I still wasn't sure, though, that I could find the language appropriate to express my belief that studying writers' lives and works could be personally useful, that the way writers worked to transform their traumatic pasts into art could help ordinary folks understand how to do that.

When I was a freshman in college, my first composition came back covered with red marks. "You write primer English," the professor scrawled across the top of the first paper. When I asked my new friend Rebecca what she thought that meant, she replied, "He means you write like a baby. It's his way of saying that in your paper you sound stupid." I knew Rebecca was right.

Though I had written well as a high school senior, in college I was so intimidated by the essays that the professor discussed as examples of "acceptable college-level writing," so afraid of the professor's promise that he would stop reading our essays at the first grammar or spelling mistake he encountered, that I wrote as simply as I could so I wouldn't make any mistakes. Through college, even when I started to do well, I carried my anger at that professor around with me; it tied me up; it stopped me from writing my best. That subterranean fear that I couldn't write well, that anything I wrote would be simple-minded, stayed with me for a long time.

When I graduated college, my prose had frozen into that disembodied, vague, pretentious, passionless prose that is encouraged on college campuses. I wanted to write a dissertation I could publish in book form that could be read by nonspecialists. And I did not yet know whether I could do that.

Through those years, as Justin learned one sound, then another, I wrote, tangled, and untangled, one sentence after another. In the acknowledgments to my dissertation (which became my first book), I wrote, in a kind of code, about how Justin had been a model "of persistence and patience for me to emulate," how, during the years when my work was in progress, I had watched "Justin learning to express himself." And I printed, in very large letters that he could understand, in his very own copy of my first book (which he insisted that I give him), "Thanksgiving Day 1980. For Justin—Who was near me while I was writing this whole book, who learned a lot in that time. I love you. Mom."

What I didn't write to him overtly, then, what I write now, is how much I *learned* from him; how, in watching the struggles of a little boy with a voice that no one could understand, I learned to be less angry with myself about how hard it was for me to find my voice. Finding my voice was, after all, not so difficult a task compared to what I saw him and others experiencing. If he had the guts, surely I did too. After all, he was made out of the same stuff that I was. As he found his voice, I too found mine.

When I am asked how an Italian-American woman became a Woolf scholar, I search my memory, and think of studying Virginia Woolf's *To the Lighthouse* with Carol Smith when I was a senior at Douglass College, where I first started to love Woolf's works. At the time, Smith was very pregnant, wearing a beige maternity dress. If you looked carefully, you could watch her baby kicking while she lectured. As she talked about the relationship between the autocratic Mr. Ramsay and his wife in "The Window" section of the novel—about who they are as parents, lovers, and people—I realized that you didn't have to stop your work if you wanted to have a family.

I suddenly remember my fascination with the figure of Cam Ramsay in *To the Lighthouse* while I was taking Smith's class. Cam Ramsay, the child Mrs. Ramsay virtually ignores; Cam Ramsay, the child who is "wild and fierce." The child who clenches her fist and stamps her feet. The child who is always running away, running away. The child upon whom a family friend presses unwelcome attention. The child who will not let anyone invade the private space that she has created to protect herself in this family with a tyrannical father who strikes out with a beak of brass, with a mother who doesn't protect her.

I remember my childhood, my adolescence. Can it be that I have seen something of myself in Cam those many years ago and that, in trying to understand Virginia Woolf's childhood, and the relationship between Cam Ramsay and her creator, Virginia Woolf, I am also trying to learn something about my past? I am in the middle of a long essay about Woolf as an adolescent, reading her 1897 diary, a tiny brown gilt-leather volume, with a lock and a key, that must be read with a magnifying glass, so tiny and spidery is the hand, an essay that has given me more satisfaction to write than anything I have yet written. And I have been stressing Woolf's capacity to cope, rather than her neurosis, in that difficult year. Can it be that in concentrating on Woolf's health, I am also trying to fix whatever is wrong with me, to heal myself?

1 9 6 3 – 6 4

Ernie and I married during his first semester of medical school, during my first semester of high school teaching. We proudly set up our first apartment in Jersey City, New Jersey, close to the medical school, in a safe-enough apartment, we thought. Brand-new Danish modern bedroom furniture, bought at Macy's, the cheapest on the floor, a generous gift from his parents: color scheme, blue and green. Brand-new Danish modern living room set, the cheapest on the floor, bought at Macy's, with money Ernie had saved from working in construction and money we got from our wedding. We had hookers who rattled up and down the stairs next to our bedroom all night long for upstairs neighbors, next-door neighbors who had screaming fights about his infidelities, a crazy superintendent, one robbery of our belongings (in the first month of our marriage), and only one murder in the building in the four years we lived there.

We quickly established our budget and our priorities. I was earning 4900 dollars a year teaching. Ernie's parents kicked in a lavish-in-those-days twenty dollars a week to help us. We would live frugally, on a strict budget, and save every penny we could. We wouldn't have a honeymoon. We wouldn't have children for four years, so we could get to know one another and travel. Our only splurges would be dinner out one night a week, on Fridays (at a pizza place, or a cheap restaurant); dinner parties, which we gave, one night a month, on Saturdays—recipes prepared from cookbooks I began to acquire; one movie night a week. We spent fifteen dollars a week for food; five dollars a week each for spending money—Ernie spent his on classical music albums; I spent mine on wool for knitting sweaters and on paperback books. Whatever was left over, we would save for travel. Neither of us had ever left the country, and we were both eager to travel. And willing to sacrifice for it.

Ernie had wanted to wait until his graduation for us to marry. I had pushed the marriage because I wanted an independent life, and the only way then for a young woman of my class and background to move out of the family home was to get married.

Our first four years of marriage were hard, yet exhilarating. I loved teaching, though teaching five classes a day, managing large classes of high school students, not much younger than I was, cooking dinner, and keeping an apartment exhausted me. Ernie did well in medical school. Though in later years he began to share housekeeping duties with me, in those early years of our marriage he didn't help much at all. But I loved being married and I tried hard to be a "good wife"—keeping a neat and well-run home, making nice meals, and entertaining well.

We soon saved enough money to take a seven-week driving trip through Europe (the first of dozens of trips we would take), using Frommer's *Europe on $5.00 a Day* as a guide, with my friend Harriet and her husband as companions. I kept a diary, filled with exclamation points and underlinings indicating how enthralled I was with everything I saw, and how naive I was. A diary entry from Paris: "Traffic in Paris is a riot. *All* the cars are small, but they are driven at a furious rate of speed. There seems to be a game here between the buses, the pedestrians, and the cars—chicken! I don't think topless bathing suits are worn here because we've seen signs saying 'Topless suits—rage in America.' American rock and roll is played here constantly. They *do* have foot-long French bread."

On this trip, I realized something important about myself: when I traveled, I became a different person. I was brave, even bold. Everything excited me. Nothing frightened me. And I realized something important about my marriage: though Ernie and I disagreed, often and vociferously, we could resolve our quarrels and we liked doing the same things—we could only take an hour in a museum; we preferred the countryside to the city; we liked small hotels, not big ones; we didn't like to shop; and we were passionate about finding and eating good food for reasonable prices; we loved having picnics.

1 9 6 8

I give birth to our first baby, Jason, in November 1967. He is born a month early, weighs less than an oven-stuffer roaster, and needs to eat every two hours. I am enduring Ernie's medical internship as best I can, on next to no money, with a baby who never sleeps and always cries. I am twenty-five. I look awful. I have deep circles under my eyes. I have no figure. I am still wearing maternity clothes.

In that internship year, Ernie and I came very close to a divorce. Your basic doctor-in-training-meets-gorgeous-nurse-and-wants-to-leave-his-wife-and-small-baby story.

What gets me through the year of misery and isolation—we live far from friends and parents, and I don't have a car and can't afford long-distance telephone calls—is my friendship with Kate and a subscription to a book club. In the precious moments I catch between feeding times, I read, take notes on my reading, and write my reflections. I try to persuade myself that I have a brain, and that it still works.

One day, I look into the bathroom mirror and decide that I will either kill myself or go back to graduate school and become economically independent as quickly as I can.

I look into the medicine chest, thinking that if my husband leaves me with this baby, I will be young, gifted, and on welfare. After wondering whether you can kill yourself by taking a year's supply of birth control pills and thinking that, the way my luck is running, I might grow some hair on my chest, but I probably won't die, I decide that I will go back to school, get a Ph.D., and go into college teaching.

I also realize that I might buy some time by squelching the young-doctor-leaves-his-young-wife-for-nurse script, at least temporarily, by announcing to my husband that if he leaves me, *he* can have the baby. Then he and his sweet young nurse can contemplate how romantic their life together will be with this baby who cries and throws up all the time.

He tells me he doesn't believe that I can part with my child.

I say, "Wanna bet?"

Shortly thereafter, he decides to hang around for a while longer.

The way I write this, the "tough broad" tone I take, is, of course, a disguise for how hurt I was, for how seriously betrayed I felt. I thought Ernie and I had a great marriage. We had the same values, had traveled well together. I had done everything I was supposed to do, the way you were supposed to do it. Clipped coupons. Made casseroles from *Woman's Day* with noodles and chopped meat and cream of mushroom soup for all his friends. I had laughed at a story of how a doctor had fucked a nurse in the linen room adjacent to the OR and how the surgeon couldn't figure out where the grunts and groans were coming from. I had done everything you were supposed to do, the way you were supposed to do it, and, still, my husband wanted to leave me.

And that disillusionment, and rage in my believing that if I did everything right for my husband, he would be with me forever, stayed with me for a long time.

I really don't know now what I would have done if my husband *had* left me. Don't know if I could have given up my son. Unlike the husbands of many of my friends, my husband *did* stay. Unlike others of my friends who went through similar episodes, I chose to stay, and I could forgive him. When asked how, or why, I have responded that a contrite husband makes a wonderful lifelong partner, and that most long relationships include an episode like the one I lived through. Besides, what he did spurred me to growth, to finding what *I* wanted.

I now wanted a career. And my own money. And access to the public world. I wanted to carry a briefcase. I wanted to carry a briefcase while walking down a path at a college, with students to my right and to my left, engaged in serious, important, intellectual discussions about literature, about what literature tells us about the lives we lead, about how it can help us. I never wanted to depend on a man again. And, I realized, that if men might leave you even if you do everything you're supposed to, then you might as well do whatever you want.

M a r c h   2 8 ,   1 9 4 1

Virginia Woolf commits suicide by walking into the River Ouse with rocks in her pocket. My mother is trying to get pregnant. That she is trying to conceive when Virginia Woolf dies is of no significance to her.

Years later, I ask her if she remembers hearing about Virginia Woolf's death on the radio. She says no. Maybe she read Virginia Woolf? *The Years*? It was a very popular novel, on the bestseller list. She says no. She never heard of Virginia Woolf until I started talking about her.

That Virginia Woolf and my mother were alive at the same time, breathed the same air, so to speak, is mysteriously significant. That my mother was trying to get pregnant with *me* when Woolf killed herself seems laden with meaning. What can explain that I am devoting a very large part of my life to this woman with whom I think I have absolutely nothing in common? She is English, purely and highly bred. I am more Italian than American, rough, tough, a street kid, out of a working-class neighborhood in Hoboken, New Jersey. We have nothing in common, except that we're both women, and that, I think, is enough.

When I first started my work on Woolf, I wasn't a feminist. I read her novels, first. And *A Room of One's Own* and *Three Guineas*, later. Reading these, while trying to earn a degree, manage a household, and raise children, showed me that many of my struggles weren't idiosyncratic: they were rooted in assumptions about how women and men should behave. These assumptions, Woolf taught me, were not immutable. Society could change if individual women made changes in the way they lived their private lives. Although my feminism has informed all the writing I do, to me the most important part of being a feminist meant changing the way our household functioned. It meant sharing everything—decision making, childcare, cleaning, cooking, financial responsibility, the works. It meant that my work and his work were equally important; it meant that each of us would have the time we required to do our work. It meant learning that our work to achieve our ideals would never be complete: we would be negotiating our need for privacy and time and what our responsibilities would be every day that we chose to stay together.

Woolf's own marriage was a model for this. She organized her daily life with Leonard Woolf to provide her with unbroken, uninterrupted stretches of time for writing and reading; she shared equally in paying for the expenses of their household. *He* took tea to her. He fussed, and made sure that unwelcome guests or calls didn't interrupt *her* work. Nor did he intrude on her privacy. Woolf didn't wait for England to change its views on acceptable behavior for women and men. In her household, she insisted on what she required for her art. And she taught me to do the same.

When I first learned that Virginia Woolf had spent seven years in the creation of *The Voyage Out*, I thought that surely she must have been mad for that, if for no other reason. But as I carried one of my books off to my editors some seven years after I began working on it, I reflected that I had come to share a great deal with this woman. I had become like her in her attitudes toward writing and art and feminism and politics. I had learned from living for years with her to take the best from her while managing, through the example of her life and her honesty about it, to avoid the depths of her pain.

She has been very good to me, this woman. And, in time, it is through her life that I begin to understand the lives of the women in my family—my mother's, my sister's. And finally, mine.

Personal Effects

Autumn 1990

SOON AFTER MY mother's death, my father gives me a small manila envelope. He finds it, tucked away in the corner of a drawer in my mother's bureau. He has been sorting through her possessions, making a package of clothes that he will donate, at my mother's request, to the local battered women's shelter.

"She wanted you to have this," my father tells me, as he hands me the envelope.

I glance at it. In the lower right-hand corner, my mother has written my name in a shaky hand. When I see her handwriting, I know that she has assembled this packet for me toward the very end of her life, before she enters the hospital, when she feels her strength waning rapidly, though she never tells us she fears that she is dying, never tells us she's been falling down, dropping things.

"Reading what's in here will tell you a lot about your mother," my father says.

Angry that he has obviously read its contents, but too tired to

242

again take up with him the issue of privacy, I tell him that, of course, I will read what the envelope contains. I am lying. I know, but can't say, that I am not ready to read whatever last message my mother has left for me. That I may never be ready. This, my father could not understand.

After my father leaves, I look at the handwriting more carefully. Examine it as I might the handwriting of an author whose work I am researching. I try to determine from its appearance precisely when my mother scrawled my name.

I remember that, near the end of my mother's life, she scrawled something on a postcard that I mailed her from Barcelona, and that the handwriting on this envelope might match. If it does, I'll know when she penned it. Determining precisely when she prepared this envelope becomes extremely important to me. It gives me something I can do. Something other than opening the envelope and perusing its contents. Something other than reading her last message.

After my mother's death, as I went through her personal effects, I found the postcard in a box on the top of the old Singer sewing machine, which my mother used as a desk, with a few letters from friends, some bills she has paid, a bank statement she has reconciled.

I run down the stairs to my basement, and riffle through a cardboard box into which I have hastily stuffed these and some other things.

My mother and I had argued about my going to Barcelona for five days during my sabbatical to attend a women writers' conference— the only trip I have taken during my leave from teaching at Hunter. I had been writing constantly. Wanted a holiday. Believed I deserved it.

"Do you have to go?" my mother asks, when I tell her about my plans.

"I don't have to go, I want to go," I snipe back at her. To me, this is a replay of every argument we have ever had about my travels, about my life. She disapproved of my going to graduate school, and leaving my babies. She disapproved of my "gallivanting," as she called it, that I had dinner with friends without my husband. That I traveled alone. It was, she thought, no way for a married woman with children to behave.

When she asks me if I have to go to Barcelona, my mother doesn't tell me she's feeling sick. Doesn't tell me to stay home because she's afraid something might happen to her when I'm gone. I'm so involved with my life, I don't notice she looks frailer, weaker, that her skin seems more pallid.

"June, 1990. Louise in Barcelona."

I am ashamed when I look at the note my mother has appended to the postcard I haven't even bothered to sign, that I have scribbled in such haste before dashing out into the magical light of an early Sunday morning in Barcelona. This postcard that I had written reluctantly, thoughtlessly, had meant so much to my mother that she saved it, dated it.

And the handwriting is the same as the handwriting on the manila envelope, not as distorted as her handwriting just before she went into the hospital; not as lucid as her handwriting in March, April, May. Surely, she had prepared it for me around the time I was away. In two and a half months, my mother would be dead. She must have suspected she was dying. Why else, I thought, would she have done this?

I congratulate myself on this bit of detective work. But I'm still not ready for this, so I get a manila folder and stick the envelope inside, labeling it "Family—Mom—Momentos." Someday, I tell myself, I'll read this. Someday, but not now.

I take it down to the basement. Stick it in a filing cabinet. And

forget it until four years later when I find it, misfiled, as I'm searching in the file drawer for an old contract.

A year after my sister's suicide, my mother calls me, shaken.

She had been crossing the street to mail a letter to a friend. The
next thing she realized she was standing in the path of an oncoming
car, unable to move.

The car screeched to a stop a few feet away from her.

The driver rolled down the window, screamed at her. He could
have killed her, he told her.

What do I make of this, she asks me.

I tell her it's serious. I say I'll take her to her psychiatrist. I'm
not surprised, though.

So, when a few months before her death, my mother casually tells
me that, when the doctor recommended she stop taking one of the
many pills she was taking for a chronic condition, she misunder-
stood and stopped taking all of them, I wonder if she is suicidal
again.

In the years that have intervened since my sister's death, my
mother's pain is clearly visible, ever present. She stops enjoying my
children. She stops enjoying our family gatherings. She stops enjoying everything. Her mouth is permanently drawn downward into a
frown. When we take family pictures, she forces a smile. She pushes
herself, each day, through her routine, through her life. She isn't
with us, though. She's with Jill.

After a gathering, I ask a friend how she thinks my mother
looks.

"The truth?" she asks.

"The truth," I respond.

"Like a zombie," my friend tells me. And she's right. Since my
sister's suicide, my mother has drifted further and further away

from us into the underworld of memory. When my sister killed herself, she took my mother with her to keep her company.

Now, when I see my mother, she often begins our conversations with a reflection about my sister. And she rarely asks me how I'm doing.

"Her checkbook, her financial papers—they were all so well organized when they came to me," my mother tells me. "She had even balanced her checkbook."

"There were hundreds of people in the chapel to mourn her. She was well loved."

"The marriage was a mistake. Maybe if she had married someone else . . . Had a baby . . ."

More than ten years after my sister's death, my mother-in-law is talking to my husband about my family.

"Did you know," she asks, "that Jill's husband used to beat her?"

When my husband tells me this, he asks me if Jill ever talked about it to me.

She didn't, I tell him. I ask him how his mother knew. He says that Jill told her. I can imagine this happening; my mother-in-law was my confidante when Ernie was fooling around. She's sympathetic, nonjudgmental, helpful.

This conversation cuts me deeply. Is this true? Why hadn't Jill told me? Why didn't my mother-in-law tell me? Were there signs I missed? Did my parents know? But my mother's support of the local battered women's shelter after my sister's death now makes sense to me.

I go back and read Jill's letters, something I haven't done since I organized them after her death. Read against my mother-in-law's words, they tell a wrenching story. Without any specific details, they allude to screaming telephone conversations, bad times, big fights, her husband's scary behavior, how he's never at peace with himself, the big problems they have to work out, starting therapy, stopping therapy, threats of separation, taking her share of the blame, trying to make the marriage work, trying not to provoke her husband, trying to believe she's not responsible for his behavior, how inadequate, incompetent, unlovable she feels, how she was so depressed she was almost catatonic.

I sit with my sister's letters on pieces of yellow, pink, white, baby-blue, and flowered stationery. As a literary critic, I can always read between the lines, find the covert story behind the story. After one class, a student tells me, "You never miss a thing, do you?" I smile at her with pride. She's right. I never miss a thing, if it's in a text, in a subject's life. With my sister, though, I missed everything. Maybe I knew, but didn't want to know.

I pack away her letters. They're too painful to read.

She's dead. I can't do anything about it now.

It took my mother six long weeks to die. My mother's dying was difficult, though I do not think it was painful. Others have taken longer, far longer, to die, I know. But, to me, my mother's dying seemed endless.

Diary entry, July 11, 1990: "Yesterday I had the most godawful day of writing. Hated absolutely everything I tried to do, and couldn't do very much at all. Dragged myself around, exhausted, probably in part because my mother really sounds sick."

Diary entry, July 24, Tuesday: "My mother is in the hospital, with God knows what, a complication, I suppose, of having stopped all her medications when the doctor intended her to stop only one. She got weaker and weaker, not saying anything to anyone, started losing her balance and took a pretty bad fall. One doctor says she seems to have many infections. They're treating her with antibiotics, and she seems better. Today she seemed stronger, and actually started joking. She joked with my father when he showed up, and he looked pretty snappy. She adores him still after all these years, I thought, as I saw her face light up when he entered the room."

Wednesday, July 25. My mother's condition mystifies the doctors. They wonder if she has a rare infectious disease.

Diary entry, July 26, Thursday: "On my regimen to try to keep myself from—what? Coming apart and crying? Running away and not doing any work? Running away so as not to deal with my mother's illness? I sit here, in tears, feeling sad, hopeless, I guess. I really think she's dying. Going to see her is agony. The woman in the next bed dying of cancer, gurgling, coughing, choking, tubes in her nose. And the nurses work and work. And the doctors come, spend seconds, minutes. You can gauge how close a patient is to death by how long the doctors spend in the room, by how close they come to the patient. Maybe this great knot inside me will untangle if I can get some of these feelings down on paper.

"I am being such a child, I guess. Wanting none of this to happen. Feelings are coming up that are difficult to deal with. Sorrow at my mother's empty life. Is mine any more meaningful? She stays in day after day, doing household chores. I stay here day after day, hacking away at a book. What difference is there? I suppose there is. But I am phobic, too, and depressed, often, and do everything I do at such tremendous psychic cost, that I wish I had another mother, and yet the only one I have is slipping fast away."

The first other mother I wanted for my very own was Happy Klein's mother. I loved the disorder of her kitchen, that she smoked, that her ashtrays brimmed over, that she ordered take-out pizza for dinner. The second other mother I wanted was Carmine's mother; I liked her wavy hair, how hard she worked, how little she said to her husband, how she was stronger than he was, how she ran the family. Then there was our neighbor Angie who raised babies and dogs as if there was nothing to it, who could rustle up dinner for ten in half an hour, while smiling and carrying on a conversation, who thought it was funny that her babies ate the dogs' food out of their dishes, who never panicked when her babies ran high fevers.

When I was little, I often thought what it would be like to have another kind of mother, one who could bundle her children and wicker baskets full of delicious sandwiches and root beer and cream soda onto a bus, and wind up, several hours later, at the seashore, for a whole day of building sand castles, swimming, and sunbathing.

I often heard the kids at school speak of these great adventures with their mothers. They reported them as something to be endured, rather than celebrated.

In my fantasy, I see us at the seashore, my mother, a bold, intrepid swimmer. She sits Jill and me on a blanket, tells us not to move while she takes her swim.

She swims straight out, into the ocean. Every so often, she rolls over, onto her back, to check the sky for storm clouds, to see that we are still on the blanket.

Jill and I huddle against each other. Our mother is now just a speck on the horizon. She swims far, far out, in the salt water, her eyes stinging, no swim hat to protect her hair from the sea. She is out, now, where dolphins play, where seals dive, where the whales sound.

Out there, so far from us, she takes off her bathing suit, and swims naked, to feel the sea upon her body. Then, she pulls it back on before she starts the long, hard pull to shore.

It takes her forever to get back. She floats to rest the bellows of her lungs, she scissors her legs to stay afloat.

I rush down to the water's edge to give her a dry towel to cover her strong and stalwart body. She wears it wrapped around her, sarong-style, until we go into the locker room to change.

When the long day is over, we are sunburnt, and as happy as we can be. Our mother shakes off the blanket, gathers our things, puts them away carefully, and asks us if we're ready to go home.

Diary entry, July 29, 1990: "We got the word yesterday that my mother has had a stroke. But it is in a part of the brain which will, most likely, regenerate. The major problem, now, is that she is too unstable to walk. We will see to it that she begins physical therapy, and I wonder if we should get a chair lift for the house. But the diagnosis came as welcome news since the alternatives were so very grisly. I went straight to the hospital because she was very upset by the news. Then a sense of relief set in and she did very well yesterday. Today, though, she's exhausted, and she'll probably be in the hospital through next week, because they want to keep an eye on her.

"I had complex feelings about everything, which hit a crescendo Thursday. A grand rush of anger springing to the surface (I never had a mother and now she's dying), jealousy (she was nicer to my kids than she was to me), rage at myself (why did I spend my sabbatical writing instead of playing). And I became infuriated with my work. Told Ernie I had gone from writing about one crazy to writing about another. From writing about Virginia Woolf to writing about D. H. Lawrence.

"But expressing those feelings was good. I went to the hospital yesterday and took along a packet of pictures of the kids and shared them with her and felt we had a good visit."

July 31. My mother seems stable, though her speech is slurred, and she gets tenses and names wrong. But she's lucid and can read. I buy her Grace Paley's *Enormous Changes at the Last Minute*. A fortunate choice, because all the stories are short, about working-class characters, set in a neighborhood my mother understands, and irreverent, like Grace herself.

My plan is to read the stories to my mother, one at a time, on my visits. On each visit, I will do something, like polish her nails, or give her a facial, or a massage, so that she can feel pampered, and to pass the time.

I tell my mother that I know Grace, that I spent time with her in Barcelona. I tell her she would love Grace because she's so down-to-earth. My mother is interested and asks me to tell her more. I realize how little of my life I share with her. Yet, when she's in the hospital, I can.

Before I leave for the day, my mother suggests that I read an article she has enjoyed in *Reader's Digest*. A Victorian spinster's recipe for fulfillment: every day do some good for someone else; do some good for yourself; do something that needs doing that you don't want to do; do something physical, something mental; meditate, mostly on your blessings rather than on your disappointments.

Well, I think, that surely is the story of a life well lived, and when I'm doing well, I try to follow something like that recipe, though I tend to dwell upon problems, complaints, and disappointments rather than blessings. But I doubt it's the way my mother has lived her life.

As I leave the hospital, I realize that, in showing me this article, my mother gives me something useful.

I choke back tears. How bittersweet that it has taken this illness for us to have such an important day together.

September 1992

Two years after my mother's death, I develop a strange, debilitating disease. I do not know it is severe asthma, but I feel as if I am suffocating.

One night, coming home from the movies, I feel myself getting weaker; I think it's a very bad flu. I'm in bed for days; I'm really sick for over a month. But I never get better.

For close to a year, I have a mysterious disease no one can diagnose. I cough. I'm short of breath. I get piercing headaches. I faint. I feel as if I'm going to die. I feel best when I'm exercising. Throughout, I continue to teach. Continue to write. I teach well, though I collapse in bed as soon as I come home. I write well. I feel as if I'm writing against the clock.

I troop from one doctor to another. Rack up thousands of dollars of doctor bills. One specialist tells me it's a chronic incurable virus, and that I'll have it for the rest of my life. Another tells me it's a runny nose and that I cough because of the mucus. A third tells me that there's nothing wrong with me, that I'm somatizing—he does no tests, and tells me to calm down, as he sends me home from the emergency room. Another tells me I might have reactive airway disease and that I should try to live away from pollution for a while to see if I get better. For a while I live away from my family, get better, then get sick again.

I haunt health food stores. The self-help sections of bookstores. I buy scores of books and read them. I read about wellness, illness, meditation, holistic healing, the body/mind connection, diary writing as an aid in chronic illness. I take up regulated breathing, visualization, yoga, body scanning, fast walking, meditation. All help, but I'm still not better.

I think that my life is beginning to resemble my mother's. I don't go out of the house except to do my exercise walking or unless I have to. I stop seeing my friends. I cancel speaking engagements. I'm afraid to go anywhere, afraid that whatever I do will precipitate a bad attack. Sometimes I think that whatever strange illness I have is forcing me to live my mother's life and that, in this way, I'm trying to keep her alive.

Sometimes, when I let myself think about her, I realize that I'm still angry with her. For not being the kind of mother I wanted. I know, though, that I held myself back from her because I was afraid that if I loved her deeply, I would become like her, but I've become like her anyway. Maybe I shouldn't try so hard not to think about her. Maybe thinking about her will help.

In the years since my mother's death, I have hardly thought about her at all, though I have felt her presence, a few times, in the laundry room, especially, where she spent so much of her time when she came to my house, helping me with the unsorted untidy mountains of laundry that were always littered across the floor of my basement, so different from the floor of hers, which had never hosted a soiled garment, much less mountains of them.

When I protested, that I didn't want her doing my housework, she brushed me off, telling me that she liked to do laundry, it gave her a sense of accomplishment.

Laundry had always been her favorite household task. It kept her busy. It gave her something to do. It took her away from us. An early memory of my mother: her head wrapped in a bandana, she stands with her back to me, rubbing laundry against a washboard set in the midst of billowing suds in the deep kitchen sink in Hoboken.

One day I'm in a health food store buying Throat Coat Tea. I spy the *Vegetarian Times*, and decide, on a whim, to buy it. I think I might go on a macrobiotic diet, a juice fast. Something, anything.

When I get home, I see an article on asthma. It's called "Breath of Fresh Air" by Lucy Moll. "Asthma afflicts millions of Americans and is claiming their lives in ever-increasing numbers," it reads. "Why has this age-old illness taken such a nasty turn? And what can be done to help asthmatics lead normal lives?"

Moll says that asthma is an underdiagnosed and misdiagnosed disease. She describes the symptoms. I have them. She describes various therapies for asthma. I call my husband.

"I have asthma," I tell him.

"How do you know?" he answers.

"I diagnosed myself from an article in the *Vegetarian Times*."

He doesn't make fun of me. This disease has been hard for our family. I've been living alone for a few months, and I'm desolate.

"Get the name of the best asthma guy in New York City," I command him. And he does.

Sure enough, I'm right. The specialist tells me mine is a very severe case, that it will take about a year to bring it under control, but that, in time, I can live a completely normal life. He tells me how dangerous asthma can be; that it can kill you. He tells me the warning signs to watch for. Then he congratulates me for keeping myself alive during the year that I've been sick, and he asks me how I've managed without medication.

I tell him about the rigorous physical regimen I've enacted. The walking and weight lifting. About my daily lengthy meditation sessions. Visualizations. Diary writing.

"Keep all this up," he says. "It can't hurt, and it will surely help." And I do, and in time become his star patient.

After I start taking my medicine, I go to an acupuncturist because I am convinced it will help me.

The acupuncturist examines me before taking a history. She feels my body.

"Your body tells me that it contains blocked grief," she says.

I haven't told her about my mother's death, my sister's suicide. I am amazed she can figure this out by touch. I'm sure she's right. I haven't mourned my mother or my sister. I've been too busy. Too busy doing my work. Too busy carrying on. This disease, though, demands that I pay a different kind of attention to my body. It demands that I take notice.

After the acupuncturist inserts the needles into their proper places, I feel a most welcome sense of relief. As she leaves the room to give my body time to let the process work, I think that I haven't yet begun to grieve because I haven't wanted to give up my mother. If my grief stays bottled up inside me, then my mother stays inside me. Can it be that the constriction of my asthma, in part, is an inability to mourn? Is all this mucus that chokes me the tears I haven't shed for her? Can it be that I am not ready to give up a mother that I never really believed I had?

I think, ruefully, of my work on Virginia Woolf's relationship with her mother. How Woolf, too, believed she wasn't feeling enough when her mother died, how Woolf felt unable to mourn her mother. I had no trouble connecting Woolf's blocked feelings at her mother's death to her mother's emotional unavailability to her—Woolf's mother, like mine, was often depressed—and to Woolf's unacknowledged anger at her mother's incapacity to protect her from being sexually molested.

It's time, I tell myself, to apply what I've learned about Woolf to my complicated feelings toward my own mother.

Virginia Woolf once said that, in writing *To the Lighthouse*, she had laid the ghost of her mother, who had haunted her, to rest. I want to write about my mother for the same reason. To see if, in writing about her, I can face how I felt about her, and put her death behind me.

Soon after I start writing about my mother, I have dreams about her and imaginary conversations.

In one dream, someone is giving me a party to celebrate my most recent book. I am trying to get there, but I am having a hard time. My legs don't seem powerful enough to carry me forward. I am like one of those cartoon characters who try to move, but can't get anywhere.

I look behind me. See that my mother is hanging on to the back of my sweater. As I try to move forward, she exerts as great a force to pull me back. I can't get to the party without her. But she won't let me get there.

At this point in my dream, I awaken. I feel frustration, anger, pain. In those moments between sleep and waking, I think that what I have to do, emotionally, is leave my mother behind, pull her off me, forcibly, if necessary, so that I can get to the parties in my life.

A few days later, I am sitting on the sofa in my study, writing about this dream, which continues to occupy my thoughts, when I hear a voice in my consciousness say, "Take the best from me, and leave the rest behind. And one more thing, take me along to the party."

I know this is my mother's voice. And the solution to the dilemma in my dream is a better one than my initial response—to leave my mother behind, to pull her off me. For she is my mother, and so a part of me. But I can invite her to come to the party with me. Take the best from her—her wisdom and compassion, her sense of justice and fair play, her ethics and morality, her dogged persistence in carrying on even in the face of tragedy and personal suffering, her respect for people, her graciousness and dignity. Yes, take the best from her. And leave the rest behind.

Diary entry for August 1, 1990, my mother's birthday: "I decided today to treat my mother to a party though she is in the hospital, and I bought a gift, and a cake, and plates, candles, napkins, the works, figuring that I could leave whatever was left over for the nurses. And it was nice. The woman in the next bed was choking, dying from lung cancer. Hideous way to die. My mother, though, looks better, feels stronger, can sit up for longer periods, and only spills her food slightly when she feeds herself. She should be home by the weekend. She wants me to buy her a new mattress. I've been putting it off."

August 6, 1990. My mother takes a bad fall in the hospital. I convince myself it's because she has been overdoing her physical therapy, that my father has been forcing her to overexert herself, to try harder.

August 14, 1990. My mother's condition deteriorates. The doctors don't know why. In the mornings, I shut off my phone and write for three hours. I treasure this time. In the afternoons, I go to the hospital. When I leave, I feel awful. My father is always there.

August 15, 1990. The strain of my mother's illness is beginning to show on my father. And on me. Driving home from the hospital, I play tapes of late Beethoven quartets. Sometimes I pull over to the side of the road to play them loud. Their soulful, mournful quality matches what's inside me, what I feel, but what I can't express. I rest my head on the steering wheel and cry.

I develop arrhythmia. Insomnia. The worst time is the middle of the night. The best time is when I'm writing. Oddly enough, my writing begins to go well.

My mother now can't walk. Slurs her speech. Can still feed herself. When I see her today, she tells me she has had a dream: we are walking together in a beautiful landscape.

"A miracle," she says. "I can walk." I can barely understand her. I take her hand. I glance down at her fingernails, notice that the manicure I have given her is wearing off. I must give her another, I think, but can't summon the energy.

"That would be wonderful," I say. "It would be wonderful if you could walk."

She looks at me as if I haven't understood her, then says something I can't understand that sounds like "Wishu."

"Wish you?" I ask.

"Wishu," she replies. "I was walking wishu."

I finally get it. Her dream has been a miracle, not only because she has been walking, but because she has been walking in a beautiful place *with me.*

The force of what my mother says is so heartbreaking that I have to turn away.

August 22, 1990. My mother wants to talk to me on the telephone today, the first time in a long time. I can't understand her. She's in no pain, and she sleeps a lot. I keep myself very quiet. Walk, work, clean out closets. I tackle the refrigerator for the first time in—what?—a year? I start getting my son Justin ready for college.

Diary entry for August 28, 1990: "My mother can't speak, has stopped eating, is semicomatose. When my father tells me, I think, but don't say, good, it goes more quickly. Just a few weeks ago, on her birthday, I thought she'd recover. So the downward spiral has been quick, really, though seeing her, daily, is agonizing.

"My father stays by her, tries to feed her. But he won't leave me alone with her. Hovers. I tell him I want time alone with her. He leaves us for two minutes.

"I want to talk to her. Tell her some things that need saying. I don't think I have much time, and there's much to say.

"I barely begin. He comes back. God forbid he should give up his primacy.

"I do what I can to help—visit nursing homes, interview the directors. See her every day. My arrhythmia, a real problem. I've been trying to make good meals. When I reread my diary and see how many words I misspell, how many words I substitute for others, I worry I'm getting her disease. That's part of this. Thinking you're going to die the same way your parent is dying.

"My feelings seem to have turned a corner, though I know they might open up again. But mostly I've accepted her inevitable death and hope, only, that it will occur quickly.

"I told her she was brave today. She could barely nod assent, could barely hold my hand."

Diary entry for September 6: "Writing about my mother's illness, impossible. I'm always exhausted. I go to the hospital every day. I cry. I rage.

"My mother had said she wanted no tubes inserted in her to prolong her life. Yet we arrive at the hospital to see a feeding tube. She can't eat. Can't swallow. Ernie says starving to death is a painless way to die, but that no hospital will let a patient starve to death. So today, with the feeding tube, she's slightly more alert, alert enough to begin suffering again.

"Modern medicine is terrified of death, I think. Unless it can be doing something, it doesn't know what to do. But sometimes doing nothing is more helpful. Isn't it supposed to be 'First, do no harm'?

"Meantime, I take a day at a time. Somehow I manage to keep writing."

September 8. My mother is totally paralyzed. Horribly, she's aware of what's happening. My father hopes she'll recover. I think he would rather have her like this than not have her at all. I spend time wondering whether I should give my mother a manicure; I think it would cheer her; I think, under the circumstances, it would be a violation. I decide against it.

September 9. I notice that my house is a mess. Everything needs to be fixed, cleaned, painted, repaired. I pick up a book about re-decorating, which is completely out of character. I take a day off from my daily hospital vigil to write out some interesting menus, shop for food, normalize my household. This day off helps me re-gain a sense of pleasure in life's possibilities.

Diary entry for Saturday, September 15, 1990: "My mother died on Thursday at around 9:30 in the evening. I had been to see her around 4 or so, and I thought she would die before my eyes, her breathing was so labored, then so shallow, and there were long stretches when she hardly seemed to be breathing at all. It was the first time during this ordeal that I couldn't touch her or go near her. She looked utterly concentrated upon the task of dying.

"I saw my mother more often in the last sixty days of her life than I saw her, under ordinary circumstances, in a year's time."

At first, I did not want my mother to die, did not think she would die, could not imagine she could die. After a time, I wished she would die quickly. For her sake. For my father's. For my children's. And for mine. I sensed that, after she died, I might get to know her better than I had known her when she was alive. That, finally, I might understand her, and, in understanding her, understand myself. And, mostly, I hoped that after she died I could release the love for her that I held tightfisted in my heart, a love she deserved.

Once, in the hospital, before she became paralyzed, as I was holding her hand, she remarked that my hands were very cold.

"Cold hands, warm heart," she said. It was a saying she often used in my childhood.

Knowing that inside I wasn't feeling toward her what I believed I should feel, that I never felt toward her what I believed I should feel, I said, "Cold hands, cold heart, in my case, I'm afraid."

She fixed her eyes on me, surprised at the fierceness of my answer, surprised that I would disagree with her in this cold-hearted way.

In the days after my mother's death, I'm very busy. My father and I go to the hospital to collect my mother's personal effects, to bring her nurses a present, to select the casket and flowers for her burial. I choose the clothes she'll wear. It's easy; she has only one good suit.

"Not too much makeup," I tell him. "She never wore very much makeup. She didn't need to. She was a natural beauty."

He nods.

I ask the mortician if he will make sure that my mother's nails are manicured. He assures me that he will.

September 1994

I am in my basement, looking for an old contract. And, instead, I find a manila envelope with my name, "Louise," penned in the lower right corner of the envelope in my mother's shaky handwriting.

I sit on the floor and open the envelope. I'm ready, I think, for seeing what it contains.

It is an odd agglomeration of memorabilia. But each piece bears a message, I feel sure. Something my mother wanted me to know.

A magazine clipping, "Three Cheers for Grandma."

Another magazine clipping from *Redbook*, dated May 1987, entitled "For You, My Children," with poems by Genevieve Smith Whitford, reprinted from *Queen Ann's Lace*. Among them, one called "From the Kitchen Door," which reads:

> *I've not gone far from my kitchen door,*
> *(the nursery is but a step or more)*
> *but I have seen love, in its shining grace,*
> *and hatred on the self-same face.*
> *. . . Tears and laughter, work and play*
> *tangle my footsteps every day.*
> *Some of drudgery, some of pain,*
> *much I could not do again,*
> *but this is life, and life is good . . .*
> *I would not change it if I could.*

A poem, typed by my sister, called "Around the Corner," its message, that you should see the people you love, often, because, before you know it, they'll be dead.

A newspaper clipping from 1988, "Hope lives amid grief and loss," by Joyce Maynard, about a woman named Hope, whose daughter had died. It concludes: "If I lost one of my children I would miss that child forever. But if I stopped living I'd be denying the very thing that having children is about—hope for the future."

Another newspaper clipping, "Prescription for a mild case of the blues," with advice from Dr. Mark Gold: "Distract yourself. . . . Lighten up. . . . Exercise. . . . Avoid drugs and alcohol. . . . Join a support group." It concludes by providing the telephone number of the National Depressive and Manic Depressive Association.

An Ann Landers Mother's Day column, "Dear Mom, a belated tribute," by an anonymous letter writer, about the many things she couldn't understand about her mother until she herself was a mother—how hard her mother worked, how lonely she was, how hurtful children can be, and how strong her mother was, though she didn't realize it when she was a child.

An article about living wills entitled "Would you choose to die?" A portion of the article, about a person's right to die, is underscored in a shaky hand.

An article by Martha Weinman Lear, "Mother's Day," describing Mother's Day as a "curious ritual for our time, filled with love and lies" and the mother/daughter bond as a "dear, murderous entanglement."

A poem, by Lynette Combs, which my mother clipped from *Modern Maturity* in 1988, called "Bloodmother Farewell."

And finally, a poem by Lynn Stein, called "Childhood," about holding one's childhood, hidden, underneath a shirt, and running to one's room, to look at it, privately: "i brushed the dust off/took my childhood into my hands, and wept."

It has been five years since my mother's death. By writing about her, I have begun to know her, and to love her, as I could not when she was alive. What I have learned alters my memories of her, transforms them, transforms her. But it changes my past, and it changes me, as well.

I travel back in time through memory. See her with her back to me, washing clothes, at the sink in the apartment in Hoboken. See her, in the window, singing "Show me the way to go home." But now I can feel her fear for my father away at war. And I know that she is not shutting me out because she wants to, but because she can't act otherwise.

How can a mother mother when she hasn't herself been mothered? I ask. And I know that what I told a friend on the day that my mother died, "I never had a mother, and now she's dead," is not altogether true.

*   *   *

In the days after my mother's death, as I pack up her personal effects, every belonging of hers that I touch makes me cry. I want to rush through this job so it will be over, but I know I must do the work slowly, for, if I do not, I might toss away something important, something special, something I should have kept, something I will regret I no longer have.

Her wallet, her watch, the key chain that my sons had picked out so carefully to give their Nana one Christmas when they were still very little—the objects my mother used every day, these are hard to pack away. The sweaters I made for her that she wore more than her others. Her meager, inexpensive wardrobe—so different from the finery of her youth.

As I sort and pack, sort and pack, I feel I will never plumb the depths of this grief. Everything I touch sends me into paroxysms of sorrow.

I go through the kitchen, come upon the kitchen tools and utensils my mother used for cooking in the years after my marriage, when she tried to reverse her own culinary history and tried her hardest to make wonderful meals for my husband and me, and then, later, for her grandchildren, though making them always flustered her. I find her recipe cards—for "wandas," an Italian cookie, for pumpkin pie, for chocolate cream pie—her measuring cups and spoons.

These powerful totems, I can't part with. I decide that I will cook with them. Make room for them in my drawers and cupboards where they can join my spoons and bowls, my sister's spoons and bowls.

The most trivial, yet the most important personal effects of the women of my family, come together at last, and mingle in my kitchen drawers and cupboards.

ACKNOWLEDGMENTS

MY GREATEST THANKS are to Rosemary Ahern, who first suggested that I write this book; to Geri Thoma, who read each version with enthusiasm and who helped me find clarity; to Carol Ascher and Sara Ruddick, who invited me to write my first memoir; to Ernest DeSalvo, who, as always, has been a source of unflagging enthusiasm and generosity.

I acknowledge friends, colleagues, and writers who have helped me conceptualize this project, shared responses to my work, or have been sources of inspiration and support: Mandy Aftel, Meena Alexander, Regina Barreca, Evelyn Bassoff, Allan Brick, Rachel Brownstein, Norah Chase, Blanche Wiesen Cook, Beth Rigel Daugherty, Cathy Davidson, Carole DeSanti, Jodi Sh. Doff, Arnold Dolin, Erika Duncan, Janet Emig, Patricia Foster, Karen Greenberg, Elizabeth Harlan, Norbert Hirschhorn, M.D., Mark Hussey, Elaine Koster, Harriet Luria Johnson, Lisa Johnson, Brooke W. Kroeger, Jane Lilienfeld, James McCourt, Nellie McKay, Frank McLaughlin, Nancy Mairs, Estella Majozo, Gulia Mallucci, Jane Marcus, Pablo Medina, Nancy K. Miller, Honor Moore, Susan Osborn, Kari Paschall, Katherine Hogan Probst, Julie Raynor, Jennifer Romanello, William Pitt Root, Susan Fromberg Schaeffer, Alix Kates Shulman, Jenefer Shute, Vanessa Smith, Maria Terrone, Marianna De Marco Torgovnick, Vincent Virga, Barbara Webb, and Robert White.

Louise DeSalvo is professor of English at Hunter College where she teaches memoir and fiction writing. She has written and edited nine books, among them the acclaimed *Virginia Woolf: The Impact of Childhood Sexual Abuse on Her Life and Work*, *Conceived with Malice: Literature as Revenge*, and *Vita Sackville-West's Letters to Virginia Woolf*. She has received numerous grants and awards for her work, among them the President's Award from Hunter College, and a grant from the National Endowment for the Humanities. She lives in New Jersey and Sag Harbor, New York.

· A NOTE ON THE TYPE ·

The typeface used in this book is a version of Sabon, originally designed in the 1960s by Jan Tschichold (1902–1974) at the behest of a consortium of manufacturers of metal type. As one who began as an outspoken design revolutionary—calling for the elimination of serifs, scorning revivals of historic typefaces—Tschichold seemed an odd choice, but he met the challenge brilliantly: The typeface was to be based on the fonts of the sixteenth-century French typefounder Claude Garamond but five percent narrower; it had to be identical for three different processes, working around the quirks of each, such as linotype's inability to "kern" (allow one character into the space of another, the way the top of a lowercase f overhangs other letters). Aside from Sabon, named for a sixteenth-century French punch cutter to avoid problems of attribution to Garamond, Tschichold is best remembered as the designer of the Penguin paperbacks of the late 1940s.

WITHDRAWN

DATE DUE

BRODART, CO.   Cat. No. 23-221-003